The
Modern
Deer Hunter

An Outdoor Life Book

The Modern Deer Hunter

by John O. Cartier

Illustrated by
Richard Amundsen

OUTDOOR LIFE

FUNK & WAGNALLS

New York

Times Mirror Magazines, Inc.
Book Division

Editor and Publisher	John W. Sill
Executive Editor	Henry Gross
Associate Editor	Neil Soderstrom
Art Director	Jeff Fitschen
Production Manager	Millicent La Roque
Editorial Assistants	Pat Blair
	Ellen Patrisso

Manufactured in the United States of America

To my wife Bernice

who long ago encouraged me to write
about the hunting and fishing sports
I've loved for over forty years

Contents

Preface

One of the best-selling general hunting books was published in 1972. In it is found these words: "Only five states have no whitetail deer, or so few as to be negligible; California, Colorado, Kansas, Nevada and Utah." Kansas deer hunters must wonder about such an out-of-date statement. In 1965 their state became the last one to open a modern deer season. Since then the state's numbers of both deer and hunters have been rising.

In another outdoor book, published in 1970 by a different author, we read that dark red-plaid is the safest color for outer garments worn by deer hunters. During the last ten years several government and private research studies have determined that Blaze Orange is a far superior color from a safety standpoint. Some state game departments have made it law that their deer hunters wear at least some outer clothing of Blaze Orange.

The same author devotes a good share of his book to stillhunting for whitetails, and adds that an entire book should be written about this single subject. Yet surveys by many game departments show that few of today's whitetails are taken by stillhunters. Except in very remote areas, the increased numbers of sportsmen and vehicles in the woods does away with the privacy needed for successful stillhunting. One of the most successful modern techniques is hunting from a stand, yet this same author devotes only a few pages to the subject.

In another recent hunting book, we read that Michigan has one of the largest deer herds in the nation, and that the state is one of the most productive for whitetail hunters. That would have been true back in the mid-1940s when the state's whitetail herd was an estimated three million. Today that herd has dwindled to about 700,000. Michigan's firearm deer hunters achieve a lower hunter-success ratio than bowhunters in several other states.

A few years ago the deer hunter using archery gear was looked upon as an oddball. Today there are over 1,250,000 licensed archers, and some of them are experts at bagging venison year after year. The gun hunter would be very wise to listen to some of their tips.

In still another recently published hunting book, is this statement: "For deer-size animals about any cartridge will do, with emphasis toward a heavier bullet at lower velocity. If the bullet goes through the animal, so much the better; it will leave a good blood trail to follow if the animal moves out of sight, and it usually does." Modern gun writers wince at such out-of-date conceptions.

Game officials have collected statistics that refute the often-repeated claim that we are killing off all of our deer. From a low point of only 500,000 deer in all of North America back in 1900, we now have over twelve million, thanks to game-management programs that hunters contribute to. We'll probably have more deer in the future because states like Michigan, where deer numbers have dropped due to maturing of forests, are initiating forest-rejuvenating plans to bring the herds back.

Some of the things I've mentioned may seem to have little in common, yet they all relate directly to your potential success as a modern deer hunter. Two of the four books I mentioned are reprints of works written many years ago. Their authors, in their eras, were top authorities whose word was gospel. They were the best of experts, but none of us have to be reminded that most things change with the passage of time. Some of the secrets of the old pros still work like charms. Some are a waste of time for the modern deer hunter. Within this book are the techniques that will work best for you today.

I don't set myself up as an expert who has developed new deer-hunting systems. Few of the principles within the following pages originated with me, even though I've been hunting deer for more than a few decades and have been an outdoor writer for most of that time. Most of the wisdom comes from experts with whom I have hunted and worked.

How do you work with deer hunters? For the past twelve years, as a field editor of *Outdoor Life* magazine, it has been my privilege to work with scores of hunters as I gathered material for deer stories and articles. I filed the best of the deer-hunting tips because I figured that some day I'd have enough to fill a book dedicated to helping the modern deer hunter, a book that has been long overdue. It is my conviction that *The Modern Deer Hunter* includes the best of the advice of old-timers as well as all the new knowledge needed to cope with today's conditions in the field.

Though some types of hunting have declined in recent years, deer hunters face a glowing future. A great deal of that future will result from scientific, modern game-management techniques that have much potential. Your future as a successful deer hunter has much more to do with your knowledge of how to hunt than it does with an *apparent* lack of deer.

John O. Cartier

The
Modern
Deer Hunter

1

Don't Lament the Old Days

All deer hunters have heard stories of the good old days when deer hunting was of such fabulous quality that it can never again be duplicated. Some of the stories were true, some enormous fabrications. The records of state game departments, old newspaper clippings, and the memories of old-timers can give clues about what deer hunters actually experienced during the past 150 years.

The stories that big bucks were far more common in the old days when there was less hunting pressure are both true and false. Some dramatic facts show why they can be false.

Mule deer have a reputation for not being very smart, plus being easier to hunt than whitetails. It might seem logical that the really big trophy muleys were all shot off years ago. So when was the world-record typical mule deer killed? Doug Burris Jr. of San Antonio, Texas, won the honors with a massive buck he took in Colorado's San Juan National Forest in 1972. Further, nearly all of the top twenty typical mule deer listed in the Boone and Crockett Club record book have been taken since 1960.

Here's another shocker. M. J. Johnson killed a typical whitetail buck in Peoria County, Illinois, in 1965. At that time it was the second-best typical whitetail ever recorded. When somebody tells you that it's too tough to bag a trophy today you might emphasize that Johnson downed his magnificent deer with bow and arrow. Johnson's second-ranked whitetail was replaced in 1971 with a buck taken near Moberly, Missouri, by Larry W. Gibson. Note that both of these outstanding whitetails were taken in heavily hunted farm country. Don't believe the stories that the big bucks were all shot off many years ago.

It's true, of course, that the deer herds of yesteryear produced more big bucks than today's herds because the average buck lived long enough to grow a big rack. But even that statement has to be qualified by making it refer to the earlier years of sport hunting. Before then—during market-hunting times—deer were slaughtered to the point of extinction in many areas. During the years of hunting for markets few male deer lived long enough to grow racks of any size. I note these highlights to point out that plenty of big bucks still exist in our deer country.

The trophy bucks of years ago received more attention because fewer people hunted deer. Hunters often camped in groups for the entire season, as opposed to today's custom of hunting for only a few days at a time. When the old-time hunters came back from camp they often brought in six to a dozen bucks which they would hang from front-yard trees to keep the meat cool. Such eye-opening sights are rare today because the modern deer hunter has his venison butchered and quick-frozen before or soon after he returns from his hunt.

But the sights of those bucks strung from camp meat poles or tree limbs have been the sources of stories of unlimited deer, and such tales originated with nonhunters who didn't have the best knowledge of what they were talking about. One of my favorite stories concerns a similar situation.

When I was a small boy, one of my older distant relatives told me that many years before I was born our local area in the northwestern part of Michigan's Lower Peninsula swarmed with whitetail deer. He told me that in the early 1900s he knew men who went out in the fall and shot all the deer they wanted just outside of town. He named some of the men, and for many years I remembered those names as if they were legend.

I learned years later that my local area actually had harbored very few deer in the early 1900s. Those men my relative named, didn't find easy hunting at all. They were seasonal farmers and teamsters who in winter used their horses to haul logs for a timber company. During the fall, however, they had plenty of time to hunt deer. Before each deer season opened they loaded their wagons with camping gear and aimed their horses toward distant boondocks. They camped and hunted strictly for the serious business of supplying their families with meat for the long winter ahead.

With their horses these men were able to get back into the remote swamps that held a few deer, and because they hunted for weeks they were able to do quite well. When they returned home they unloaded their largest bucks from their wagons, hung them from a tree limb, and let admiring townsfolk take photos. As the years passed, those photos were

Meat-pole photos like this one give many people the mistaken idea that deer were generally more plentiful in the old days. But these North Dakota deer were taken before hunting limits had been established. If hunting laws were suspended today, such photos would be common again.

handed down through generations of family members until, when I first saw them as a boy, the stories were well-established that deer were all over the place in the good old days.

I have another Michigan story that stretched the truth even more. When I first started hunting deer back in the early 1940s I always regretted not having a way of hunting in the state's Upper Peninsula (U.P.) In those days that's where the big bucks were. The Mackinac Bridge that now links the two peninsulas wasn't even a dream then; you had to get your car across the few miles of water on one of several small ferry ships. So great was the appeal of Upper Michigan deer hunting, and so limited the carrying capacities of the small ferries, that lines of cars stretched for miles back of the loading docks during the few days preceding deer season.

Many of the old-timers I talked with when I was a boy told me stories of the great hunting in the Upper Peninsula. I about cried when one old man said, "The good hunting is fading in the U.P. Too many hunters now and the habitat is diminishing. I've nailed my share of good bucks, but the

hunting is getting tougher every year. When Upper Michigan was in-
habited by Indians there were big bucks all over the place. I've heard stories of how the Indians killed deer with arrows as easily as we killed them
with rifles."

At the time I believed the old man but now I know better. The truth is
that before the coming of the white man there were almost no deer in
Michigan's north country. Records of explorers and fur traders mention a
few moose and caribou, but none of the early journals made mention of
deer. The reason is obvious to anyone who has studied the habitat and
habits of whitetails.

Deer are browsing animals. During the Indian era there was no browse
because all the timber was mature. Deer also will eat in grain fields and
truck gardens, but there was little agriculture before the white man arrived. The equation is simple: no habitat, no deer. Northern Michigan
didn't show deer until after the lumbering companies began cutting the
pine forests. In cutover areas the slashes fed fires that left the land de-
nuded, but in perfect shape to begin producing second-growth browse.

Hardwood sprouts and cedar began growing and the area became attractive to deer. The late George Shiras III, a leading authority on the
early history of Michigan deer, recorded that the animals migrated into
the U.P. from southern Wisconsin by the thousands as top habitat became
available. By the early 1800s about 80,000 deer were killed annually on
lands in the U.P. where 50 years earlier no deer were found.

As more and more of the timber was logged, some of the cutover land
was sold to early settlers. As land clearing developed so did the deer herds,
until the arrival of the market hunters who considered 200 deer per man
per season only average hunting. Such slaughter drastically reduced the
previously exploding numbers of deer. In sharp contrast to the previous
beneficial slash fires, huge forest fires followed the rape of the pine stands
by lumber companies. The fires consumed the new browse required by
deer. The effects of market hunting and ravaging fires did in the whitetails.
By 1920 Michigan's U.P. had few deer left. Farsighted citizens then de-
manded legislation to prevent complete extermination of the remaining
whitetails.

A buck law was passed and forest fire control began to be serious business. With the absence of raging fires, browse growth exploded all over the
U.P., and control of the deer harvest by hunting laws gave the whitetails a
new lease on life. Their numbers boomed. By the 1940s deer hunting in
Michigan's north country reached its peak. Since then it has been declining because the browse that produced the enormous herds has now itself
become mature forest. Michigan's Department of Natural Resources is en-
gaged in a ten-year program to bring back the habitat and rebuild the
whitetail herds. The program's goal is to increase the annual current statewide harvest from 75,000 whitetails to 200,000.

HOW DEER HERDS DEVELOPED

The history of building deer herds is a fascinating story because deer, in almost their present forms, existed in prehistoric times and lived among other forms of life that have long since become extinct. Deer have survived because they are able to adapt to change so long as they have suitable habitat. Another factor, their ability to prosper in proximity to man, means that deer herds can be built in conjunction with modern land-use plans that would spell extinction to such species as wild sheep, buffalo, and wolves.

An interesting example of how deer and concentrated human activity can go together is found in Delaware, a small state surrounded by the eastern megalopolis.

"Our deer herd thrives despite increasing pressures from urbanization," H. Lloyd Alexander, Jr., the state's Supervisor of Wildlife, told me. "The only deer-management problem we face is one of under-harvest. As areas become closed to hunting because of urbanization, deer populations build to considerable levels. Deer management in Delaware has always included either-sex hunting. We feel that either-sex hunting is the only way to control our herd, and that it is essential to modern management."

The key to all of today's healthy deer herds is modern management by knowledgeable deer biologists. Consider the situation in Kansas, where both whitetails and mule deer once were common. With the plowing of native grasslands, extensive grazing of livestock, and the lack of adequate legislation protecting deer, the population declined until both species were considered extinct between 1904 and 1933.

The following years saw a limited number of introductions of deer by private individuals and by the Fish and Game Commission. Undoubtedly some deer migrated into Kansas because of stocking and redistribution programs in neighboring states. With a complete ban on hunting, the herd grew slowly until 1956 when there were an estimated 3,000 deer in the state. Then the population increased at the rate of about 30 percent per year till 1964, with deer being found in every county. The rapidly exploding population began to cause local crop damage problems and the highway kill was becoming a major headache.

An effort had to be made at some kind of control and the only logical approach was a hunting season. In 1965 an archery season was authorized for October 1 to November 15, and a firearms season from December 11 through December 15. All hunting would be on a permit basis. Archery permits were mailed to all applicants, but gun permits were limited to 4,575. After the planning was over and the permits were issued, game officials and hunters alike wondered what would happen to deer that had never been hunted.

The result was that the deer herd continued to increase even though many of the animals ended up in hunters' freezers. As the years passed the hunting continued to improve. In 1973 Kansas hunters harvested nearly 4,100 deer. That's startling when you recall that as late as 1956 the state had only 3,000 deer. Statewide deer hunter success in 1973 averaged 39 percent, an impressive figure anywhere in the nation.

And the boom continues. The 4,575 gun permits offered in Kansas in 1965 expanded to 10,065 in 1974. The herd is in excellent shape and continues to produce bumper crops of fawns. The Kansas story shows what can be done by deer managers, and why your future as a deer hunter looks far better than the future of other big-game hunters.

Another success story comes from Missouri. Both the deer harvest and the number of hunters in that state have doubled in the past decade. Still, deer biologists feel that at least part of the state, the timbered Ozarks, could double the deer herd that was present in 1974. In that section hunters take less than two deer per square mile of forest. Biologists believe there is potential for perhaps twenty-five deer per square mile in the Ozarks where now there might be five to ten. In 1973, for the first time in Missouri's modern deer-hunting history, the northern part of the state topped the Ozarks in harvest. How do biologists feel about that? For one thing, they acknowledge that northern Missouri has progressed farther than anyone would have believed possible when the first deer were stocked there. Statewide, in 1975, Missouri deer hunters took 38,149 deer through the first two days of the state's 9-day season, nearly 5,000 more than the highest previous total for an entire season.

Unlike northern Michigan, Kentucky was loaded with deer during the era of early settlers. Daniel Boone never had trouble living off the land, and much of the meat he ate was venison. Years later, Audubon often mentioned the vast numbers of deer he saw in Kentucky.

However, for reasons only partly known, Kentucky's deer dwindled rapidly from the early 1900s to shortly after World War II. By that time the total whitetail herd numbered only a few thousand animals. Open seasons had by then been outlawed. But though most of the state contained no deer at all, Mammoth Cave National Park had so many of the animals they were considered a nuisance.

Kentucky's modern deer-management program got off the ground when hundreds of deer were live-trapped in the Park and relocated in groups of about fifty in scattered areas around the state. Biologists hoped the nucleus herds would adapt to the new territories and multiply. The deer did just that, and the program was so successful that Kentucky went from a non-deer to a deer-hunting state in little more than a decade. The state's first modern deer season was held in 1956. In 1961, 11,650 hunters killed 2,710 deer. By 1973 the numbers of deer hunters had increased to 40,000, the herd had multiplied to 60,000, and the harvest had jumped to 6,500.

Deer-management programs have been great successes in many states, but what has happened in Texas is almost enough to boggle the mind.

From the early 1900s through the late 1920s there were few deer left in Texas. The future for deer hunters looked dismal. Today, the Texas herd numbers 3,500,000 whitetails and 150,000 mule deer, far and away the largest of any state in the nation. The deer bag limit is two per license in most parts of the state, and the season lasts for over a month. Texas has so many deer it's begging for hunters. How could such an astounding circumstance take place in just a few decades? I got most of the details from research carried on by Eugene A. Walker of the Texas Game and Fish Commission.

Years ago, as the human population in the state increased, the great and famous cattle empire was founded. Cattle production reached its peak between 1880 and 1890, with the result that many of the major cattle ranges in the state were overgrazed. Sheep and goats were brought in to utilize the scant forage that remained.

With the introduction of sheep and goats came a need for predator control, and ranchers turned to traps and hounds in efforts to reduce losses to livestock. But the hounds much preferred to run deer than the wolves, coyotes, bobcats, and cougars at which control efforts were aimed. To prevent this, deer were shot on sight. Thus, wide areas in the state were virtually depleted of deer.

By the 1920s the deer population in Texas had reached a very low level. But by this time a few conservation-minded landowners and sportsmen initiated efforts to preserve existing deer and provide means for increasing their numbers. Legislation was enacted to afford greater protection to deer in certain portions of the state, while in others the processes of elimination of the deer continued.

With the increased protection of brood stock, and disappearance of the big livestock empires, deer began a comeback. By the late 1930s they had reached saturation in one or two isolated parts of the state.

The Texas Game and Fish Commission initiated its first attempt to trap and transplant wild deer in the mid-1930s in Mason County. Trapping techniques later were improved, and since the program's inception more than 20,000 deer have been moved from areas of overabundance to suitable locations all over the state. The success of this transplanting program is indicated by the large number of deer now present in areas of the state where they were virtually absent in 1938.

The Federal Aid to States in Wildlife Restoration Act, the so-called Pittman-Robertson Act, was enacted by the National Congress in 1937. Under the provisions of this act a 10 percent excise tax was levied on sporting arms and ammunition. These monies were gathered in Washington, D.C., and reallocated to qualifying states. Texas was one of the first states to become eligible to receive these funds and immediately undertook the vast job of wildlife management work.

The state hired its first trained wildlife biologist and studies were immediately initiated to determine the distribution of native game species. Research work on life histories of game animals and birds was begun. Since the whitetail deer is the most important big-game animal in the state, this species has received much of the federally assisted research effort.

The first recommendation by a biologist to harvest antlerless deer along with bucks was made in 1941, but it was twelve years later, in 1953, that the first legal antlerless deer were killed by hunters in this state.

Wildlife biologists soon recognized that deer management closely parallels livestock management and that deer numbers must be controlled just as are livestock in order to prevent range depletion and subsequent extensive die-offs. A rancher who owns a thousand acres of ranch land may conceivably be able to run 100 head of cattle on such an area. At the same time, a given number of deer will be able to prosper on the same land with the cattle. Such a rancher knows that he must remove the annual increase of both sexes in his cattle herd in order to prevent overstocking. The same reasoning applies to the deer on the same area. Once the carrying capacity has been reached for either livestock or deer, the annual increase must be removed in order to protect the rancher's investment in livestock and the sportsmen's and landowner's investment in the deer.

By 1961 deer had increased in Texas enough to cause overpopulation in a large number of counties. At that time there were approximately 125 counties in the state in which the harvest of surplus antlerless deer could be allowed if the need became evident. The program for antlerless-deer harvest was carried out in 48 counties in 1961. Deer had reached extremely high numbers in 24 of these 48 counties and provisions were made for the taking of a third or bonus deer in these counties.

There still are too many deer in Texas even though the state's annual harvest is nearly 400,000. Are you welcome to hunt in Texas? I put the question to Richard A. McCune, Information and Education Director of the Texas Parks and Wildlife Department.

"We welcome all the deer hunters we can get because our harvest should be much higher in many areas," he told me. "But the problem of hunter access to the deer supply gives cause for real concern. Most of Texas is private property, and that makes it difficult for the average gunner to find a place to hunt. The harvest could be greater if we find ways to increase landowner-sportsman cooperation. That's one of our modern problems of efficient deer management. Ways and means must be found to permit the taking of 25 to 30 percent of the total deer population in normal years to insure a healthy herd."

SOME PROBLEM STATES

At this point you should understand very well why I titled this chapter "Don't Lament the Old Days." I've painted a pretty bright picture for modern hunters so far, but not all states have the deer-management programs, the lands, or the abilities to follow the examples I've mentioned. This chapter wouldn't present a true picture if I didn't discuss the situations in some other states.

As this book goes to press, one has to wonder about what's going on in California. Though the state's game officials say California harbors 1,500,000 deer (second highest figure in the nation) many of its hunters don't believe the claim.

California game officials say that early state records show deer were plentiful in the valleys and foothills during pioneer days. After the gold rush ran its course deer populations declined rapidly. The use of meat and hides by settlers was unrestricted. Free grazing on public lands caused a livestock buildup that resulted in severe overgrazing by domesticated animals.

The cycle changed when deer hunting laws were enacted and more browse became available through the ever-increasing clearing of mature stands of virgin timber. By 1940 California's deer herds numbered more than one million animals. But, by 1950, the trend reversed again because of urban development created by the demands of the state's 20 million people. In addition, second-growth timber was maturing and crowding out much of the browse required by deer.

Some California game officials privately admit that the state probably doesn't harbor as many deer as it did in the 1940s. Yet the official estimate of the number of deer in the state given by the Department of Game and Fish is 1,500,000 animals. If the herd is obviously decreasing in numbers how could it total 500,000 more deer in 1974 than in 1940?

However, the situation may be turning for the better. The evidence comes from Ray Arnett, Director of the California Department of Fish and Game, who made some enlightening statements at the National Rifle Association annual meeting in March 1974.

"Deer populations throughout the West are decreasing and their habitat condition is worsening," Arnett said. "The decline has been particularly evident along the western slope of the Sierra-Nevada Mountains. Deteriorating range conditions and poor fawn survival are considered to be the major reasons for the decline. In addition to loss of habitat, deterioration of habitat must also be considered.

"Poorer hunting opportunity is directly translatable into hunter dissatisfaction. For the first time in memory we are getting indications of hunter disenchantment with our programs and hunting opportunities in California. The number of complaints is now significant. We are doing something about it.

"We have manipulated some 5,500 acres of deer range in California," Arnett went on. "Our controlled burning results have been encouraging. Deer use of treated areas has increased and even doubled in some areas. Our goal is to manipulate some 25,000 acres of key range. We are developing a deer-management plan to rebuild deer populations and to improve hunting opportunity to maintain and enhance habitat, and to educate the public on deer-management principles."

Other problem areas exist in portions of the prairie states, the Great Lakes states, and the East. The North Dakota story is a good example of what's going on in prairie country.

Game and Fish Department records in that state go back to 1881. The first year a hunting license was required was 1897. A bag limit of five deer per person also became law that year. In 1909 the daily and seasonal bag limit was reduced to two. By this time the once-great deer herds were already being shot off. In 1913 the deer season was closed, and it remained closed through 1920. How's that for the good old days?

Enough deer were present in the state in 1921 and 1922 to allow hunting (1 buck bag limit), but without a deer-management program the animals were shot off in a hurry. The season was closed again from 1923 through 1930. From 1931 through 1939 a deer season was held every other year. From then to 1953 there were closed seasons during six years. Permit hunting for both mule deer and whitetails was initiated in 1959. Deer management has taken hold well enough in North Dakota to permit hunting during each year since 1954.

The problem on the prairie is that deer habitat is limited, so, therefore, must be the number of deer. During soil-bank years the numbers of deer increased because habitat increased. When the program was dropped, deer became fewer. Coupled with this situation is another problem: the ever-increasing number of deer hunters. In 1945 there were only about 15,500 deer hunters in North Dakota. By 1971 that number had exploded to more than 53,000. When you consider that the deer-hunter success ratio on the prairie consistently runs about 60 percent, it's easy to realize that biologists are doing a good job of deer management. But, unless ways are devised to expand habitat, deer hunting on the prairies probably will remain the domain of a relatively few special-permit holders.

Lack of habitat is the problem in the Great Lakes states, too. But unlike the prairie states where deer licenses are limited, Michigan, Wisconsin, and Minnesota sell unlimited licenses to both residents and nonresidents. During recent years, in Michigan and Wisconsin, deer license sales numbered over a half million in each state.

The history of deer hunting in the three states closely parallels the situation in Minnesota, so I'll mention some facts from the old records of that state.

Whitetails were all over southern Minnesota when the white man came, but the human population rapidly exploded. In 1850 the state held only a little more than 6,000 people. By 1860 that figure jumped to 172,000, and it boomed to 440,000 by 1870. The entire population was categorized as rural and was concentrated in the southern and western areas. Coupled with that were unrestricted use of game for food, market hunting, and loss of deer habitat due to the clearing of land.

Still, there were so many deer that their numbers held up well. It wasn't until 1895 that a bag limit of five deer was established. In 1899 a hunting license was required for the first time. It cost 25 cents. By 1900 the southern Minnesota deer numbers greatly increased due to timber-cutting operations and the resultant growth of much browse. The situation in the north developed along the same lines I mentioned earlier in this chapter while discussing the early boom of deer populations in Michigan's Upper Peninsula.

Great changes in Minnesota's deer-management ideas occurred between 1900 and 1936. The bag limit was reduced to one deer in 1915. Market hunting had been stopped, and many restrictions were applied to sport-hunting methods. In 1923 a law was passed allowing deer hunting in only even-numbered years; it remained in force through 1941.

What happened between 1951 and 1963, compared with the 1964–1971 period, is a dramatic example of what can happen to deer in the snow states. The first period showed only one severe winter. Deer populations boomed and carried over into the beginning of the second period when a series of hard winters hit the state. The whitetail harvest neared 100,000 for 10 years in a row, and it hit an all-time high of 127,000 in 1965. Following that, the hunter take showed a marked reduction, dropping to 45,000 animals in 1970. In 1971 the season was closed. There is no better example proving that when deep snow covers the browse required by whitetails, many of the animals simply starve to death.

Minnesota's solution to rebuilding its whitetail herd is the only solution biologists say will work in the heavily forested states: creation of new deer habitat by intensive range management. The tools are increased logging (which is coming naturally because of paper shortages), controlled burning and bulldozing with enormous dozers equipped with cutting blades. Such operations open the mature forest canopy of trees and enable new browse to begin growing. If the job is done properly, just two back-to-back fawn crops with good survival would provide enough animals to double the hunting-season herd in a managed area. That's how prolific deer can be on ideal range, and that's why the future of deer hunting in states now having habitat problems could be far superior to what it is today.

The situation in New Jersey is typical of the eastern states with high human populations. Here's the picture as put together by George P. Howard, Assistant Chief of the state's Bureau of Wildlife Management.

In the early 1900s deer herds as we know them today were nonexistent in New Jersey. The deer population consisted of a few family groups of whitetails scattered through the pine oak woodlands of South Jersey.

During the period 1900 to 1915 an effort was made by the then Board of

Fish and Game Commissioners (the forerunner to the present Fish and Game Council) to increase deer populations statewide by the strict enforcement of regulations pertaining to deer, together with the reintroduction of deer in various sections of the state. Deer were purchased from Pennsylvania and Michigan, as well as from private deer preserves in New Jersey, and released in suitable habitat.

The fact that habitat conditions at that time were highly favorable and could support a much greater deer herd, plus the effects of an expanded law enforcement effort resulted in a rapidly increasing deer population which probably reached the carrying capacity of the deer range as early as 1935 in certain areas of the state (the central pines area of Ocean and Burlington counties).

The state's first modern season was authorized in 1909. The first statewide harvest of antlerless as well as antlered deer since 1915 took place in 1961. Still, the herd continued to grow. Today, practically all deer habitat in New Jersey is presently supporting a deer herd either at or in excess of its carrying capacity. But the state is losing an estimated 45 square miles of deer habitat each year to housing and development alone.

So the problem in the East and some other areas I'll discuss in Chapter 3, is more a problem of people management than deer management. If, in the future, people value wildlife more than they do today, deer hunting may get better. It will get worse if the increasing human population continues making more and more demands on the habitat. It should be noted that diminishing and deteriorating deer habitat is a nationwide problem, even though it's most serious in the East.

Though I've concentrated on telling how much of the future of better deer hunting keys on habitat problems, we may also produce more deer with improved technical knowledge in such fields as disease control. One of the greatest examples of the possibilities has been the successful screwworm control program in southern states. Developed by agriculture interests, this breakthrough made the livestock industry more profitable and at the same time made possible the dynamic deer restoration program across the South. Today, many of the southeastern states have some of the largest deer herds in the United States. Nationwide, regardless of our problems, we now have more deer than when the Pilgrims landed.

By 1885, according to the National Shooting Sports Foundation, there were only some 350,000 whitetail deer south of Canada. Today there are at least 12,000,000 in the lower 48 states. That's reason enough not to lament the old days.

2
Your Odds on
Bagging a Buck

During the past several years I've encountered some interesting examples of what's happening to deer hunting. Last fall I couldn't get it out of my mind that some of the best hunting techniques of years ago have become far less successful. It also seemed apparent that some of the better hunting states of decades past aren't so hot today.

During the winter I wondered how I could determine if my ideas were valid. I decided the answer was in getting opinions from hunting experts and game officials.

I developed a three-page questionnaire with questions pertaining to the how-to of today's deer hunting and where the best action is found. I mailed the questionnaires to game officials and deer-hunting veterans in each of our forty-eight contiguous states and our neighboring provinces of Canada.

Before I get into the answers to my questionnaire I should mention some experiences that prompted development of the project.

My son Jack turned fourteen in 1972. That's the legal age for deer hunting in Michigan, my home state. I had a tough time deciding where I should take him for his first deer hunt. One day during the summer I discussed the problem with Warren Holmes, a veteran of more than three decades of chasing whitetails. Warren owns a cabin and 300 acres of remote woodlands along the headwaters of the Pere Marquette River 50 miles from my home.

"I'll put you and the boy on a stand," he told me. "I've got some good spots, you'll see plenty of deer."

I didn't particularly like the idea of putting Jack on a stand. Teenagers don't have the patience to sit still long, and that's a must when taking a stand. I assumed the relatively remote area would be lightly hunted, so I told Warren it might be better if we did some stillhunting.

He laughed as if I'd told a joke.

"Look," he told me, "this area will be crawling with hunters. The deer become spooked as soon as the hunting army moves into the woods. There's little chance of getting a shot while stillhunting. The trick is to take advantage of other hunters moving deer through the area. If you sit long enough in a good spot Jack will get his chance. The old-time stalkers and stillhunters couldn't kill a buck in this area today."

Jack did get his chance. The first deer we saw was a six-pointer that was spooked past us by other hunters. He didn't offer a very good shot. The boy missed him.

Later that day another member of our four-man hunting group killed a fine buck from a stand. Warren got his opportunity the next morning. I won't forget what he said when we looked at the venison hanging from the buck pole near his cabin.

"The average hunter-success ratio in this area is about 10 percent because there are more hunters each year. Three of the four of us have had good shots at bucks in only 1½ days. That should tell you something about the value of hunting from stands in heavily hunted country."

Ten years ago I took a mule-deer hunt in Wyoming. We worked the thickets along creek beds and draws in the bottom of valleys near a ranch. We jumped plenty of deer. I killed a fine three-pointer (western count) the first day of the hunt.

Two years ago I hunted similar terrain in Montana. The rancher who was hosting me said that between 50 and 150 deer could be seen in the huge field behind his house on moonlit nights. I expected to hunt near that field the next morning. I was surprised to learn that easy hunting was out. We would have to climb far up into the foothills long before dawn. Why?

"Mule deer aren't as dumb as they used to be," my host explained. "Lots of hunters come out West now. The deer are reacting to the pressure. They'll leave that field before dawn and climb the mountain to bed down. We've got to be up there to intercept them when they move up the canyon trails. We don't get much shooting in the valleys any more."

That statement emphasizes another trend of modern deer hunting.

Twenty years ago when I'd ask a local hunter where he got his buck he'd invariably mention some area close to home. In recent years a good share of my townsmen have come up with an answer something like this: "I don't hunt deer in Michigan any more. Now I head for the western states where game is plentiful."

Last year during a Colorado deer hunt I began discovering that the popular opinion, "The West is where the deer are," might not be all that correct.

One of the hunters in my group was Ken Callaway, an outdoor-movie producer from Houston, Texas. He surprised me when he said, "We've got so many deer in Texas our bag limit is three per season in the area I hunt. The only reason I came to Colorado is because I've never hunted mule deer."

A few months later I talked to another hunter who brought up the subject of deer hunting in Florida, a state not many gunners would recognize as good deer country. "Tell you what," the man told me. "Deer hunter success ratios in Florida average 30 percent. We've got about half-a-million deer in our state."

Those are the types of experiences that made me ponder some questions. Could it really be that Florida has more deer and a higher hunter success ratio than some of the more well-known deer states? Is it true that hunting from stands produces more deer in heavily-hunted country than any other system? Further, what are the best systems to use in various parts of the United States?

Such questions led to others. I wondered what states have the largest deer herds and the highest hunter-success ratios. Do game departments in the best states encourage nonresident hunters? Where can a nonresident get information on any given state's deer hunting?

I reasoned that if I had the answers to such questions I'd have a pretty good picture of what modern deer hunting is really all about. What follows is the information gleaned from my project.

Let's start with the question of which states harbor the most deer. The answer may surprise you. Texas leads the list with a herd of 3,500,000 whitetails and 150,000 mule deer. Next in line, and far below Texas, is California with 1,500,000 mule deer. The only other state with more than 1,000,000 deer is Alabama. Thirty-two states boast herds in excess of 100,000 and—another shocker—ten of those states are in the Southeast. It's interesting to note that some of the western states, well-known for their great deer hunting, don't harbor the largest herds. Colorado, for instance, ranks 14th on the list.

Does the above information suggest that the states harboring the largest herds are *not* necessarily the best states to hunt? You bet it does, with the exception of Texas which reflects a special situation which I'll discuss later. The hunter success ratio in California is only 11 percent. Some eastern states have gun-hunter success ratios of less than 10 percent, and that's another shocker when you consider that the *bowhunter* success ratio in 10 states is 10 percent or better.

A few years ago the Midwest states of Michigan, Wisconsin, and Minnesota offered some of the best deer hunting in the nation. Not any more.

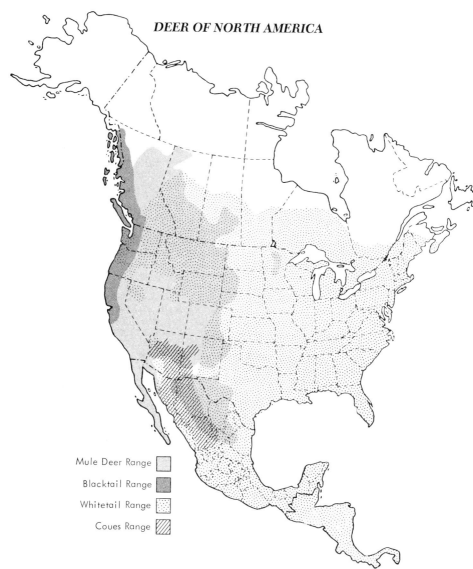

DEER OF NORTH AMERICA

Mule Deer Range
Blacktail Range
Whitetail Range
Coues Range

This shows the ranges of 1) the basic mule deer, 2) the Columbian blacktail, a mule deer subspecies of relatively pure strain, 3) the basic whitetail, and 4) the Coues deer, a small whitetail subspecies of relatively pure strain. Naturalists recognize many other distinct subspecies within the overall ranges shown, but these four are the ones recognized in the Boone and Crockett Club system within the North American Big Game Awards Program. For all except the blacktail, awards are given in both "typical" and "nontypical" (abnormal) categories. Due to the comparatively low harvest figure for blacktails, there have not been enough nontypical heads to merit a separate trophy category.

WHITETAIL   **COUES DEER**

The photos show the antler and tail features that distinguish the four hunting categories of deer.

    The basic mule deer and the blacktail subspecies both display the bifurcated (branched) antlers on each side and a brow tine that normally measures only an inch or two in length. Each of the branches forms a "Y." The tail of the mule deer is white except for a black tip, and the underside is hairless. The blacktail's tail is dark with a white underside.

    The basic whitetail and the Coues deer, a smaller subspecies, display a distinctive main beam on each side, from which tines extend. On older bucks, the brow tine may be as long as many of the other tines. Generally, the whitetail's main beams sweep outward and forward. Whereas, those of the Coues buck tend to hook forward, toward one another, and form a more compact rack. Both deer sport a tapered tail, broad at the base, that is white on the underside. When alarmed, both deer normally hold the tail high and flair the rump patch—thus, the name "whitetail."

MULE DEER   **BLACKTAIL**

Michigan gunners recently posted a measly 11 percent success ratio. Wisconsin ranks slightly higher, and Minnesota's figure of 25 percent reflects that state's any-deer laws. Hunters in the deer-rich southeastern states don't do too well either, except where hunting with dogs is permitted. Florida is the top example. Game officials in that state told me that 70 percent of their deer harvest goes to hunters with dogs.

The ten top states, from a deer-hunters success standpoint, are all west of the Mississippi River. With the exception of Oregon they're all in the prairie and intermountain area. Most of the best states allow nonresident deer hunting by quota only. This last fact points out two important aspects.

One, deer are easier to hunt in the prairie and intermountain states. Two, game officials in those states are well aware of the value of their deer herds and they're not going to permit over-harvest by unlimited numbers of hunters. In fact, the picture isn't too bright for nonresidents.

"Our nonresident deer license quota has been declining in recent years," said George Kaminski of the Wyoming Game and Fish Department. "In 1971 it was 50,000. In 1972 and '73 it was 48,000. We're dropping it to 39,820 for 1974. The drops are results of declining mule-deer populations in some areas."

In 1973 Utah cut its nonresident deer licenses down to only 20,000. In Saskatchewan nonresidents have been restricted to hunting in specified zones. South Dakota's Harvey H. Pietz, Executive Assistant of the state's Division of Game and Fish, told me, "We will go to a limited number of permits in the Black Hills if we get too much hunting pressure from nonresidents. Out-of-stater permits are already very limited in our prairie zone."

In most of the best deer-hunting states the demand for hunting opportunity already exceeds the supply. That's a very important point to remember if you plan to hunt in one of the top hunter-success ratio states.

The key to getting a license is to plan a year ahead. Write the game department in the state you wish to hunt and ask for details on how to apply for a nonresident deer license, then get your application in as early as it will be accepted. Consider this: Many Wyoming nonresident deer licenses are sold out in spring, months before hunting seasons begin.

The picture in Texas is so different from other states that it warrants special mention. If you can work out some "ifs" your odds of bagging a buck in Texas zoom to about 80 percent. Parts of the state have so many deer it's no problem for a good hunter to score, *if* he can find a place to hunt. Most of the good deer country is privately owned. Many of the ranchers book deer hunters on a fee basis, many others lease deer-hunting rights. If you can make contacts—best bets are chambers of commerce in the south-Texas brush country from San Antonio to Del Rio to Brownsville, and in Llano and Mason counties—you'll have great hunting and you won't have to worry about getting a license.

"We welcome all the deer hunters we can get" Richard A. McCune, of the Texas Parks and Wildlife Department, told me. "Our harvest should be much higher for proper management of overpopulated herds in many areas. Licenses are unlimited and good for taking up to three deer in many parts of the state."

The only more astonishing bag limit than that is the one offered in Alabama. Buy a deer license in that state and you can shoot one deer each day of the entire season. The catch is that Alabama's deer aren't very easy to hunt, and only 17 percent of the state's deer hunters go home with venison. That statistic brings us to the question of why relatively few hunters score in the deer-rich southeastern states. I put the question to some experts.

Jack Crockford, Director of the Georgia Game and Fish Division, had this to say: "Many property owners in the South won't allow hunting except by family and friends. That means a lot of good deer country is underhunted. Also, our terrain is difficult to hunt. The swamps and woods are thick, the advantages are with the deer."

Charlie Elliott, Southern Field Editor of *Outdoor Life* magazine, brought up another important point "There are more novices in the woods today," he began. "Most people have more money and more leisure time. Some guys figure they'll go out and shoot a deer with little idea of how to go about it. The expert will get a deer in the South because he knows how to hunt our spooky whitetails. It takes a lot more skill to score here than out West where the novice has a better chance."

The section of my questionnaire dealing with best deer-hunting techniques brought other suprising replies. The answers blow some large holes in many of the popular theories on how to hunt deer.

I asked the experts to rate the harvest in their states in terms of percentage of total kill taken through use of the following techniques: stillhunting, hunting from stands, stalking, driving (including gang drives), calling (including horn rattling), hunting with dogs, snow tracking and hunting from horseback. Note that I did not ask how most deer hunters hunt, but rather which method the successful hunters used.

Though I suspected that hunting from stands in heavily hunted whitetail areas of the East and Midwest would rate high, I was astonished at some of the final figures. In Missouri, for instance, Dean Murphy, Assistant Chief of the state's Game Division, reported that 95 percent of the Missouri deer harvest was taken by hunters working from stands. I thought Murphy's figure was an error, so I asked him to verify it.

"I stand by the 95 percent," he replied. "Many unsuccessful hunters use various techniques, but the vast majority of our deer are taken by hunters on stands. Our aerial surveys show that most hunters sit quietly on stands till abouut 8:00 a.m., then start stillhunting, walking along roads and moving to cars. The fellow who goes on a stand before dawn and stays there when other hunters begin moving around is the fellow who takes a deer. Most of the deer are moved by impatient hunters."

Results of my survey show that all game officials in the East and Midwest states except Maine and Iowa rate hunting from stands as responsible for over half of their deer harvests. In the same states the driving technique ranked second with about 25 percent, except in Iowa where it scored 70 percent. When it's realized that most deer taken on drives are downed by standers ahead of the drivers you realize how important it is to know how to select a stand and how to hunt from it.

Statistics supplied by William C. Mincher of Maine's Department of Inland Fisheries and Game show that 60 percent of that state's whitetail harvest is taken by stillhunters. Standers ranked second at 30 percent. Because of the heavy influence of Maine, stillhunting in the Northeast accounts for 25 percent of the deer harvest. By contrast, stillhunting rates only 11 percent on similar terrain in north-central states. Stalking in all of the northern whitetail states is mostly a waste of time, accounting for only about 8 percent of the harvest.

Stands get the nod in southeastern states too, by a whopping 65 percent except in areas where hunting with dogs is legal. Stillhunting and stalking account for about 10 percent of the harvest. Driving rates about the same at 11.8 percent.

All of these figures point out that the average gunner going after whitetails east of the Mississippi River had best forget about stillhunting, snow-tracking, and stalking techniques and concentrate on learning how to hunt from a stand. If you can't put up with sitting still your next best bet is to organize a drive, especially in the snow-belt states.

The picture changes west of the Mississippi, especially in mule-deer country where the terrain is more open. In prairie areas your odds on nailing a buck are about even, regardless of the major hunting technique in which you specialize. Here's how my composite figures came out: stillhunting, 20 percent; stands, 26.5 percent; stalking, 29.8 percent; driving, 20 percent; snow-tracking and horseback hunting combined, 4.7 percent.

This is as good a place as any to mention that the techniques of snow-tracking and horseback hunting, very popular years ago, don't account for many of the deer killed today. The highest ratings I got for both systems came from the intermountain states at 5.8 percent and 7.4 percent, respectively.

Unless you hunt in Texas, you can forget deer calling—including horn rattling—as a good means of collecting venison. For some reason Texas rates by itself in this category. Many of its whitetails are taken by hunters rattling antlers. Even so, 50 percent of Texas deer are taken by hunters working from stands.

Stillhunting rates as the best technique in the intermountain states where it accounts for 42 percent of the deer harvest. The next best system is stalking at 27.4 percent. In this area only 10.3 percent of the deer are taken from stands. Driving rates about the same. So if you hunt the top deer states in the West it's best to learn how to stillhunt and stalk.

Some of the most surprising statistics showing up on my questionnaire were the high success ratios for archers in Midwest and intermountain states. I followed up my survey with some questions. Here's a typical answer:

"I think the archer success in mountain states is high because of the many opportunities bowmen have to shoot at deer," said Gary T. Myers, Big Game Supervisor for Colorado's Division of Wildlife. "Once while I was bowhunting on the Uncompahgre Plateau I saw thirty-six bucks in one day. A fellow from New York hunted near my camp and he couldn't believe the number of deer he saw. In the West a man has a chance to see lots of deer, and he usually has a chance to stalk them."

The archery take also rates high in such midwestern states as Iowa, South Dakota, Kansas, and Nebraska where wooded terrain is often found in small patches. It's relatively easy to scout these small-cover areas, determine deer travel routes, and ambush the animals from stands. Archer success ratios are low in the heavily forested states east of the Mississippi for the opposite reason: It's simply too difficult to pinpoint deer and get close to them. It's interesting to reflect that years ago just about all deer hunters felt that trying to kill a deer with an arrow was simply too difficult anywhere. Today, hundreds of thousands of successful archers know better.

Another trend of the times came on strong as I tallied results of my survey. Years ago the game departments in the better deer states did plenty of promotional work to attract nonresident deer hunters. Not so today. Many state game officials are now worrying about too many deer hunters, rather than too few, and the quota states no longer have any problems selling their high-priced nonresident deer licenses.

Costs are up in game departments as they are everywhere else. As a result, public-relations divisions in many game departments are no longer supplying the reams of information to prospective nonresident hunters that they used to. Some of your best bets now are tourist associations, state travel agencies, and—in western states—outfitters and guides.

The increased numbers of nonresident hunters in the West has meant increased numbers of outfitters and guides. The good ones are more than anxious to supply you with all the information you need. Game departments in most western states continue to supply names and addresses of licensed guides and outfitters for the asking.

STATES AND PROVINCES WITH OVER 100,000 DEER

TEXAS	3,279,000	MINNESOTA	450,000	MAINE	225,000
CALIFORNIA	1,500,000	ARKANSAS	420,000	S. DAKOTA	220,000
ALABAMA	1,000,000	MISSISSIPPI	410,000	S. CAROLINA	215,000
OREGON	973,000	NEW YORK	410,000	SASKATCHEWAN	212,000
MICHIGAN	875,000	LOUISIANA	375,000	UTAH	200,000
WISCONSIN	675,000	COLORADO	352,000	W. VIRGINIA	200,000
PENNSYLVANIA	600,000	VIRGINIA	330,000	GEORIGA	200,000
FLORIDA	540,000	WYOMING	325,000	ARIZONA	180,000
N. CAROLINA	500,000	NEW MEXICO	300,000	TENNESSEE	140,000
WASHINGTON	470,000	IDAHO	250,000	NEVADA	135,000

PERCENTAGES OF HUNTER SUCCESS IN STATES AND PROVINCES

This chart shows percentages of hunter success in states and provinces. Note that the top ten areas are all west of the Mississippi River. The Texas figure may be misleading since the best hunting is often done on private property. For license-holders who find good places to hunt in Texas, the success rate is about 80 percent. Figures were not available for Louisiana, New York, or Oklahoma.

MONTANA	79%	CONNECTICUT	24%
UTAH	76%	ILLINOIS	22%
S. DAKOTA	63%	S. CAROLINA	20%
WYOMING	60%	VIRGINIA	20%
NEBRASKA	55%	ARIZONA	18%
SASKATCHEWAN	54%	MISSOURI	18%
COLORADO	52%	NEW BRUNSWICK	18%
N. DAKOTA	51%	ALABAMA	17%
MANITOBA	50%	DELAWARE	15%
OREGON	46%	WISCONSIN	15%
IOWA	43%	KENTUCKY	14%
NEVADA	42%	ARKANSAS	11%
TEXAS	40%	CALIFORNIA	11%
NOVA SCOTIA	38%	GEORGIA	11%
BRIT. COLUMBIA	37%	MICHIGAN	11%
MARYLAND	35%	QUEBEC	11%
N. CAROLINA	33%	INDIANA	10%
FLORIDA	31%	PENNSYLVANIA	9%
NEW MEXICO	31%	NEW HAMPSHIRE	8%
IDAHO	30%	OHIO	8%
KANSAS	30%	VERMONT	8%
MISSISSIPPI	29%	W. VIRGINIA	8%
MAINE	25%	TENNESSEE	7%
MINNESOTA	25%	NEW JERSEY	6%
WASHINGTON	25%	RHODE ISLAND	6%

WHAT HUNTING METHODS WORK BEST IN DIFFERENT SECTIONS

Drives		Stalking	
NORTHEAST	18.2%	NORTHEAST	8%
SOUTHEAST	11.8%	SOUTHEAST	6.9%
N. CENTRAL	28.8%	N. CENTRAL	7.5%
S. CENTRAL	10%	S. CENTRAL	10.2%
PRAIRIE	20%	PRAIRIE	28.8%
INTER-MT.	9.8%	INTER-MT.	27.4%
FAR WEST	32.4%	FAR WEST	26%

Stillhunting		Stands	
NORTHEAST	25%	NORTHEAST	44.1%
SOUTHEAST	5.5%	SOUTHEAST	65%
N. CENTRAL	11%	N. CENTRAL	53.5%
S. CENTRAL	30%	S. CENTRAL	49%
PRAIRIE	20%	PRAIRIE	26.5%
INTER-MT.	42%	INTER-MT.	10.3%
FAR WEST	22%	FAR WEST	16%

3

Your Future as a
Deer Hunter

If your experiences are anything like mine, you're seeing more and more of your hunting opportunities going down the drain. Will the future get worse?

I live in a small town in the northwestern section of Michigan's Lower Peninsula. This part of the state is considered to be top deer-hunting country. Let me tell you what has happened to some of that country.

When I was a teenager I hunted whitetails along river flats outside of town. Those flats are now dumping grounds for a chemical company. Another area that contained acres of wild blueberry bushes always harbored deer. Today the blueberries have been replaced by ranch homes.

I shot my first three whitetails in a section of wildland along the shore of one of our nearby inland lakes. If I fired my rifle in those woodlands today I'd be asked to leave in a hurry. The area is now all private and is dotted with expensive summer homes, posted, and patrolled by a caretaker.

Nationwide it's obvious that game habitat has diminished. The last annual Environmental Quality Index released by the National Wildlife Federation reports that more than one million acres of wildlife habitat are lost each year. If you're a long-time hunter you know of many places where you used to hunt that are now out of bounds. Even if they weren't out of bounds the deer may be gone. And there are some important reasons other than the boom in subdivisions, increased agriculture, and growing human populations.

Ray Lyons, a past president of the Colorado Guides and Outfitters Association and a knowledgeable conservationist, points out one reason why deer are becoming fewer in some areas. "In the West we have lands that are overgrazed and waters that show poor fishing," he told me. "If the fish-and-game boys want to rejuvenate a mountain lake they can poison it out, restock it, and produce great fishing in a year of so. But if they want to rejuvenate overgrazed land it will take ten to fifteen years to bring the range back to where it's suitable habitat for deer. It's far easier to produce good fishing than it is to produce good hunting."

An even more discouraging subject came to light during a discussion I had with a game official in a midwestern state who asked me not to identify him or his state. "I don't want our deer hunters to become alarmed yet," he told me, "but we're going to be facing a new situation if the number of deer hunters continues to increase. Our herd is getting close to being overshot. If the trend continues we'll have to eliminate nonresident hunting and we'll have to license residents on a lottery basis. That will come as a shocker because this state has offered unlimited numbers of deer licenses for many years."

Let's look at the situation in some other states.

In 1970 there were 32,300 deer permits authorized in Nebraska. For the 1974 season that number dropped to 25,000. In 1970 more than 1,000 permits went unused because no hunters requested them. When it came time for nonresidents to apply in 1974, only three of the sixteen management units remained unfilled and permits were issued to very few nonresidents.

To get more details on what is happening to the state's deer-hunting picture I asked Jon Farrar of the Information Division of the Nebraska Game and Parks Commission to put some questions to Karl Menzel, the commission's big-game specialist. Here are the questions and Menzel's answers:

The number of permits authorized has been declining for three years now. Last year hunter success increased 11.7 percent over the 1972 season. Do you think that lowering the number of permits will mean better hunting and bigger bucks taken in the future?

"It could, but the primary reason for the jump in hunter success during the 1973 season was ideal weather conditions. The weather was poor during the 1972 season. Good hunting weather always means a larger harvest. However, as for the fewer permits, bigger bucks theory, I don't have much doubt that it will work. It's one of the signs of the times."

Is the day of the nonresident deer hunter in Nebraska gone?

"Last year we had four or five units with permits left over after the resident application. I guess we had fewer than 400 nonresident deer hunters

An increasing number of women are hunting deer. Many of them have become expert in all phases of the hunting art.

last year. This year there were only three units with any permits available when the nonresident application period opened: Sandhills, Platte, and Upper Platte. A few years ago applications used to string in slowly over several months, but in recent years most of them have come in the first few days after they can be accepted. I would say that nonresident hunting for deer in Nebraska is out unless we offer more permits. Even if we did return to the peak number we have a greater resident demand now."

This year, 1974, is the first year that deer hunters in Nebraska have been legally ineligible for a permit in the Wahoo, Elkhorn and Blue units if they held permits in those units the previous year. Do you expect this regulation to spread to other units, and that sometime in the future most deer hunters will be subject to alternate-year hunting in their favorite units?

"Yes, very definitely. Based on current guidelines we can expect other units to be included, perhaps in the next year or two. We simply have more hunters applying in some units than we can satisfy fairly without going to this type of regulation."

Do you think the time is coming when there may be a 2-year waiting period between eligible years in some of the high-demand units?

"I wouldn't expect it to get to the point where a hunter will be excluded for more than one year, unless it would be in one or two very specific areas."

What does the deer hunter have to look forward to 10 years from now?

"I look for it to be hard to find a place to hunt, hard to get a permit, and in some places, lower deer numbers because of loss of habitat due to increased demand for agricultural products.

"Most of the land in all units but the Pine Ridge is privately owned. Generally, permission to hunt deer is harder to come by than permission to hunt upland or small game. Modern landowners regard deer on their land a little more personally than they do pheasants or squirrels. The difficulty in finding a place to hunt, coupled with a greater demand for fewer permits, makes getting into the field almost as difficult as finding a deer. The day of sending in for a permit a couple of weeks before the season, driving out to your unit, and uncasing the rifle is gone from Nebraska."

Sounds bad, doesn't it? Here's more bleak news from another prairie state.

"Several problems have been plaguing North Dakota's whitetail herd," a game official told me. "Of most importance, the number of deer hunters has been increasing each year. A record 58,434 deer licenses sold in 1973. As the numbers of hunters have increased their success ratios have decreased. This means that more hunters are going without a deer each year.

"Another problem is rooted in the fact that as more hunters are forced to hunt bucks only there are fewer bucks to go around. A recent winter survey showed the ratio of bucks per every 100 does was only 13. The 12-year average has been 36 bucks for every 100 does. There are fewer adult bucks in the whitetail population.

"Also adding to the problem every year has been the loss of wintering areas and general deer habitat because of increasing agricultural programs, strip mining, oil development, and overgrazing of pastures."

In the far West the situation isn't a lot different, particularly in California. Consider the following letter I received recently from Ray Arnett, Director of that state's Department of Fish and Game:

"California is particularly concerned with the future of the deer hunter. The deer in California is our most important species as far as the hunter is concerned, and we are faced with some real problems in losses of deer habitat, decline in deer herds, and reduced hunter success. Our Department has been looking into this problem to determine what can be done to reverse the downward trend in deer numbers.

"Our history shows that deer numbers in California were very low at the turn of the century. After about 1910 the population began building, stimulated by such occurrences as clearing for homestead, forest fires, logging, and other events that opened mature forests and created conditions which supported good deer forage.

"This buildup continued until the 1950s and 1960s. Since then a combination of known factors—increased fire control, drought, reservoir and highway construction, increased highway traffic, mountain subdivisions, natural succession—have combined to reduce the quantity and quality of deer habitat as well as deer numbers. Declines have taken place in herds subject to all levels of hunting.

"In spite of increasing numbers of deer hunters the hunter success stayed about the same up to 1960 because of the increase in deer numbers. However, in the last six to seven years there has been a significant drop in hunter success. Although the number of deer hunters in California has been relatively stable during the last ten to twelve years we have had problems of heavy hunting pressure in certain populated areas, and serious thought is being given to the possible need to regulate the number of hunters on a unit or area basis.

"As for the future of deer herds in California, we just do not believe that it will be possible to bring deer numbers back to what they were in the late 1940s and 1950s. However, we are hopeful that through working with the large land-management agencies, particularly the U.S. Forest Service, and through better land-use planning, where full consideration is given to the needs of deer, we can halt this decline in deer populations and improve deer numbers, deer-herd condition and hunter success."

Though some of what I've written here may sound contradictory to material in the first two chapters of this book, I mention it so that you may draw a clear picture of what is happening to deer hunting in some states. Earlier, I pointed out that deer census data tells us we have more deer in the United States today than we had when the Pilgrims landed. Well then, how does that information tie in with the gloomy picture I've painted so far in this chapter?

The point is that we do have more deer in total because some deer-management plans have been extremely successful. Management plans in some states have not been successful, but should they become successful we'll have more deer than we have today. The overall problem is that the army of hunters is increasing more rapidly than the deer herds. Overshadowing everything else is the increasing problem of finding a place to hunt as habitat decreases and parcels of posted land increase.

So what's going to happen? Let's take another look at Missouri, a state whose deer herds have boomed in recent years.

Because all species of wildlife are affected by weather conditions, land use, community growth, and pressure from sportsmen, game biologists are generally reluctant to forecast future wildlife trends. But when asked to make a long-range prediction on the future of deer hunting in Missouri, Mike Milonski, Chief of the Wildlife Division, proved optimistic.

"Knowing there is going to be a continual increase of the human population over the next twenty-five years, and that there is going to be a decrease in forest cover, I still believe the outlook for the deer hunter is excellent," Milonski said. "Our native whitetail is a hardy animal.

"I'd guess that twenty-five years from now we are going to be managing people more than we're managing deer. We'll have stricter quotas enabling us to put the gun pressure where we want it. Hunters will still be able to hunt, but the number of hunters in certain areas will be controlled.

"And, some way, we have to control the poaching problem. This isn't just a Department problem. It's a problem that has to be partially handled in local courts. There has to be a change in public opinion on the local level to make poaching an unpopular activity. The law-abiding hunter has to get more involved and make his feelings known. After all, for every deer poached the legal hunter has one less potential target. There's nothing romantic about deer poaching. These guys are the counterpart of metropolitan thieves, they contribute nothing and take what they can. In the future the average deer hunter won't stand for this nonsense."

From all of the foregoing it seems apparent that herd-management headaches and people-management headaches are definitely the trends of the future. If such problems are solved we'll have good deer hunting in most areas, and exceptional deer hunting in others.

Hunting regulations are more complex today than they were twenty-five years ago, but it seems definite that they'll get more complicated as the years go by. The more hunting pressure there is the more complex the regulations have to become. The reason is basic: the major way to avoid overharvest is to control gun pressure. Make up your mind that you're going to have to put up with more forms to fill out, more regulations to read, and more laws by which to abide.

I queried many game biologists and deer managers for their thoughts about more restrictive regulations while I was preparing the material for this chapter. Here is a representative reply from James J. McDonough, Game Biologist for the Massachusetts Division of Fisheries and Game:

"By issuing a regulated number of permits per county it will be possible to control the number of deer harvested and enable manipulation of the deer population within a county for the benefit of all hunters," began McDonough.

"I do not enjoy regulating and restricting deer hunting, but to allow an unlimited and uncontrolled number of deer hunters into limited deer range is to invite disaster to the sport. I believe it is the duty of the Division of Fisheries and Game to impose rules and regulations.

"I believe that one of the limiting factors of future deer populations will be water and/or access to water. Watersheds and reservoirs may be potential deer-hunting areas in Massachusetts. In such limited areas, it will be necessary to limit the number of deer hunters."

But McDonough, like most other deer biologists, is optimistic about the future of deer hunting, even in the East where human populations are high.

"Looking back over forty-two years of deer hunting, I cannot say, other than natural plant succession, there have been any drastic changes in the deer producing-counties, with a few exceptions. The changes that I note were slow and required some readjustment. For instance, in the mid-1950s the Massachusetts Turnpike was built through the heart of some of our best deer range. The harvest dropped for a couple of years, but we will never know whether the declining harvest was due to the influence of the Turnpike or poor deer management such as unregulated harvest of deer of either sex. Plymouth County used to produce good deer harvests; today we have more deer reported killed by cars than by legal harvest. Sure there are more people, homes, shopping centers, dogs, and roads today, but the backbone of our deer range is still intact.

"Cape Cod (Barnstable County) with its summer traffic and people is still producing a healthy harvest of antlered males each year and should continue. I expect the deer harvest on Nantucket and Martha's Vineyard islands to level off in the next two years. Both islands should produce a sustained harvest for at least the next twenty years, if a limited number of hunters are allowed to harvest the deer on a controlled basis.

"The backbone of the Massachusetts deer herd is located in Berkshire, Franklin, Hampshire, Hampden and north Worcester counties. I feel that at the present rate of amoebic urban sprawl in Massachusetts, deer hunters can continue to enjoy deer hunting in these counties. However, it may be necessary to limit or control the number of hunters."

In short, deer biologists all over the country told me that deer can be managed for population growth to a much higher degree than most other species of wildlife. Game managers, given an adequate degree of hunter control, can insure that deer hunting will be with us far into the future.

The key part of that last paragraph is *"deer can be managed for population growth."* Mismanagement can have a devastating effect.

To cite one example of mismanagement, in 1906 President Theodore Roosevelt, who also was one of the country's top hunters and foremost pioneer conservationists, set aside the beautiful Kaibab Plateau area on the rim of Grand Canyon in the northwest corner of Arizona as the Kaibab National Game Refuge.

In 1906 it was excusable that people—from those in the White House on down—should be unaware that the simple and obvious mathematics of cows in a pasture applied with equal relentlessness to deer. In less than twenty years deer the Kaibab would create one of the worst game disasters this country has ever seen.

Between 1906 and 1910 some 600 mountain lions plus hundreds of smaller predators were done away with in the Kaibab. And during those years the refuge was kept closed to hunting, as game refuges were supposed to be. When warning signs of an impending disaster became clear, no one heeded them.

By 1910 the deer herd had climbed to about 4,000. Fourteen years later it numbered 100,000, and the food supply was gone. In the next two winters 60,000 Kaibab deer died of starvation.

Today the range is still far from what it was when the whole disastrous chain of events began in 1906, and there is little likelihood that it will ever make a complete comeback. Over the years thousands of tons of the Kaibab's best topsoil have been washed down the Colorado River and added to the mud and silt at Lake Mead and has shown up as far away as the Gulf of California.

Something could have prevented the whole tragic mess: hunting—legal, regulated hunting. It's the primary tool in the management of all wildlife populations. If hunters had been allowed to hold the Kaibab deer herd in balance with its available food supply, as they should have, that herd would still be prospering today.

This juniper shows the effects of overbrowsing in the Kaibab National Forest on the North Rim of the Grand Canyon, during the 1920s. The results included mass starvation, severe plant damage, and extensive erosion.

Such disasters no longer occur where modern game managers can maintain healthy deer herds, but we still haven't been able to control habitat destruction in other ways. Want to know how to destroy deer habitat at taxpayers' expense? The question sounds ridiculous, but consider this:

In 1972, 363 acres of private land in Modoc County, California, were sprayed at government expense, achieving a 100 percent kill of the brush, and subsequesntly of the deer habitat. In 1973, in Nevada, taxpayers' money was used on a brush-removal project on land administered by the Bureau of Land Management. In another instance 1,150 acres in northeast California, which happened to be prime winter deer range, were treated with a low-volatile solution of 2,4-D herbicide at a cost of $6.50 per acre. The taxpayers paid for that habitat-destruction project, too.

These are examples of one of the ways that deer habitat can be destroyed needlessly. The "public-be-damned" attitude still does rear its ugly head with enough regularity that citizen surveillance is highly advised. It's good news that ordinary citizens, as well as deer hunters, are becoming more opposed to such habitat destruction. Our voices are being heard with more and more authority, and that's a definite trend of the future.

It also looks as though we may be licking some of the image problems the hunter has with the 93 percent of the public who do not hunt. Consider the following statements made by Cotton Gordon, President of the International Professional Hunters Association, during his speech to the National Rifle Association Annual Convention in 1974:

"I would like to express my very optimistic views of the future of hunting in this country. I am quite certain that this sort of an attitude comes as a shock to many of you and will be contrary to what you have been hearing, reading and seeing in this last decade . . .

"For years now we have heard that the young people in this country seriously oppose hunting. In a recent survey of college students across this country of ours, Dr. Dale Shaw of Colorado State University found that only a small minority did actually oppose hunting, but that a great majority opposed the hunter—not hunting but the hunter. They seriously object to the slob who shoots water tanks, signs, livestock, and who leaves his litter from plains to mountaintop. So, here again, we hear of the hunter image. . . .

"The slob image, if not taken seriously and if not soon corrected, will be the image that every hunter in this country bears. You and I can correct it by not tolerating the illegal or unethical practices that we see in the hunting field. We can correct it by calling them slobs and not hunters, and most certainly never referring to them as sportsmen. We can correct it by reporting all such incidents to law-enforcement people and by testifying when they go to trial. We can correct it by seeing that our individual states have strong laws that will keep these slobs out of the woods by not issuing licenses to those habitual offenders that jeopardize our sport. We must make the public understand that there is a vast difference between the sportsman who loves and respects this sport of hunting and the slob with a gun in his hand."

All of the foregoing material in this book should lead you to some conclusions about your future as a deer hunter. In summary, game managers in some states are producing more deer than was ever thought possible. In states where herds have declined, managers are finding ways to bring them back. In the future we may have more deer than ever before, but there will be more hunters who want to share in the harvest. This means there will be more regulations and controls on hunting. One more change we can expect is an increase in the cost of hunting. Though modest license and permit fee increases will be a sign of the times and will produce more deer, it's likely that you'll be shelling out more money in the future if you want the best hunting. The handwriting is already on the wall. Ray Lyons, the Colorado big-game outfitter I mentioned earlier, expressed it this way.

"You take a rancher out here who has fifty head of deer on his place," he began. "If he could get rid of those deer he'd have food for maybe ten more head of cattle. Those deer are costing him money, so he's reluctant to let hunters go after them for free. More and more ranchers and landowners are realizing that they have money invested in the game they produce. We'll never get rid of deteriorating hunter-landowner relationships till gunners realize it's only fair to pay for good hunting. When the day comes that a landowner makes money on the deer he produces he'll produce more deer and he'll be happy to have hunters. Like it or not, the providing of hunting as a profit objective is a trend of the future."

A hidden blessing in lease or fee hunting is the positive control of the slob hunter who has largely contributed to the hunter's image among non-hunters. A landowner who sells hunting rights knows the names and addresses of his hunters, and they know he knows them. Such hunters don't cut fences or shoot at signs and livestock. They behave themselves.

In my surveys of the trends of deer hunting one of my questions was this:

Do you feel that the modern trend is toward less "free" hunting on public lands? In other words do you feel that more hunters are finding better hunting through:
  A. Deer clubs where members buy or lease land and manage it exclusively for their private hunting?
  B. Leased lands where ranchers or landowners lease their hunting rights to groups or outfitters?
  C. Hunting fees charged by ranchers or landowners who now recognize their deer herds as cash crops?

It was surprising to learn that over one-third of the game officials in the lower forty-eight states said that, as yet, there is no trend toward any of these systems.

Deer clubs have come on strong in areas where fairly large tracts of private property—usually worthless for most other purposes—have been purchased by groups of deer hunters. Top states in this category include Alabama, Arkansas, California, Delaware, Georgia, Michigan, Minnesota, New Jersey, North Carolina, Virginia, West Virginia, and Wisconsin.

The advantage of belonging to a deer club can be tremendous, though expensive. Only club members are allowed to hunt, which means a drastic cut in competition. Also, hunting is far better because most club properties are managed by members to produce the best hunting. One example should serve to illustrate:

In my local area I do most of my deer hunting on public lands where the average annual deer hunter success ratio is 10 to 15 percent. My cousin is a member of a deer club whose property borders some of the country I hunt. Last fall forty-six members of the club hunted during the opening weekend of deer season, and they harvested twenty-seven bucks. That's nearly a 60 percent success ratio, and it was achieved in only two days of hunting.

Members of the club use their dues to produce this great hunting. They cut timber to produce browse, they plant crops which are left unharvested to serve as food for deer, and they hire a caretaker to protect their property from poachers.

A cheaper way for a deer-hunting groups to purchase good hunting is to lease a block of land for exclusive hunting rights. Under this system no deer-management practices are involved. The theory is simply to lease land that is already good deer country. The owner maintains all rights to his property except the hunting rights which are controlled by the leasing group. The system is coming to the forefront in Colorado, California, Delaware, Montana, Nebraska, New Jersey, New Mexico, Virginia, Wyoming, and Wisconsin. In Texas practically all deer hunting is controlled through leasing.

I've already mentioned that straight-fee hunting is a sign of the times. This system involves no more than the landowner charging a nominal fee for the right to hunt on his property. Numbers of hunters are usually unlimited. You just pay your fee and take your chance. Only sixteen state game departments told me that fee hunting will probably never gain a foothold in their states. In all the rest of the states it's likely to come on stronger as the years roll by.

4

Are Deer
Really Smart?

The subject of this chapter causes heated arguments among the best and most experienced venison-chasers. It's a simple question: How smart is a deer? Is an adult buck, particularly a whitetail, the craftiest quarry you'll find anywhere in the outdoors? Or are deer in general really pretty stupid?

All any hunter can do is develop his own ideas. I can reflect only the sum of of my own observations tempered with what I've read and what I've learned from other hunters.

Just recently I spent an evening talking over the subject with a hunter who has killed many deer in Texas. He came up with a statement that condenses my thoughts.

"My opinion is that deer are not smart, but they can be fantastically clever," the veteran hunter began. "Look up the two words in a dictionary and you'll see what I mean: The *American College Dictionary* offers one definition of smart as meaning shrewd or sharp, as a person in dealing with others. Note that your inference here relates to human beings who deal in facts. There are two definitions of clever that are not restricted to human activity. One means to be dexterous or nimble with the body. Another means showing adroitness or ingenuity. Both meanings could apply to animals as well as humans. I think a wise old buck can be extremely clever, but I've seen a lot of

36

them pull stunts that sure weren't smart, stunts that put them into some-body's freezer."

Whenever I get into an argument on the subject I ask: "How come so many deer are killed on highways by cars?" "It's a fact that about half a million deer are killed on highways each year. Now if deer were smart they'd know enough not to run into a vehicle they see coming and have every chance to avoid. A deer has to be pretty stupid to get knocked off by a car, especially in daylight."

That's one example of plain stupidity. Let's consider another that would seem to indicate an even greater lack of brains, at least where whitetails are concerned.

In northern states, during winters of heavy snow, whitetails herd into ce-dar swamps or other lowland thickets to escape the worst effects of bliz-zards and extreme cold. These areas are termed "yards" and they are used traditionally year after year. The problem is that herds are confined to very small areas where available food is rapidly consumed. If the winters are hard and long many of the younger and weaker deer die of starvation.

The horror of all this is that in many instances there would be no star-vation if the deer were smart enough to reason things out. Game biologists tell us that in many starvation areas deer die only a few hundred yards from lowlands harboring plenty of browse that isn't utilized. Why weren't these deer intelligent enough to travel a short distance and save their lives? Biologists claim it's habit for the animals to yard in specific areas regard-less of the consequences. That's certainly not being very smart.

But being clever is something else. Let me mention some examples of just how clever deer can be.

A bowhunter friend of mine spent four days last fall hunting a section of local woodland. During those four days he saw sixty-seven deer, thirteen of them bucks. During the rifle season he spent another four days hunting the same area and he saw only four deer, all does. A month after the rifle sea-son closed he was back in the same area hunting rabbits.

"John," he told me, "you wouldn't believe the number of deer in there. "Snow was pawed up everywhere under the oaks where whitetails were turning up acorns. I saw more than twenty deer and I wasn't even looking for them. Now where the hell were all those deer during rifle season?"

To find a possible answer let's turn to another fact from deer biologists: on good range a whitetail may live its entire life in a one- or two-square-mile area. Most deer select a relatively small home territory and stay in it. So, to answer my bowhunter friend's question, his disappearing deer prob-ably remained in the same area he hunted, but they were clever enough to stay out of sight during the firearms season. Why just during the firearms season?

All wild birds and animals react dramatically when somebody starts hunting them. In all the whitetail states most of the deer harvest is taken during the first few days of the gun season, then the kill drops drastically. Mule deer that fed in valley fields close to ranch houses all summer are gone shortly after rifles begin roaring in fall.

It seems to me that wildlife which survives in proximity to man has learned there are times to avoid human beings, and those times come with the echo of gunfire. For instance, deer are frequently almost tame in summer, exhibiting entirely different behavior patterns than in fall.

I'm writing this in my office which is on a lakeshore backed by several hundred acres of woodlands. These woods are loaded with fox and gray squirrels. Most of the year they raise havoc with my bird feeders. They become almost brazen, refusing to retreat more than a few yards up the closest tree even when I run outside in efforts to chase them away so the birds can feed. In fall, however, when I hit the woods with my .22 rifle in search of the makings of a squirrel dinner, those little varmits become very elusive.

The lake outside my office window is a good area for attracting a few diving ducks in fall, but you should see the enormous flights of ducks that pile in during April while the spring migration is under way. The fall ducks raft in the middle of the lake and will flush a quarter-mile away from an approaching boat, the spring birds swim along shorelines and pay much less attention to human activity. Why?

Is wildlife getting smarter? Can it be that through recent generations of ever increasing gunning pressure our hunted species have developed built-in alarm systems that say "be clever" in fall?

It seems to me that as the years go by our heavily hunted game is becoming increasingly clever all the time. The easily killed birds and animals don't last long enough to breed. The ones that stay alive do the breeding and they pass on their own genes.

A few months ago I brought up the subject with Lyle Laurvick, a gunsmith in Superior, Wisconsin. Lyle is a deer-hunting addict. He has hunted whitetails almost every day of each Wisconsin season since 1946. He doesn't quit hunting when he gets his buck; he puts aside his rifle and helps other hunters by participating in drives. A man with that much experience is worth listening to.

"No question about it, deer hunting is a different ball game today and is played by an entirely different set of rules than years ago," he began. "The older bucks with the big racks didn't get that way by being stupid. The stupid ones have all been through meat grinders. These modern bucks are of a much more clever strain than the ones we hunted years ago.

"This is one of the hardest things for today's hunter to accept. But I can tell you dozens of personal experiences proving that today's bucks don't make the mistakes made by the bucks of yesteryear. It seems as though there can be only one explanation: today's deer are much more clever because of heredity. Their basic trick today is to hide instead of running.

As evidenced in this copse of cedars, overbrowsing destroys habitat. White-tails commonly hold to traditional winter "yards" that offer poor browse even though nearby areas may offer good browse. Malnutrition and starvation often result.

"I'll tell you a story that should convince some skeptics. I had a buddy, Bob Gainey, a pilot who flew two or three months of each year, mostly crop dusting. He wasn't much of a hunter, but every day during deer season when he could fly he was in the air. In the evenings we would sit down over a pot of coffee and discuss how the deer were outwitting hunters. Bob watched all sorts of goings-on from his very high vantage point.

"Time after time Bob told me about big bucks he saw bedded in sunny weeds close to a jungle of cover," Lyle went on. "He'd circle slowly and watch when he'd spot hunters moving toward the deer. Most of those bucks never budged an inch, even when hunters passed within 30 feet. The clever old boys would watch the men till they walked past, then resume napping as if nothing had happened.

"As I mentioned, Gainey wasn't much interested in hunting. But he'd buy a deer license and keep a rifle in his car just in case an easy opportunity presented itself. One afternoon he had the manager of our airport along for a ride. They were heading home when they spotted an enormous buck bedded in thick alder brush no more than 40 yards from a gravel road and less than three miles from the airport. Bob decided that nailing that buck in his bed would be a cinch.

"He put his plane down on the runway, then headed for the buck's hiding spot in his car while the airport manager flew back upstairs to watch the show.

"Gainey figured he knew exactly where the buck was lying. All he had to do was drive to a spot opposite the deer's bed, find him with his riflescope and shoot him on the spot. He parked his car, shoved a cartridge into his rifle, climbed to the top of his vehicle and searched in vain for the enormous rack.

"He then crawled down very quietly and tried sneaking toward a particular poplar tree near which he was sure the buck was bedded. When he got to the tree he looked for the bed that had to be a few feet south of the poplar. No bed. It then entered his mind that he had chosen the wrong poplar, so he attempted to climb it for a better look into surrounding brush. The 180-pound man and the skinny tree didn't go well together and Bob put up quite a commotion.

"About that time the buck had seen enough. He exploded out of the brush near a similar tree and bounded toward the road. Gainey was disgusted that he'd picked the wrong tree, but he was even more upset when he got back to the airport and heard the manager's story of the episode.

" 'Bob,' Bill said, 'you could have killed that buck easily after he jumped. He hit the ditch on the side of the road in a few bounds and he froze right there because he spotted a woman walking toward him down the road. He waited till she walked by, then carefully tip-toed across behind her. She never knew he was there. If you had hurried after him you would have had an easy shot.' "

It depends on how you analyze this incident whether you'll claim that buck was smart or clever. I'll contend that the whitetail wasn't smart at all. If he could reason like a human, he wouldn't have wasted one second trying to avoid being seen by an unarmed woman when he knew there was a man with a rifle just three jumps behind him. He simply reverted to cleverness to avoid a new situation that suddenly presented itself.

It's not the purpose of this chapter to tell you about the hunting techniques necessary to cope with the traits of modern deer. You'll find all that information detailed in other chapters. My purpose here is to mention the changed reactions of today's deer so you'll understand more readily why the how-to tricks work as well as they do.

I've harped on the theory that modern bucks have learned it's much more clever to hide than to run, but I can't resist mentioning another of Lyle's stories that may do much to cement the theory. Here's the way Lyle tells it:

"One recent fall there were few deer shot in my area because of extremely poor hunting weather which, in my book, is the Number 1 reason for a low harvest. My buddy Bob Gainey was shook up about the fact that so many hunters were positive the herd had declined. He had been flying all season and he had spotted plenty of deer from the air.

" 'You know, Lyle,' he said, 'you could make a pile of money betting disgusted hunters that you could show them twenty deer in twenty minutes. I'd take them up in my plane and we'd see deer by the dozens.'

"Well, a while later George Constance walked into my gun shop. I got him all shook up by saying that anybody who couldn't spot deer couldn't call himself much of a hunter. He was hopping mad when I bet him $10 I could show him twenty deer in twenty minutes. He about broke his arm reaching for his wallet. He figured he had been conned when I told him Bob Gainey was waiting at the airport, but he drove out there.

"When he came back he was amazed. Not only had he seen a lot more than twenty deer, he had seen at least twenty big bucks. And Bob never did fly more than fifteen miles from the airport, which is in the huge Superior, Wisconsin-Duluth, Minnesota metro area."

WHEN DEER ACT DUMB

We can only draw conclusions from the actions of deer in different situations. If a buck were smart he would never lose all of his instincts for caution. With man or animal it's possible to be clever one day and not so clever the next because cleverness isn't an instinct. I doubt if there's a veteran deer hunter anywhere who won't agree that a mature buck can exhibit the heights of stupidity during the rut. That's not being smart, but it is instinctive.

I shot my best whitetail buck, a Saskatchewan giant, because that fool deer wouldn't leave three does. My guide and I spotted the four deer in broad daylight in a willow swale and we made a successful stalk. I fired my first shot at the buck while he was still unaware of our presence. The range was only 150 yards, but my .243 slug hit a willow branch and deflected.

The four whitetails lit out on a run straight away and I missed two more shots. In that prairie country you can see a long way so after the animals were out of reasonable range I ran to the top of a knoll and watched them run in the distance. Through my scope I saw the buck break away from the does several times and head for heavy cover. But each time he noted the does weren't staying with him and he rejoined them. Eventually they trotted into a small pocket of brush. They didn't come out the far end.

"Okay," my guide said, "it'll be quite a walk but we've got that buck dead to rights if he stays with those does. We'll circle around a couple of miles then come in on that brush from downwind."

That's what we did. When we got close to the brush my guide walked around to the south end and I stationed myself near the north end. As soon as my guide began crashing through the cover that giant whitetail exploded out with rush. He ran right in front of me and I piled him up.

That buck did a lot of things that weren't smart at all. First, he allowed himself to be caught out in the open where he could be seen in daylight. Mature whitetail bucks just don't do that except during the rut. Second, though he wanted to escape to heavy cover where he would have been safe, he couldn't resist staying with the does. He still could have saved his skin if he'd had enough sense to watch his back track from just inside that pocket of cover where his lady friends decided to stop. He didn't even do that, which is a common stunt pulled by bucks during seasons other than the rut.

There's one trick deer try that makes me wonder if they have any reasoning power at all. That's their idea of trying to escape notice by freezing motionless even if they are in scant cover. I've had many experiences with this act; one yielded my best mule-deer buck, a real bruiser that I nailed on the western slope of the Colorado Rockies.

Why have modern deer developed the strong tendency to hide rather than run when confronted with approaching hunters? Usually this is a clever tactic for two basic reasons: Because of ever-increasing numbers of hunters, a running deer is likely to blunder into more trouble ahead. Also, if he jumps and runs the hunter who jumped him is suddenly aware of his presence and may get a shot. This is especially true in mule-deer areas where the country is relatively open. So a clever deer doesn't jump and run. He freezes and hopes to go unnoticed.

My guess is that this tactic works exceptionally well when there is no snow on the ground. I'd bet that for every deer a hunter sees there are at least twenty more that see the hunter but are unseen themselves. Deer are so successful with this trick that they use it year-round. If they had real mental ability they'd realize most of their camouflage is gone when there is snow on the ground.

Anyway, I was on horseback that morning in Colorado when I happened to spot the big buck silhouetted against a snow background in some aspens. The buck was watching me, and if he'd had any common sense he'd have run over the top of the ridge he was standing on as soon as I made my first move to dismount. But he didn't. He stood still as a statue all during the commotion I made yanking my rifle out of its scabbard and dismounting. By that time I realized the buck figured he was hidden. I took my time with my shot and dropped him in his tracks.

Some hunters to whom I've told the story claimed that buck didn't move because mule deer are used to horses. Well, they shake their heads when I tell them another story. It concerns the time I was coming down a mountain in Montana during an elk hunt.

It was late in the afternoon and turning dusk. A group of us were in two four-wheel-drive vehicles. We were driving slowly down a winding snow-covered trail. Suddenly my guide said, "Look at that fool buck standing over there in that sagebrush. He thinks we can't see him. You might as well take him. He's a good three-pointer."

Our casual attitude about shooting the deer was born of the fact that many hunters don't bother with deer when concentrating on elk. My general big-game license that year included two permits for deer, and I intended to fill at least one. Since we were finished elk hunting for the day my guide thought I might as well nail that buck,

I stepped out of the vehicle, jerked my rifle out of its case, jacked in a cartridge, took aim, and knocked the buck flat. Can anybody convince me I outwitted a super-smart animal? No way. But it could be that I shot a clever buck who was too clever for his own good. If he'd been smart he'd have known he couldn't hide against a snow background even though he was standing motionless in brush. He'd have been safe if he'd bolted as soon as the vehicles stopped. The reason he didn't is the same reason that thousands of deer are killed every year after snowfall. You will hear about similar incidents any time modern deer hunters discuss their success stories.

My guess is that deer will freeze motionless against snow backgounds because the seemingly clever stunt works so well when there is no snow on the ground. In any event today's deer use it so extensively that the art of seeing deer—or parts of deer—is one of the most important abilities the modern hunter can develop. For that reason I've devoted an entire chapter in this book to the subject of seeing deer.

The frequent reaction of a deer shot at and missed is another reason to question his mental ability. If you're a veteran you probably, at one time or another, missed a shot at a buck and had him stand right there as if nothing had happened. One time years ago my brother fired five shots at an eight-point whitetail buck standing broadside less than 70 yards away. They had no more effect than if he'd been shooting blanks. The sixth slug from the old rifle took that buck in his lung area and dropped him as if he'd been sledged.

Why will a mature buck occasionally do such a crazy thing? Perhaps it's partly because he's not smart enough to recognize gunfire for what it is. My gunsmith friend Lyle Laurvick has some theories about this.

"In today's woods there is a lot more gunfire than there used to be," he told me. "I'm convinced that deer have no fear of noises that they hear frequently. I've been on hundreds of stands in trees, places where I've been able to look down on deer and watch their reactions when rifles roared nearby. Invariably they'll look immediately in the direction of the shot, then go back to whatever they were doing before the noise occurred.

"The incidents that really convince me of their lack of fear of gunfire have been my experiences on my rifle range. I fire hundreds of rounds through my customer's rifles on that range, and it happens to be located in good deer country just outside town. I've had scores of deer feeding within 200 yards upwind of me while I'm shooting. They'll look up when I start a new round of shots, then go back feeding with an apparent 'so what?' attitude.

"Two days before our season this year I'd just finished firing a string of twenty-one shots," Lyle continued. "Right then I happened to spot a six-point buck standing 150 yards away. One of the customer's rifles lying on my bench was an H&H Magnum equipped with a 15x scope. I viewed that deer through the scope and he didn't seem the least bit frightened or alarmed. It's obvious to me that it takes more than gunfire to spook a deer."

I believe that Lyle is right when he says, "It takes more than gunfire." It's my guess that deer depend upon more than one specific sense to detect danger. Of the three senses, sight, sound, and scent, it's likely that scent is the most important because deer seldom tolerate human scent. It would appear that no deer would stand still and let a man shoot at him if he could detect human odor unless the animal was sure he was hidden. But caught by surprise a buck is not likely to try being clever. He may not bolt till he sees the hunter or smells him, but add one of those senses to the sound of gunfire and the animal probably will panic. I'd bet that a buck shot at and missed isn't unusually alarmed until he sees or smells the man shooting at him. Many fine bucks have been bagged because they waited too long to make sure they were in trouble, and that's not being very smart.

Add to these thoughts the knowledge that deer behavior is often controlled by habit and curiosity to the point of stupidity. Deer are extremely curious about unfamiliar sounds. They will not hesitate to investigate when something new and unusual happens in their home area. Though I've never tried calling deer with a varmint call I've heard and read that the technique is quite successful in some parts of the country. Why a deer, supposedly smart, would be curious enough to run to a varmint call is beyond me. A fox or coyote will eagerly respond to a call because he thinks he will get something to eat; what does a buck think he will get?

As to being controlled by habit, deer habitually use the same runways, feeding and bedding areas, and they favor certain watering spots. One of their most stupid habits is their tendency not to expect danger from above. They just don't have the sense to look up, and that's precisely why tree stands are so effective.

Most hunters claim that whitetail deer obviously are super-smart because their populations are higher now than when the Pilgrims landed in America. They say that an animal smart enough to survive the drastic conditions of modern civilization and greatly increased hunting pressure has to have a great amount of brains. Serious students of the principles of game management know better. They're aware that the original whitetail populations in many of our states were virtually wiped out by overhunting back around the turn of the century. Even the mule deer in our western mountains were nearly exterminated by meat and hide hunters.

We don't have more deer today because the animals know how to take care of themselves; we have our millions of deer because of controlled hunting and the knowledge applied to deer-management programs by modern game biologists. The principle is basic: Give a wild animal the habitat he needs and his populations will multiply as long as he gets the required protection.

The reason the majority of hunters don't bag a buck seems to me to be fundamental. Every hunt is a contest of wits with only two possible outcomes: either you get your deer or you don't. Usually the hunter loses the game because he is a lot smarter but far less clever than his quarry. The odds highly favor the deer because they know every inch of the relatively small area they live in year-round. The hunter is in the same area only a few days each fall. He normally doesn't score because he makes mistakes, does something wrong, and doesn't hunt hard enough.

We can be thankful that deer make mistakes too, and I hope this chapter has convinced you of that. Perhaps it will make you hunt harder next fall. If you hunt the way you should you may very well cash in on a small error made by your buck. Many hunters go at the game of wits half-heartedly because they figure they're no match for a "smart" buck in the first place. That is a mighty stupid attitude to have.

5
Whitetail Deer

The top secrets of the successful whitetail hunter are silence and knowledge of deer habits, traits, life history, and habitat. This chapter contains information that should make your hunting skills more productive.

The normal life span for unhunted whitetails in the wild is ten to fourteen years. In captivity where excellent living conditions are provided these deer can live to the age of twenty. A legal buck will have his first set of antlers at 1½ years of age. This means that every buck in most woodlands will be dodging hunters each fall for his entire adult life. These facts should point out dramatically why a mature whitetail buck is a pretty clever character, especially when you consider his physical capabilities.

SENSES

Much has been written about how well a whitetail can hear. But just how acute is a deer's hearing? In a test, a whitetail buck heard the clicking of a man's fingernails 75 yards downwind. I once had an experience that was even more enlightening.

I was on a stand when I spotted three deer approaching me. They were 100 yards upwind of my position and walking straight on at a steady pace. Suddenly they stopped, looked toward me, and cupped their ears. I was sure they couldn't see me and I hadn't made a sound since long before I'd spotted them. Still, they wheeled and trotted out of my view. Several minutes later I heard another hunter walking up behind me. It was obvious those deer had heard the man long before I did even though I was much closer to him.

To sum it up, a deer's hearing is so superior to yours that sneaking up on a whitetail in normal hunting terrain is extremely difficult. But forget the noise factor for a moment and concentrate on a whitetail's eyesight.

Though deer are color blind, that's about as far as their blindness goes. Regardless of what you may have read or heard, a deer sees exceptionally well, especially in semi-darkness. Dawn and dusk are the periods when whitetails move the most, and those are the periods when most shooting opportunities are offered. During these periods their eyesight is far superior to yours. Even during midday deer can see astonishingly well. They sometimes don't notice motionless hunters, but they can spot movement from incredible distances.

I've often moved into a suitable position for glassing hunting terrain and then spotted deer which were far out of rifle range. In just about every instance those deer were staring at me. They'd seen me before I saw them, even though I was using a spotting scope or binocular. So don't ever base your whitetail hunting plans on the notion that deer don't see well. If you do you won't be successful.

When alarmed, whitetails normally show their flags, that is, raise their tails exposing the white undersides. But this is not always the case. One of the lead bucks shown here flees with his tail down.

Which gets us to the question of a whitetail's sense of smell. It's unbelievably sharp. It's so sharp that a buck relies more on discovering danger by scenting than by hearing or seeing. With a favorable wind or thermal current a deer can smell a man from far away. If you get upwind from even a distant buck there's no way you're going to fool him unless you use special techniques we'll discuss later.

SPEED

Okay, so if a buck does get wise to you through sound, sight, or scent, how fast can he escape by running? The answer isn't so surprising to veteran hunters who have seen deer blitz away from danger, but it's still interesting to know that whitetails can run at 30 miles per hour for several miles. Bucks have been clocked at 40 miles per hour during sprints. This still doesn't sound so impressive till we make a comparison.

Ruffed grouse are often found in whitetail country. The explosive, rocketing flight of these birds seems so fast that the average hunter would state flatly that a grouse can escape faster than a deer. Not necessarily so. Flight speeds of ruffed grouse have been clocked at 25 to 40 miles per hour. This means a deer can run as fast as a grouse can fly if he really wants to pour it on.

Another shocker is the whitetail's phenomenal jumping ability. There is a record of a deer jumping an eight-foot fence without even taking a preliminary step. Broad jumps of around 30 feet are common. A downhill jump of over 100 feet was observed by a naturalist.

Whitetails are great swimmers too, especially during hunting seasons when they wear their hollow-haired winter coats. Wisconsin researchers clocked deer many miles from land swimming at thirteen miles per hour. So a buck won't hesitate to escape by swimming if he figures that's the best way out. And this brings up another interesting item regarding a whitetail's physical capabilities: in northern states, during late November deer seasons, the water is so cold that a man would perish in it in minutes, yet a deer can swim in the same frigid water for miles with no ill effects at all.

SURVIVAL INSTINCT

There's one thing about deer that I've never found discussed in print, but which I've heard promoted as an important point among a few veteran hunters. Let's call the subject "instinct for survival." From my experience this instinct is well-pronounced in deer, though all birds and animals have it to some degree.

For example, if we put a smart man in an uncharted wilderness, leave him without a compass and tell him to find his way back to his starting point, he will be confused and lack a sense of direction. On the other hand,

Unlike mule deer, which migrate many miles with seasonal change, white-tails tend to live their entire lives within a few-square-mile area. But they may migrate from marginal range.

you've probably heard stories of dogs or cats that were lost on family vacation trips far from home, yet which traveled long distances over unfamiliar country to return home. How did they do it? The answer has to be that they used an instinct unknown to man.

Man can learn to do many things well, but he does these things by thought processes or constant repetition of the act, not by instinct. What makes birds migrate unerringly from a specific summer area to a specific winter area thousands of miles apart? Much of it has to be instinct. Even the most experienced jet pilot couldn't make such a trip without benefit of dozens of scientific instruments, yet birds do it with no problems at all.

Years ago, whitetails had natural enemies such as wolves. Today, except in places such as northern Minnesota where some wolves still kill deer, the whitetail finds man and free-ranging dogs as his only predators. Is it any wonder that the whitetail's instinct on avoiding human hunters is being honed to an ever-finer edge as the years pass? This edge isn't as developed in mule deer because muleys have less contact with man than most white-tails; they are still killed by mountain lions in many areas; and they react more out of habit than does the whitetail, which has more capacity to adapt to the world of man. If you go along with the instinct concept you'll have to conclude that today's whitetail is more difficult to bag than were his ancestors.

Everything I've mentioned so far points out that the whitetail is much superior to man in physical endowments and instinct. With this knowledge the smart hunter recognizes that the only advantage he has over deer is his far greater ability to reason things out. The guy who consistently scores on whitetails is the guy who takes advantage of a deer's relatively small degree of reasoning power.

MORE INSIGHTS

But that's a subject for other chapters in this book. Let's go on and discuss a few other facts that should help you gain additional understanding of the whitetail's nature. The more a hunter knows about how his quarry functions, the more appreciation he has for the best ways to hunt.

Adult bucks in the northern states are in breeding condition from September to February, but does are receptive to these bucks only from October through December, during "heat" periods which last twenty-four to thirty-six hours and which recur every twenty-eight days until a given doe is bred.

This cycle is important because it shows why a buck will travel out of his normal home range during the rut. He doesn't collect a harem as does a bull elk, and if he can't find readily available does in his local terrain he'll go looking for them. If your deer-hunting season falls during the rut you may find bucks in areas where you never saw a sign of them during scouting trips before or after the breeding season.

Deer biologists tell us that a wild buck can service six to eight does without trouble. (A penned buck can service up to twenty does.) This generally means that some does will get bred despite heavy hunting pressure. Habitat is the all-important factor in determining survival of the species. On good range having few deaths from disease or winter loss, the whitetail herd nearly doubles between the pre-fawning and post-fawning periods. Even many doe fawns get into the act by getting pregnant at the age of six months. They have their own fawns at the age of twelve to thirteen months. Also, studies have shown that wild does seldom become too old to bear fawns. Females more than ten years old have been observed with their youngsters.

However, you should keep in mind that although all does get bred, the breeding may be accomplished by few bucks or many. In an area holding few bucks each male will service many does. So it doesn't follow that an area automatically harbors lots of bucks just because it may harbor lots of deer. An area that produced a tremendous buck harvest last year may not be so good this year because a lot of the bucks have been shot out.

This is why it's not always a good idea to hunt the same place year after year as tradition called for in the old days. Years ago, deer hunters didn't have the mobility they have today; now there is no reason to suffer through the ups and downs of buck populations in a given area. The secret is in pre-hunt scouting for the definite signs of bucks. I'll get into all the details of this technique in Chapter 9, "Why Stands Beat the Odds."

Research shows that male deer outnumber females about 110 to 100 at birth. Buck fawns are also usually stronger and heavier than their sisters, about seven pounds to five. They have the best odds for staying alive after birth, so hunting pressure often is the only reason buck populations may be low in a given area.

Yearling does usually produce one fawn. Thereafter, on good range, healthy does produce an average of two. Occasionally a doe will produce three fawns, rarely four. The gestation period is about 200 days.

In either-sex hunting areas, and in those areas where does may be harvested on special permits, it's common for some hunters to claim they killed dry does. They assume from this that such does did not produce fawns that year. The assumption is usually wrong because fawns nurse heavily for only about two months and are weaned at about twelve weeks. A doe can "dry up" about one month after nursing stops. So a doe that is dry in November could easily have had twin fawns in June.

Though even novice hunters are aware that bucks shed their antlers each year in winter, many beginners claim there are few bucks in a given area because they don't find dropped antlers in the woods. The real reason they don't find them is because the racks usually don't last long. They quickly become bleached and softened by the elements, then they're gnawed by rodents. Most dropped antlers are completely devoured. In northern states whitetail bucks shed their antlers in December and January. They begin growing new sets in April. Growth is finished by September, and polishing is usually complete by mid-October.

A deer has no gall bladder, but, like cattle and sheep, it does have a four-sectioned stomach. The first stomach (called the rumen) stores rough-chewed food which is later regurgitated and chewed as cud, swallowed again, an then passed on through the other three sections. A whitetail licks its coat frequently. This habit accounts for the hair balls hunters sometimes find in deer stomachs. These leathery-surfaced spheres can be two to three inches in diameter. Hunters who find such balls need not be concerned that the deer are diseased. Hair balls are normal occurrences.

When I discuss deer-hunting techniques later I'll point out that the normal home range of a whitetail buck living in ideal terrain may cover only a mile or two from place of birth. Unlike mule deer, whitetails are basically nonmigratory. But exceptions occur and the hunter should be aware of them. Today's deer biologists have facts about whitetail movements that the old-timers could only guess at.

Winter hunger may force deer to abandon their normal furtive ways. This photo was taken at midday in a grain field.

Speed of escape is a whitetail hallmark. Whitetails can average 30 mph for several miles. Bucks have been clocked in 40 mph sprints. Broad jumps of 30 feet are common. Jumps over eight-foot fences, with no preliminary steps, have been recorded.

Whitetail does can become pregnant at age six months, and they may continue to bear fawns after they are ten years old. The old doe shown here tends twins, the usual number of fawns to a doe on good range.

53

In northern states, where yarding of these deer is common, movements may be greater than in southern areas where snow creates no problem for deer. Still, a Wisconsin study showed that most deer were bagged less than 3½ miles from their winter yards.

The rule of thumb is that where terrain conditions are best you'll find comparatively minor movement patterns. In less suitable areas, movements may be extensive. You should consider this fact if you hunt in marginal deer country, or if you hunt in an area where whitetails occupy various habitats on a seasonal basis. In agricultural states, for example, grainfields may provide good food from July well into the hunting season. But when the produce is gone, deer will pull back into the cover of stream courses or other permanent vegetation areas.

Where habitat is good only in widely scattered areas, deer may move long distances while seeking better homes. A good example of this is Nebraska, where tagging studies have shown movements which are considerably greater than normal. Recoveries of twenty-three whitetails which were tagged in the poor habitat of the Sand Hills showed an average movement of 38 miles. A yearling buck tagged southwest of Valentine, Nebraska, was killed the following year near Clearwater, 137 miles away. Another whitetail buck, tagged south of Valentine, traveled 125 miles before being killed the next year west of Lewellen.

The implications are obvious: find the best whitetail habitat your area offers during deer season and concentrate your hunting efforts there. Where are the top spots in your state? You'll find the best tips I can offer in Chapter 23, "How to Get Hotspot Information."

Some of the better whitetail hunters I know kill their bucks close to towns and cities. One reason is that whitetails have learned to live near man and will prosper in good habitat no matter how close it may be to population centers, but another reason is far less recognized.

Practically all land near populated areas is privately owned. You can't hunt it unless you have permission. I learned long ago that landowners are much more likely to give permission prior to hunting season than later when they may be swamped with requests. This is one of the great benefits of pre-hunt scouting. Most landowners also allow only a limited number of hunters on their property, so if you're the first to ask you're more likely to get an okay. What this boils down to is that some hunters get their bucks simply because they have hunting rights in good habitat that's unavailable to other hunters. The principle doesn't apply in public-hunting areas of the West, but it can make all the difference in the world in the East, Midwest, and South. Make friends with rural landowners and you'll up your odds on whitetail-hunting success significantly.

If you like to hunt on your own this principle takes on even more weight. Landowners will grant hunting permission to a loner much more readily than they will to a group. When a property owner grants permission to only one loner this guy can hunt a farm which, in effect, is a private hunting preserve. Not only that, but farmers watch their deer all year and can offer advice on the animals' habits and where they're most likely to be at any given time. The most meticulous hunters will tell farmers where they will park their cars and what type of clothes they'll be wearing so the landowner will be aware of trespassers.

Still another advantage is that some of the biggest bucks are found in farm country. This is true because the weather is usually milder than in the northern forests, food is more plentiful, and the same limestone fertilizer that grows crops also can promote exceptional body and antler growth. Further, the deer herds of farm country aren't so subject to the population cycles of forest deer. They're apt to increase more than decrease. A case in point is Michigan.

Hunters seldom find dropped antlers even though an area may contain many bucks. Dropped antlers quickly become bleached and softened by the elements. They are then gnawed by rodents for the calcium, phosphorous, and salts they contain.

Michigan deer biologists say that back in the old days there were only a few hundred deer in the thirty-four southernmost counties. During the 1940s the herds had grown to several thousand whitetails. By 1963 the overall population of the area was estimated at 50,000 animals. Now those southern Michigan counties hold over 100,000 deer and provide some of the state's best whitetail hunting. But practically all of that hunting is on private land. I know of no better example pointing out how important it can be to get hunting permission long before the day of the hunt.

One of the reasons farm-country hunting can be so productive is that alien sights, sounds, and smells upset whitetails very easily. In forests, where deer are not used to people or human activities, the opening-day crowds of hunters make whitetails spooky in a hurry. Deer in farm country are used to human activity year-round. Thus, a farm-country buck seldom considers a hunter as an alien to his environment because he doesn't know the difference between a man with a gun and a man with a rake. This advantage is one of the few that whitetail hunters have over mule-deer hunters, and it's found only in farm country.

Whitetails find little feed in mature forests except when mast crops such as acorns or beechnuts are available. They favor the combination of browse and protection afforded by country with mixed cover, such as woodlands, grasslands, thickets and tangles.

Proof that whitetails can accept man as part of their natural environment is the existence of many deer farms holding deer for tourist attractions. Most whitetails on these farms are completely tame.

Once a whitetail hunter has settled on a general area, the next step is selecting the best territory within that area. Whitetail hunting anywhere is only as good as the country hunted. Most of the best country contains the mixed cover of timber, grasslands, croplands, and lowland thickets which join together in all-important brushy terrain type referred to as "edge." Whitetails are often thought of by beginners as animals of the deep, unbroken forest. They're not; they far prefer lower, brushier vegetation. And they prefer this type of cover most of all when they find it bordering fields, clearings, swamps, lakes, timbered hills, and so forth. These fringes of thick cover are the "edge" areas that produce the best whitetail hunting.

Such cover is the precise reason why deer herds in agricultural states have exploded in numbers. The "edge" in farm country affords ideal habitat for whitetails. It's also the reason why whitetail numbers boomed in the northern states after the mature timber was logged off in the early years of this century. As the tall trees were replaced with low brush (more browse) deer moved in and multiplied because habitat conditions became ideal.

Whitetails feed very little—except when mast crops are available—in heavily timbered areas because thick top foliage discourages the growth of browse. But these deer don't favor one type of food to the exclusion of any other. They prefer a varied diet, which is why edge in wilderness areas is as attractive to the animals as edge in farm country. In agricultural areas whitetails will utilize wheat, rye, corn, or other crop fields so long as the safety offered by brushy edge is nearby. Likewise, in wilderness areas, they'll move into forest areas to feed on beechnuts and acorns if they can escape quickly to edge when danger is present. You'll always find the most whitetails where there is a mixture of food types including much edge between the different types.

The main thing to keep in mind is that it's normally quite useless to look for whitetails in heavy timber. Right here, so I don't confuse the issue in the following chapter, I want to point out that there can be a difference in defining edge depending on whether you hunt in the East or West.

Edge in whitetail country usually means brush or low trees growing as tall as 20 feet. You'll seldom find these animals in brush so low that it won't cover their outlines when they're standing. It's a different story with mule deer. They'll often feed and bed in brushy areas so low it's necessary for them to bed down before they're out of sight.

But edge in the West, can also mean brush and small trees growing high above a man's head. Edge in whitetail country is always high enough to hide a standing deer; it may or may not be so in mule deer country.

Heavy hunting pressure has more effect on whitetails than mule deer.

When the pressure gets heavy, whitetails become almost exclusively nocturnal in all their activities. About the only chance you have of seeing them then is very early and very late in the day when they're moving to and from feeding areas. This is another reason why hunting edge is very important. Deer will take a chance on moving in fringe cover as dawn or dusk comes on, but they'll seldom be caught in clearings, fields, or openings in heavy timber during hunting season.

How to get a shot at your buck is covered in following chapters. The next chapter, "Mule Deer," contains still more information on the successful hunting of whitetails that I didn't include in this chapter because it becomes more useful and enlightening when we examine the traits of the two species simultaneously.

6
Mule Deer

The first mule deer I ever saw astonished me because it was so strikingly different from a Michigan whitetail. This one came many years ago as a friend and I were driving into Wyoming on our first hunting trip in the West. It was shortly after noon on a mild, sunny day. We drove around a curve in ranch country and spotted several cattle grazing on a hillside clearing 100 yards to our right. Suddenly I noticed a deer among the Herefords.

"Look," I stammered to my companion. "There's a deer out there in the open. It's a buck. A six-pointer."

We pulled off onto the shoulder of the road and stopped to stare at the deer. He paid us no heed for several moments.

"Hard to believe," my partner said. "Back home in Michigan we'd never see a whitetail buck feeding in the open during broad daylight. Look at the enormous ears on that critter. No wonder they're called mule deer."

We got our next surprise when the buck finally decided we couldn't be up to any good. Away he went, bouncing into the air and coming down stiff-legged on all four feet in a kind of pogo-stick gait we'd never seen. He didn't seem to be in any hurry heading for cover. A Michigan whitetail would have flashed across that clearing on a dead run.

We were also surprised to note that the muley was

much grayer than a whitetail, that his tail was far smaller. He didn't hold his tail high as he ran, and that his antlers appeared higher and much less inclined to curve than those on our deer back home. Then the buck pulled another stunt that left us shaking our heads.

He pulled up to the top of a knoll 200 yards away, stopped in his tracks, and turned to look at us. We couldn't believe it. A jumped whitetail usually runs till he's out of the immediate area and he never stops to look back. Broadside to us, the muley stared in our direction for a few moments, then calmly walked over the knoll and melted from view.

Eastern deer hunters making their first trips to mule-deer country often have similar experiences, which emphasize that the muley has a far different make-up than the whitetail. And to hunt him successfully, there are many other considerations you should be aware of.

Mule deer are far less abundant than whitetails, and their range is much more restricted. Only eleven states offer good mule-deer hunting, and only six others offer even poor to fair hunting for this species. On the other hand, most mule-deer hunters enjoy a success ratio that's twice as high as that for whitetail hunters. In areas showing the best mule-deer hunting, the success ratio may be four times as high. This shows that mule deer are easier to hunt.

There are two general reasons for this. One, mule deer are usually hunted in much more open country than are whitetails. This means that shooting opportunities are easier to come by simply because you'll see more deer. Second, mule deer generally aren't as cautious or as clever as whitetails. This, again, means that shooting opportunities can come more often.

The above statement has been challenged in recent years by some veteran mule-deer hunters who claim the western deer is adopting the habits of the eastern whitetail by hiding in deep thickets, showing himself less in daylight and becoming far more clever. They say that many hunters are unsuccessful because they're taken in by the tradition claiming mule deer are easy to hunt. These veterans insist that modern hunters should go after muleys as if they were going after whitetails.

I agree—if we're talking about trophy bucks, those monarchs who have made it through a few hunting seasons and have lived long enough to learn the ways of hunters. I've had a few big mule-deer bucks make a fool of me when they used evasive tactics in thick cover which they refused to leave. These bucks are adopting the traits of whitetails for the same reason the whitetails have: ever-increasing hunting pressure.

But it's a different story with the younger bucks that most hunters bag. There are all kinds of facts to prove the point. The most obvious is hunter success-ratio statistics. Take a moment to go back to the deer-hunter-success chart, shown in Chapter 2. You'll note that the states showing the top ten hunter-success ratios are all west of the Mississippi River, and

Mule deer are far less abundant than whitetails, and their range is more restricted. Only eleven states offer good mule deer hunting. Six others offer poor to fair hunting. Yet, most mule deer hunters enjoy a success ratio of 50 percent or better. That's twice as high as in many good whitetail states.

Here the author poses with an exceptionally long-tined three-pointer he took in a foothills feeding area. Mule deer often feed in the foothills and bed on the slopes.

they're all in mule-deer country. You'll also note from an accompanying chart that the top mule-deer states, in terms of deer-herd numbers— Wyoming, Colorado, New Mexico and Utah—harbor far fewer deer than the top whitetail states east of the Mississippi River. The conclusion is obvious: It's much easier to bag a deer in good mule-deer country than it is in good whitetail country.

Another fact that sheds a lot of light on the subject is the availability of deer-hunting licenses. In most of the eastern deer states licenses are unlimited to residents and nonresidents alike. Anybody can hunt deer in these states by paying the fee for a license. The reason this situation exists is that it's almost impossible to over-harvest bucks in the typical whitetail states of the East. These bucks are just too clever to be killed easily.

Not so in the West. The majority of the best mule-deer states limit the number of nonresident hunters; some of the "fair" hunting states limit the numbers of *resident* deer hunters. Lottery or drawing systems determine which applicants get a chance to hunt. The reason? Mule deer herds can be subjected to overharvest by too much hunting pressure. This again points out that it's generally far easier to score on mule deer than whitetails.

I've seen many examples of how easy it can be. One time I killed a fine buck in the mountains of Colorado during a late season when there was deep snow on the ground. My guide told me time and again before our actual hunt started that I shouldn't take the first buck I saw unless it was a trophy because there were plenty of big bruisers in the area. "These deer are migrating at this time of year," he told me. "The area we're going to hunt is a concentration area where the muleys gang up on their migration route before moving down to lower elevations. It's not really hunting up there, it's more a matter of picking the buck you want and nailing him."

Years ago, Ben Gregory, a local deer-hunting partner of mine, and I planned a Wyoming hunt with several other friends. Just before we left home for the drive to Wyonimg, business matters forced Ben to postpone his trip. As it turned out, the business problems were solved sooner than Ben expected. He packed his gear in a hurry and made the drive to Wyoming to join us and utilize the two-deer license he had purchased by mail months before.

As Ben drove into the general area the rest of us were hunting, he spotted a herd of mule deer crossing a knoll behind some ranch buildings. He drove into the ranch, asked and received permission to hunt, loaded his rifle and took off on foot for the hills where he'd seen the deer. A half hour later he peeked over the top of a ridge and saw two fine bucks in a clearing 100 yards below him. He dropped them both with quick shots from the same spot.

Hunting mule deer with pickup trucks has been common procedure in the plains and foothills of the West. You simply drive cross-country in good deer areas till you jump deer. A few years ago the system got so out of hand in North Dakota that it's now illegal for hunters to drive off established roads and trails in that state. This is as it should be. Hunting from a vehicle is no sport and no challenge. Such things just don't happen in the East because no self-respecting whitetail buck will allow himself to be killed so easily.

I'll concur, however, that it's standard practice in the heavy brush country of the South Texas to hunt whitetails by pickup truck. This is a special situation. Some of the ranches there are hunted so lightly the whitetails aren't overly cautious. But the main reason for using a vehicle in some areas is that the brush is so thick a man can't see a deer from ground level. So the pickups are specially rigged with platforms built about six feet above the beds of trucks. Hunters, while riding or standing on the platforms, can look down into the brush.

Regardless of these factors I certainly don't want to imply that hunting mule deer is always easy. On the contrary, most of my mule-deer hunting has been far tougher than my whitetail hunting, especially from a physical standpoint. A mule deer is much more of a wilderness animal than the whitetail. The latter has learned to cope with man's civilization and is often hunted on flat country along the edges of towns and cities. You'll seldom find mule deer in such places because they are fundamentally animals of the mountains, canyons, draws, and slopes. If you want a good buck you'd best figure on getting back into the wilderness away from the beaten track.

This does not contradict the notion that mule deer are easier to kill than whitetails. It simply points out that once you get into good mule-deer country—which often requires hard work in the form of backpacking, going on horseback, or hiking over rough country—your chances of downing a buck are better than if you were hunting whitetails. Beginners at mule-deer hunting are always encouraged by learning that their odds of taking a buck are high, but their enthusiasm often fades when they make their first hunt and find that the work involved in getting a mule deer can be a lot tougher an adventure than they anticipated.

Mule deer have several personality traits that make them vulnerable once you get into a good hunting area. This deer is a far more placid animal than the whitetail. His personality is deliberate. He'll react more out of habit than the impulsive whitetail, which is nervous and jumpy and far more clever. I've already mentioned that jumped mule deer will often move off a short distance, stop, and then look back at a hunter. They also frequently run across openings, they bed down in spots where they can be spotted easily, and they can be driven along predictable escape routes. Whitetails seldom exhibit these traits.

Mule deer are far less suspicious of man. Many times I've watched these animals, caught by surprise in the open, stare at me for a few moments

Mule deer bucks are more gregarious than whitetails. Though whitetail bucks are usually loners, it's not uncommon to see three or four muley bucks traveling together.

then walk slowly away as if I presented no danger at all. Bedded muleys also have the unhealthy (for them) habit of jumping up and looking at a hunter before taking off. When you combine all these factors with the realization that mule deer are found in more open country than whitetails it's no wonder that a lot of them are shot at.

Mule deer are far more gregarious than whitetails, and this is another great advantage to the hunter. It's not unusual to see herds of ten or more muleys feeding on a single ridge or slope. And, except during the rut, bucks of this species are often found in groups. It's not uncommon to spot three or four bucks feeding together. This is one reason why proportionately more trophy muleys are taken than whitetails. When a hunter comes upon a group of these bucks he'll naturally try for the best head. The whitetail hunter normally sees only a single buck at a time. He'll usually take the first one he sees, and the odds are good the animal will be a younger, less-clever buck without much of a rack.

64

Successful hunting of the muley often involves knowledge of the animal's migration tendencies. Mountain deer will range high in summer and low in the dead of winter. During hot weather these animals range near timberline to avoid heat and insects. The really big bucks—in an attempt to escape hunters—will often stay high till snow becomes belly-deep. (Unlike elk, which graze off the ground, deer are browsing animals and can find food above deep snow.) If you want those big bruisers you'll have to go up there after them.

Still, as I touched on earlier when I told about one of my Colorado hunts, mountain mule deer tend to migrate down along general migration routes and they tend to concentrate in given areas. The experts who know the general boundaries of these routes and areas have little trouble killing fine bucks each year. Migration is another trait that's insignificant to whitetail hunters.

The top periods for hunting deer are dawn and dusk. This principle holds true for both mule deer and whitetails. All deer are basically nocturnal animals. By dawn they are moving from feeding to bedding areas. At dusk the reverse process begins. You're likely to see the most deer by being in hunting country during these two periods.

However, you should be aware that some big mule deer bucks tend to be quite active—especially in oak brush and other thicket areas—during the period from about 10 a.m. to 1 p.m. I've never heard any reasonable explanation for this, but if you'll check a lot of kill records you'll discover that a considerable number of trophy muleys are downed during this midday period by experts at stillhunting. These fellows move quietly through the brush looking for the browsing bucks who seem to feel an urge to feed during midday. It's a tendency that whitetails don't have.

Another trait that distinguishes a muley buck from a whitetail buck is the former's desire to watch his back track. Though I've mentioned in several places in this book that I believe modern tracking is mostly a waste of time, here is another good place to point out one reason why I feel this way.

A hunter-wise mule deer watches his back track because he has learned it's one of the best ways to stay alive. Consider that a deer has far better eyesight, hearing, and sense of smell than you do. Consider further that a buck watching his back track is doing so from a stationary position behind at least some cover. Is it any wonder that a moving hunter is easily detected? You have practically no chance at all to get a shot at a mule-deer buck by following his track if he has the least suspicion you're after him. I shake my head every time I meet a hunter in the West who tells me he's tracking a big buck he jumped. The man is usually wasting his time.

The only time tracking may work—note that I say *may* and not *will*—is when there's enough snow on the ground so you can see your buck's tracks from a considerable distance. If you follow the tracks from 100 yards or more to the side it's possible you may surprise the animal before he's aware of your presence, especially if you move in from behind cover above the deer. Being on the uphill side of the trail accomplishes two purposes. First, deer seldom look up so you're less likely to be seen. Second, you'll be able to see a deer's tracks in snow a lot better and from a greater distance if you're above the trail, which means you can stay farther away from the back track area your buck is watching.

It's been my experience that mule deer pick up movement a bit better than whitetails. This is probably because movement, rather than sound or scent, is a more common warning of danger in the open country of the West than in the thick forests of the East. This is why it's important for the mule-deer hunter in open and semi-open terrain to avoid getting into places where he can be seen easily. Never walk along the top of a ridge where you'll be skylighted. If you want to go high it's best to work along just below the top of ridges. Never go up or down an open slope if you can pick another route that offers some cover. When you're stillhunting or stalking it's best to stick to the heaviest cover available.

Being inconspicuous often has a good deal to do with your equipment. Don't use anything that will shine or glitter. In some areas it seems to be a fad today to have shiny instead of blued rifle bolts. This seems to me to be a mistake simply because a shiny bolt will glitter. So will other items such as the cheaper grades of Blaze-Orange shooting vests. Purchase the better quality, which is soft, pliable, and nonreflective.

Back in the late 1800s mule deer were almost wiped out across the West by settlers who hunted for meat and by market hunters who hunted for hides. Today this species is well-established in so many different types of terrain and in so many different climates that there's no such thing as typical mule deer country. I've hunted them along creek bottoms at low altitude and far up on the slopes of mountains. The one generality I have made is that muleys like rougher and more open country than do whitetails. We can narrow this down a bit by adding that the mule deer tends to inhabit brushy coulees and draws while the whitetail prefers taller cover.

One of the greatest attractions of mule-deer hunting is the possibility of coming up with a real trophy rack. This species grows the largest and handsomest antlers of all North American deer. Even a young mule-deer buck will boast antlers far larger than young whitetail bucks. The difference is even greater as each species matures.

To make the record book in the North American Big Game Awards Program, you'll have to take a typical whitetail scoring a minimum of 170 points. But to make the book with a typical mule deer you'll have to take a rack scoring 195 points. If you study the latest record book (published about every six years) you'll find there are well over 200 mule deer listed scoring 195 or better, but very few whitetails score above 195. I'll discuss the record book in Chapter 21.

The rack of a typical mule deer is dichotomous, which means that it is

This young mule deer buck is still in velvet. Note the two "Y" branches on each beam that characterize the "typical" rack for trophy scoring purposes.

The antlers of this aging monarch show many long, abnormal points in addition to the two basic "Ys" on each antler. For trophy scoring of this head in the "typical" category the total length of abnormal points would penalize the score. In the "nontypical" category, the abnormal points would improve the score. Scoring aside, this is a very impressive head.

evenly branched. The antlers are basically "Y" formed, and the upper ends form into two smaller "Ys." The points of a whitetail buck all come off one main beam, much as the points on a garden rake. A branched rack can, of course, be much more massive. Mule-deer antlers also curve inward less than whitetail racks, which means their size can be more impressive because they tend to be higher and wider. These facts are probably the basis for the somewhat confusing terminology on how many antler points a buck actually has. Hunters in eastern whitetail country count all points on both the left and right antlers. Thus, a buck with four points on each side would be an eight-pointer. In mule-deer country this same buck would be a four-pointer because western hunters count only the points on one antler. A whitetail buck with antlers measureing 20 inches across the outside spread could very well be a candidate for the record book, but veteran mule-deer hunters don't consider a muley a top trophy unless the buck boasts an outside spread in the 30-inch bracket.

Though mule deer in general are easier to harvest than whitetails, these big bucks with the enormous racks can be very difficult to fool. The antlers of a mule deer reach their greatest size when the animal is at least five years old. A five-year-old has seen plenty of hunting pressure. The only reason he's still alive is that he learned how to be clever.

These bucks seek terrain that is not overrun by hunters. When hunting season comes on they normally bed in areas hunters find almost impossible to reach without being heard or seen. Choice areas are just under rimrocks. That's why these crafty old bucks are often called "rimrockers." They'll also bed at the upper ends of canyons or draws offering a screen of brush or weeds.

Such sites are ideal for safety because the hunter who tries approaching from below is readily seen. Sometimes trophy bucks consider the wind direction when picking these bedding spots. They like to have the wind at their backs so they can smell or hear an intruder approaching from behind.

One way to outsmart these bucks is to cash in on the mule deer's trait of seldom allowing a hunter to approach closer than 100 yards. Where a whitetail may lie in hiding while a hunter passes within a few steps, the muley will jump and move out when he figures you're getting too close. The hunter who moseys along about 100 yards or so below rimrocks or the tops of canyons and draws often lulls a buck into thinking he isn't seen. The ones that decide they're not in trouble till it's too late get shot at. The principle to remember is to take your time, move slowly in zigzagging directions and never walk straight toward a spot a buck may lie up in. If he thinks he's been seen while you're still several hundred yards away he'll slip out behind cover or go over the top.

If you have a partner you can try ambushing a buck if you already have spotted him. One partner sneaks in behind the animal and takes a stand along the route the buck will likely use when escaping the downhill man.

Mule deer will often bed down in areas that offer little concealment. Contrasting snow thus makes them easy to spot.

In this case the lower hunter simply moves uphill toward the buck in a straight-on approach designed to make him scared enough to try escaping. When he moves out he may get waylaid by the hunter in hiding.

Another trick is to hunt from above if you have the wind in your face or at least quartering into you. This technique takes advantage of the knowledge that deer seldom look up. Also, they expect danger from below and consequently they'll bed in a spot harboring some cover that screens them from below. Often this cover affords little or no camouflage from above. A buck picking such a spot will be in plain view of the hunter above. In addition, the hunter who works high while looking down can see anything that moves over a considerable area.

This last trick is almost sure death to a buck if you discover his hiding spot while you're still so far away you don't worry him. This is the reason why spotting scopes and good binoculars are of far more value when hunting mule deer than whitetails. Experienced hunters know the types of areas where mule-deer bucks are likely to lie up and they glass these areas thoroughly. When they spot a buck they then decide which of the tricks I've mentioned should work best.

Because of the vast terrain and distances where mule deer are hunted they usually are not driven with the same techniques used so successfully with whitetails. However, a partner can help in much the same way when you're hunting small canyons or draws. The accepted procedure is for one hunter to circle around in advance and post himself on a stand at the head of a canyon or draw where deer are likely to emerge when jumped. The other man then zigzags up through the cover as he tries to jump deer. Another good system is for each man to work opposite sides of the depression, moving slowly and on the same elevation. Deer jumped by one man will often run across the depression with the idea of escaping out through the other side. Therefore, any game moving out is likely to be seen by one or the other of the hunters.

To avoid hunters, mountain mule deer often stay high up until the snow becomes belly deep, making food scarce. Clever bucks are the last to migrate down, yet most travel along established routes, just as the bucks in this photo are doing.

A good trick for a single hunter working these depressions is to select a spot at the top where he has a fine view of the terrain below him. Then he pitches or rolls rocks down into the cover where deer may be. The noises so produced are very irritating to mule deer. They'll take only so much of it, then out they go. This trick again takes advantage of the fact that muleys just won't take a chance on hiding with the tenacity of whitetails.

Though the watering habits of mule deer are no different than those of whitetails, it's good to keep in mind that watering holes are fewer and farther between in the West than in the East. This means that taking a stand by a known watering area in mule-deer country can be quite productive simply because a lot of deer are likely to be using the spot.

I have a rancher friend in Wyoming who kills his buck every year near the overflow puddle produced by one of his windmills. He takes a stand 100 yards from the puddle and waits for deer to come down out of the hills at dusk. It's an easy way to kill a deer, and it's very effective. Smart western hunters keep their eyes open for watering areas used heavily by deer.

As a general rule mule deer will water—and feed—at lower elevations, then move high to bed down as dawn comes on. It follows that a good hunting technique is to climb above feeding and watering areas under the cover of darkness and take a stand along the edge of game trails leading up through canyons, draws or gullies.

Good binoculars are almost a must for this type of hunting. From an outcropping of rock or other high vantage point a man can glass a lot of country. He may see deer moving directly toward him, but it's more likely he'll spot animals bedding down somewhere below. In this case he can switch to one of the hunting methods I described earlier. In any event, if you get above the animals before they start moving up you'll be in a far better position to spot them than if you hunt the low country.

If your favorite technique is stillhunting, don't expect to hear alerted mule deer snort as whitetails often do. And, as I pointed out in the beginning of this chapter, muleys don't run with their tails erect, which is standard whitetail procedure. But they do move out in various gaits, and these gaits can offer clues as to what the deer intends to do.

If your buck takes off with the peculiar pogo-stick gait I described earlier, it usually means he is alarmed but not quite sure of what to do next. Chances are he will cover a short distance, then stop and offer a standing shot. If a buck starts off this way it's often best to hold off shooting and wait for the best opportunity.

If the buck really wants to blow out of there he'll move with astonishing speed and power in a dead run. But even then he may not go far. He may flee wildly for 100 yards or so, then stop on top of a knoll or ridge to stare back at you. Though I've never tried the trick, I've heard many veterans tell how they stopped a running mule deer simply by yelling or whistling at him. The unusual noise apparently makes the the deer curious enough to stop and wonder what's going on.

If you jump a buck in thick cover and he takes off running, you'll probably have no chance to score unless you try a quick shot. But if the terrain is relatively open, chances are your buck—especially if he's a young one—will stop before he goes far. Even if he doesn't, it's very possible you can get another opportunity to shoot. Once a mule deer runs over a ridge or knoll, he's likely to stop when he has the hunter out of sight. These deer seem to have an out-of-sight, out-of-mind attitude.

Unlike whitetails that thrive near towns or in lowlands, mule deer are essentially animals of mountains, canyons, and slopes.

In relatively open country, mule deer favor brushy coulees and draws that afford food and cover.

Once in Wyoming I jumped a herd containing two bucks. The six animals ran over a knoll and disappeared. It was a small knoll, which I circled in several moments. When I came around to the other side the herd was standing dead-still in wide-open prairie watching their back tracks. I lined my rifle on the larger buck and dumped him. Such incidents are common in the West, but they're almost unheard of in whitetail country. Once a whitetail buck starts running, he's long-gone.

Another dramatic example of the differences between the two species is shown in their requirements for bedding spots. A whitetail buck will always select a dense thicket or other heavy cover while a muley buck may bed in cover so scant the average hunter would never believe a deer could be there. I've seen them bedded near a single bush in otherwise open terrain. I've already pointed out that muleys like to bed high—primarily because a high spot offers the best view of potential danger—but once they're high, they'll often bed with scant thought of cover. This, again, is why good binoculars can be such an important hunting tool in the West. The careful glassing of any slope or ridge during midday hours may turn up a bedded buck. And don't overlook the vast rocky areas that course these types of terrain. They may seem incapable of hiding deer when viewed from below, but once you climb up you'll find endless crannies in which the muleys find ideal bedding sites. The best mule-deer hunters spend far more time glassing than do the best whitetail hunters.

And many of these same mule-deer hunters make a point of knowing what the deer feed on in the areas they hunt. The chief forage of deer can vary drastically from region to region. Concentrating your hunting efforts in an area of top food supply can often be the major factor contributing to a successful hunt. If you don't know what the favorite plant species are and what they look like, you can get the information from local game wardens or veteran hunters. Keep in mind, however, that mule deer are migratory in states with mountainous terrain. A forage area heavily used by deer in December may not harbor a single animal in October. Be sure you're hunting the right area at the right time. A big muley buck needs over seven pounds of food per day, he isn't going to use an area unless the range supports the best menu he can find.

One theory that has carried over from the old days is that a mounted man can get closer to game than one on foot because game isn't alerted by four-footed critters. Don't put much stock in this theory today. Too many mule deer have been shot at over too many years by hunters who stepped off horses and blazed away. Modern bucks have been bred with the instinct to be wary of anything that isn't a normal part of their habitat. It's best to accept the principle that a horse only helps get you up to where the game is. From there on, you'll usually be more successful if you hunt on foot and employ the techniques I've discussed.

When to go hunting during deer seasons isn't nearly as important for mule deer hunters as it is for whitetail hunters. In whitetail country most of the deer harvest is cropped off the first few days of each season. Many whitetail bucks, especially the young ones that haven't yet learned the ways of hunters, are caught by surprise on opening day when nimrods flood the woods. It may take the survivors a couple of days to find hiding places, but when they do, they become exceedingly difficult to hunt.

Hunting pressure in mule-deer country isn't usually as heavy; consequently, the deer aren't as spooky. Also, as I have mentioned several times, mule deer in some areas are migratory. A whitetail buck, not being migratory, is in danger all season in the same small and usually quite accessible area he calls home. But a muley often moves out of a given range and into another. When he does this he loses some caution because of his tendency to think he has moved away from trouble. This is one reason a good share of big muley bucks are taken late in the season.

So your chances of success with mule deer are just about as good the last day of the season as the first. They may be a whale of a lot better if you hunt late when there is snow on the ground, especially in the deer-concentration areas utilized during migration, or if you use the glassing technique. A deer bedded in snow is far easier to spot than one bedded on bare ground.

Furthermore, early-season hunting in the West can be tough because deer seasons get underway much sooner than in the East. September hunting can be hot, which restricts your physical activity. The rut has not started, which means the big bucks are off by themselves and are cagier than they are when the rut begins. It's a fact that mule-deer hunting may be at its worse when the sun is shining, the temperature is hot, the ground is free of snow, and the most hunters are out.

A last big distinction between eastern whitetail hunting and mule-deer hunting is the readily available guided hunt in the West. The guided mule deer hunt is tailor-made for the man who is too busy to learn hunting techniques, and who has little time to spend on the adventure itself. Guides and outfitters are few in whitetail country, but numerous in the West. The busy hunter, for a price, can probably get his mule-deer buck with little more preparation than sighting in his rifle. This type of deer hunting has become so prevalent today that I'll devote much more emphasis to the subject in a later chapter.

7

General Tips

The title of this chapter may seem odd in view of the fact that this entire book is filled with tips. But all the other chapters relate to specific phases of deer hunting, this one covers tips that all deer hunters should be aware of regardless of which hunting technique they may be using. Some principles of our sport are universal.

GAME TRAILS

The most important general tip is that the basic nature of all deer is to use game trails in all types of weather and on all types of terrain. Game trails should always be your primary consideration when going into deer-hunting territory anywhere. The one thing that all experts have in common is an intimate knowledge of deer trails whether they take a stand, participate in drives, stillhunt, or stalk. For the most logical thing for a deer to do from all the standpoints of safety, ease of reaching feeding and bedding grounds, and protection from the elements is stay on trail. The only exception to this principle is a wounded deer, for he may go anywhere.

Even when danger threatens, a clever buck will seldom panic and move out through openings just because he can get away faster. He'll almost always sneak along a game trail leading to security cover. Unalarmed deer almost always move along trails to get to wherever they want to go. Your hunts must be based on this all-important prin-

Deer use trails in all types of weather and terrain. Thus, your odds improve if you can locate these trails and hunt near them by means of stands, stalking, stillhunting, or drives.

ciple to be consistently successful. In many other places in this book I'll get into the details of how deer trails relate to the various hunting techniques; I just want to emphasize here that whenever I mention trails I'm talking about one of the deer hunter's most important concerns.

BLAZE ORANGE

With the coming of the Hunter's Moon the foremost thought in the minds of all deer hunters is getting a buck. This is as it should be, but the objective should also include getting through the hunt safely.

In the old days, hunting accidents were more common than they are to-day for a single reason: the old tradition among deer hunters of wearing red and black checked wool outfits, or a simple red covering, which really was sort of stupid. A hunter dressed in red is not wearing an "awareness" color. If you're clad in red your movements could be mistaken for a deer, or you could simply be behind a deer and not be noticed as the animal is fired upon.

You'll always be noticed if you wear some outer clothing of Blaze Orange, also called hunter's orange or fluorescent orange. Nature has nothing to offer that comes close to the brilliance of the modern safety-minded outdoorsman who is wearing Blaze Orange.

The truth is that nature does offer plenty of variations in red. Dress in red and you may not look out of place at all under certain conditions. Studies have shown that red fades on cloudy days, especially in thickets where light penetration is less. Red needs good light to be highly visible. At dawn and dusk—the two prime deer-hunting times—red fades into oblivion.

Blaze Orange does not. It is always visible, even in the first or last moments of daylight. Hunters wearing it, even if it's just a cap, are not mistaken for deer. And if a nearby hunter swings on a running animal, that orange registers in his eyes immediately as the gun swings past its wearer.

That's reason enough why many states have passed laws making Blaze Orange mandatory for deer hunting. The scientific data on Blaze Orange is supported by a wealth of practical experience.

The Pennsylvania Game Commission recently reported: "There has never been a person shot in Pennsylvania who was wearing fluorescent orange and who was mistaken for game." In 1973 alone, there were twenty-five accidents in the Keystone State involving hunters who were wearing the traditional red, and an additional thirty-one mishaps involving hunters who wore no safety color at all.

Kansas passed a mandatory Hunter Orange Law in 1965; they haven't had a single fatality in the mistaken-for-game or in-the-line-of-fire categories there since. Georgia passed its law in 1973 and reported its first season without a hunting fatality in twenty years. The list goes on and on.

Even in states where legality is not a factor, nimrods who know the score are retiring the drab red plaid deerstalker's jacket. And why not? With the exceptions of waterfowl and wild turkey, game couldn't care less if the sportsman looks like a neon sign to other hunters. Visibility is not a factor in spooking deer. All big-game animals are color blind.

It all adds up to a single simple fact: Being seen by other hunters is being safe. So, whether you are hunting where it is required or not, get into Blaze Orange this year if you haven't already done so. A small investment in fluorescent-colored deer-hunting outerwear can pay big safety dividends, and you'll be doing what a lot of other smart deer hunters are doing. Here are some more facts:

A Wisconsin Department of Natural Resources (DNR) survey during the 1974 deer hunting season showed that 63 percent of the hunters observed were wearing some form of Blaze Orange clothing.

According to DNR Hunter Safety Supervisor Homer Moe, the survey was conducted in sixty-one counties during one day of the nine-day hunt and included 16,269 hunters.

"This 63 percent is a significant increase from the 49 percent observed the previous year and 29 percent in 1972," Moe told me. "And, not only did the total use of Blaze Orange increase, but more hunters wearing it wore a vest or jacket in addition to a cap."

Moe also mentioned that none of the firearms accidents during the season involved a victim dressed in Blaze Orange. In addition, many DNR field personnel commented on the high visibility of hunter orange and its obvious safety value.

Investigation of a shooting death on the first day of Minnesota's 1974 deer season convinced a Beltrami County deputy sheriff of the virtues of modern Blaze-Orange hunting clothing.

In his report of the accident to the Department of Natural Resources, Deputy David L. Bergstrom said the dead hunter was shot by another member of his hunting party who was shooting at a deer and did not see the victim. The victim was wearing the old-style red clothing and was in dense cover.

Reconstructing the accident, Bergstrom said he placed two of his assistants on the spot where the victim was shot, one in Blaze Orange clothing and the other in red.

He then stood where the shooter had been at the time the fatal shot was fired, a point about 150 feet away.

"From this position," said Bergstrom, "I could clearly see the Blaze Orange jacket worn by one man, but the red jacket worn by the other man was extremely difficult to see, even with the knowledge that he was there."

Orange clothing—not just any orange but a special orange color—is the key. The effectiveness of hunter orange depends to a large degree on its fluorescence, or termed differently, its ability to actually emit light rather than just reflect it. Since most substances absorb some of the light that strikes them and reflect the rest, they cannot match the brightness of a fluorescent object, which actually gives off more light than hits it. For example, a pure white card will reflect only 90 percent of the available light hitting it. Fluorescent orange has a reflective index as high as 200 percent.

What this means to the deer hunter is that he should do a little shopping around to compare the degree of fluorescence of the various items available. Some hunting clothing now on the market is orange, but is not truly fluorescent. The hunter's margin of safety will be increased if he chooses the brightest, most garish item he can find because it will have the highest degree of fluoresence.

CHECK RESULTS OF EVERY SHOT

Last fall during the second weekend of our Michigan deer season, I was attempting to drive deer out of streamside thickets toward my son who was on a stand. While fighting my way through a particularly thick clump of brush I spotted a dead deer only a few yards ahead. It proved to be a fine forkhorn buck that had been shot through the heart. The animal had probable died the previous weekend because it was now bloated and partially spoiled.

Through the years I've found other dead deer in the woods, and every time I've come upon the sight I get mad as hell. A lot of prime meat is wasted every fall by deer hunters who shoot at bucks and assume they have missed when they actually haven't. There are many reasons for this. Many hunters go after deer with rifles and ammunition which combine far more firepower than is ideal for killing deer. I'll get into the details in Chapter 16, but I just want to mention that the guy shooting a heavy slug in, say, a .30/06, is likely to put his bullet straight through a deer before it has a chance to expand.

Expanding bullets that blow up inside a deer produce the extreme shock that kills. Bullets that don't do their expanding jobs usually produce fatal wounds if the animal is hit in a vital area, but he may run a considerable distance before dying. And even a buck that is hit properly with a proper bullet may show no immediate sign of being mortally wounded. I once shot at close range a mule-deer buck in Montana which didn't even flinch when my slug blew up in his lungs. I couldn't believe it when he turned and ambled toward some thickets. I put another 100-grain bullet into his lungs just as he was walking into cover. That one didn't seem to phase him either.

The buck didn't go very far before caving in, but from all appearances it seemed as if I had missed him with both shots. The same thing happens all too frequently with deer hunters, especially on long shots. Never take it for granted that you missed. Deer have amazing stamina. If you haven't heard stories of bucks running off with their hearts exploded from bullets you haven't been deer hunting very long. Some deer, especially those frightened before the shot, refuse to go down. They'll run off and die while running before they'll drop. This is common when a deer is hit in a vital area with a bullet not appropriate for the job. Such bucks don't go far before piling up, but they can begin a dash with strength enough to convince you that your bullet missed.

So it's common sense to check the results of every shot. Carefully mark the spot where you last saw your buck. Go to that spot and look for blood or hair. If you find no indication of a hit it's best to cut 20- to 30-yard arcs across the last direction the animal was headed. Look for blood as well as looking for tracks. If you find nothing return to the original spot and repeat the search through bigger arcs. If you still find no signs of a hit you can be reasonably sure you missed.

The reason this system should be employed is that deer do not always drop blood immediately upon being hit. Often they'll move off some distance before the bleeding starts. When you do find blood you can often tell where your deer was hit. Bright frothy blood with visible bubbles indicates a heart or lung shot. A buck hit in these areas won't go far. Dark beet-red blood usually means a bullet through the liver. A liver shot usually puts a deer down quickly, too. If the blood contains bits of yellow or green matter you're faced with tracking a gut-shot animal. Such a wounded deer will often travel a considerable distance before dying. Clear, uniform blood of medium color almost always means a muscle wound that does not penetrate the body cavity. Animals so wounded are usually not found and generally recover.

Sometimes a mortally wounded deer will drop no blood at all. In this case his tracks may be a clue that he has been hit. A wounded deer will usually leave game trails and other deer he may have been with at the shot. He wants to be alone and will go off by himself. If a deer's tracks suddenly deviate from his original course it could mean that he's been hit. Be especially suspicious of deer that head for nearby water. It's instinctive for wounded deer to go to water. They feel that water will cool and heal their wound. In any event, smart hunters consider as wounded every deer that moves away after the shot. Only after careful checking should you conclude that your shot actually missed.

HOW TO CHOOSE BINOCULARS

In the next chapter I'll point out why binoculars can be a tremendous aid in spotting deer, but here I'll discuss choosing the right pair.

The first decision to make is what magnifying power is best for you. The basic reason for using binoculars is to make things look closer. This is accomplished by magnifying the image. A glass that makes an object look six times closer is termed a six-power glass and is marked 6x. In addition to power you should also consider light-gathering ability, field of view, size, weight, and cost.

A glass anywhere from six to eight power is preferred by most deer hunters. If you go beyond 8x you should remember that increased power has its drawbacks. The larger-power glasses are heavier and therefore less steady to hold and have reduced fields of view and poorer light-gathering qualities. When you're trying to focus in on deer in brush or at long distances, the problem of holding a high-power pair of glasses steady is important. This is one reason why it makes little sense to go beyond 8x.

Remember that each little tremor or shake is multiplied in direct proportion to the power of your glass. Six-power binoculars will multiply each shake six times, so it's obvious you'll get a clearer picture in terms of shake with a 6x glass than you will with a 10x.

Field of view—the amount of landscape you can see through your glasses without moving them—decreases as power increases. An 8x glass has only three-fourths the field of view that a 6x has. Increased magnification also cuts down relative brightness. A 6x pair of binoculars has four times as much light-gathering brightness as a 10x. Since deer hunters often find their best action in poor light conditions (early and late in the day) it again makes little sense to choose binoculars beyond 8x.

If your glasses are marked with the numbers 6x30, the "six" is the power and the "thirty" is the size of the objective lens in millimeters. The size of the objective lens has a big effect on performance. The larger the objective lens the brighter the image will be. So it's obvious that a 6x15 wouldn't serve you nearly as well as a 6x30.

From my experience I'd say that most of the deer hunters I know who have had a lot of experience with glassing use either 6x30 or 7x35 binoculars. Maybe I have odd eyes, but my favorite pair is 8x40. Anyway, this is the range you should choose from. You can buy binoculars for as little as $50, but you won't get much quality for that price and you won't get fully optically coated lenses. Expect to pay $125–$175 for a good pair.

Until recent years, good binoculars have been pretty much standard in size. Now you can get good-quality glasses that weigh as little as six or seven ounces. They're so small they fit easily into a shirt pocket.

HOW TO CHOOSE A HUNTING KNIFE

The more experienced the hunter, the smaller the knife he carries. Why? Because you don't need a blade longer than four inches or so to perfectly execute the gutting, skinning, quartering, and caping of your deer. A good knife is small, sharp, and handy. Those Bowies with the 10- and 12-inch blades may look good swinging from your belt, but when it comes to field dressing a deer they are nothing except awkward.

Further, all you need is a sharp blade. You don't need long finger guards, blood grooves, saw backs, finger grips in the handles, double edges, double hilts, or any of the other gimmicks which range from silly to downright dangerous. Get a top-quality knife with a blade of four inches or so and you'll be perfectly equipped. Anything bigger is excess weight.

SHORT TIP ON THE COMPASS

A compass should always be carried in wild country for the obvious reason that it may prevent you from becoming lost. Strange as it may seem, some hunters don't lose their way—but they lose their deer after they have killed and field dressed it. This happens when they leave a deer in the woods to get help in dragging it out.

Remember that a compass does nothing more than point north. It won't tell you where your deer is and it won't lead you back. You must take a compass reading on the direction you're going when you head out. Note all the major features of the terrain where your deer is, and all the major features on your way back to camp or vehicle. Base your return trip on compass heading and observance of the familiar terrain features. Nothing is more discouraging than to lose a prime field-dressed deer simply because you can't find it. This compass trick is even more important during changing weather conditions. Snow or rain can change the looks of even familiar country in a hurry.

FROM FIELD DRESSING TO FREEZER

On the surface, dressing out a deer sounds like a difficult and messy job. It really isn't if you go at it correctly. Veteran deer hunters wipe the last blood off their knives about 15 minutes after they walk up to their downed buck.

The first step is to drag the carcass to sloping ground and place it on its back with the head uphill. This is because the carcass will drain best from its rear end after it's cut open. Then follow these steps in order:

1) Cut a circle around the anal vent with your knife point going about one inch deep. Pull the vent out an inch or so and tie it off with a piece of cord. A boot lace will suffice if you don't have a cord. (It's best to keep a short piece of cord in one of your pockets for this specific purpose.) The vent is tied off to prevent droppings from coming into contact with the meat.

2) Begin the abdominal incision at the V formed by the breast bones of the rib cage. Your purpose is to open the animal without puncturing any of the intestines, so this cut is critical. Make the cut with the blade edge up. Guide the blade between two fingers of the left hand which should hold the skin up and away from the gut pouch. Slit the skin and belly membrane down the belly and around both sides of the genitals to the crotch. Some veterans don't bother cutting around the genitals, they just slash them off and make a straight cut from breastbone to crotch. Many guides do this. I've never had any reason to feel that slicing off the genitals has any effect on the taste of the meat, and it seems to me to be a little neater to cut around them.

But don't waste your time cutting the glands from a deer's legs. Years ago it was believed these glands would taint the meat if not removed. It's now known that this isn't true. Deer have glands not only on their legs but between their toes and at the corners of their eyes. All of these glands become inactive after death.

3) Tilt the carcass sideways, then reach inside and pull the abdominal contents out far enough so you can cut away the diaphragm, which is a wall of thin muscle tissue separating the chest area and the belly.

4) Reach into the chest area with your free hand, grasp the windpipe as far toward the head as possible, and cut it free.

Steps 1 & 2

Step 2a

Step 3

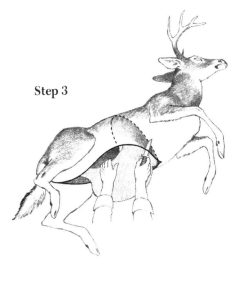

Step 4

5) Roll the carcass on its side and pull out all the innards. The rectum and its contents will come through the anal cut with gentle tugging. Be careful. The bladder lies within the pelvis and you don't want to cut or break it.

6) Separate the heart and liver from the pile; cut them free; wipe them clean; and lay them on a rock, a log, or the grass to drain. After they have drained, put them into a plastic bag carried for the purpose. These parts of the deer should be eaten fresh.

7) Check for bloodshot muscle or shattered bone and cut these parts away from the carcass because they spoil quickly and will taint the meat.

8) If your deer was gut-shot and water or snow is available, wash it out carefully. Don't use water unless the intestines were shot, broken, or cut, because moisture hastens spoilage of an otherwise normal carcass. The best bet is to tip the deer on its belly to drain puddles of blood then wipe the inside of the carcass with grass, ferns, or anything dry.

9) Prop open the belly cavity with a stout stick to hasten the cooling.

10) What you do next depends on your situation. If you have partners it's best to drag the deer out to camp or vehicle and hang it as soon as possible. Animal heat is what spoils game. A deer will spoil as quickly in cold weather as in warm weather if the carcass isn't lifted off the ground and hung as soon as possible so air circulation can cool the meat. If you can't get help till the next day, get the carcass off the ground by hanging it, dragging it over brush, or working poles under it.

Some lone hunters skin and quarter their deer immediately. Then they hang the quarters, go back to camp or vehicle, and return later with a packboard. It is far easier to make two trips with a packboard than to drag a deer out in one.

Most hunters have help available to get their deer out of the woods soon after the kill. It's at this point that two basic mistakes are made, and they're both hangovers from the old days. Years ago it was custom to hang a deer by its head and to leave the skin on during the aging process. A quick look into any slaughter house will show you that modern meat handlers know better.

Hanging a deer by its head tends to allow whatever blood remains in the carcass to drain into the hindquarters, which contains most of the best cuts. Conversely, a deer hung by its hind legs will allow the remaining blood to drain into the neck and head, which contain little edible meat. Commercial meat cutters also skin their carcasses immediately after killing because skin holds in the animal heat that taints the meat. My primary objective after getting my deer field-dressed is to get it skinned as soon as possible. My second objective is to have the carcass aged three or four days before the meat is cut up and frozen. This isn't always possible if I'm hunting away from home, but aged meat is always more tender than non-aged meat.

In my opinion, venison chops and steaks are far more tasty than venison roasts. I tell the guy who butchers my deer to get every last steak and chop out of the carcass, cut them one inch thick and forget about roasts. The remaining scraps of meat go into deerburger. The old custom was to have pork mixed into deerburger. I don't do this because pork needs thorough cooking. I like my deerburgers and meatloafs on the medium-rare side.

Good quality freezer paper is ideal for wrapping deer meat for freezing. Wrap similar cuts in packages large enough to provide a meal for you and your family. In my case I have one teenager left at home, so I wrap enough meat in one package to feed three people. I mark all my packages with identifying words such as: "Venison—round steak." This enables me to get the type of meat I want for any particular meal. I don't date my packages; my family loves venison so much that it doesn't last long around my house.

Many deer hunters don't bother saving their animals' hides for clothing or crafts, but if you want to utilize your deer's hide, the first step is to coat the flesh side with salt. The following day remove this coating and the accumulated moisture, then re-salt. Fold it with the salted side in and take it to a taxidermist for tanning.

WATCH YOUR MANNERS

Once in Wyoming, I struck up acquaintance with some other Midwest hunters. These guys asked me to join them one afternoon. They seemed like nice fellows so I went along. I'll never live long enough to get over regretting that decision.

It turned out that these fellows hunted by pickup truck. They drove through cottonwood cover along creekbeds and flushed deer with the vehicle. Whenever a buck jumped up these nitwits would blaze away from the truck's bed. The lack of sportsmanship was bad enough, but the clincher came late in the afternoon when another pickup roared onto the scene and stopped our vehicle by braking right in front of us. Out jumped an irate rancher.

"Who the hell told you bums you could hunt on this ranch? This is my land and you never asked permission to hunt it. Get the hell out of here and never come back. You nonresidents don't even have the manners to act like gentlemen."

Never again will I hunt with companions I don't know or hunt on property that I'm not sure is open to me.

Another breach of conduct that I consider just about unforgivable is to bang away at someone else's buck. A couple of occasions in the West found me stalking bucks to get within surer shooting range. One nitwit noticed my obvious sneaking tactics, aimed at my buck and blazed away at a far greater range than I would have. The buck ran off unharmed.

The other time I got into good shooting range and was laying my rifle over a log when some jerk opened up on my buck from a hill behind me. On both occasions I was wearing a Blaze-Orange cap and vest. There's no question that the other so-called hunters had spotted my activities and tried for my deer before I could shoot. Not only were these guys trying to get my buck, but they were shooting out of range and spoiling the action for me. This type of conduct gives hunting a black eye.

Even worse are the hunters who have no respect for the land. The bums that strew it with empty beer cans, cigarette packages, cardboard cartons, and other assorted garbage do so with an extreme disregard for the rights of others. The man who owns the land no doubt takes pride in it in addition to paying taxes on it. The ill feeling between landowners and deer hunters in some areas is caused to a great degree by the selfish and inconsiderate hunter. In most cases the landowner who grants hunting permission does so out of the goodness of his heart. The only way a hunter is going to get back onto such property is to leave it as he found it.

The good guy not only doesn't litter, but he also does his share of the work during a hunt. Good manners are especially appreciated by all when a group makes a camping hunt. Cutting wood, cooking, washing dishes, and such chores should be shared in one way or another. There's no such thing as social status in camp. The guy who does his share will be asked to go again.

The well-mannered deer hunter observes the spirit as well as the letter of the law. He doesn't chase deer with vehicles, he doesn't let a small buck rot in the woods if he suddenly gets a chance at a better trophy, and he never takes unfair advantage of deer. The sportsman works at his hunting because cutting corners robs his hunt of its honest joy.

In short, good manners in the field are the sure way to the most enjoyable hunting. Remember too that the greatest enemies of the sport of hunting are those thoughtless characters who misbehave in the field.

TAKE CARE OF YOUR RIFLE

Because of modern design, today's rifles require less care to keep them in working order than their counterparts of years ago. They're designed so that the parts regularly needing special attention can be reached or removed quickly and easily. Actually, a modern rifle can be as ruined by too much care as by too little. Most grit and grime builds up on a gun because it has too much oil and grease to stick to. An over-oiled gun operates stiffly in freezing temperatures, too. Don't lubricate your rifle any more than is necessary to keep the parts operating efficiently. Stubborn gunk is easily removed with a rag dipped in gunpowder solvent.

Many hunters think they should oil the trigger mechanism to get a smooth trigger pull. The opposite is true. Modern rifle trigger mechanisms are quite complex and function best when they are absolutely clean and dry. If you oil them you beget crud which, in turn, makes trigger-pull rough and inconsistent. So not only should you avoid oiling your trigger mechanism, but you should be very careful to keep oil out of it when you oil other parts of your rifle.

All you need to clean your rifle is a cleaning rod with a bronze-bristled brush, solvent, an old toothbrush, oil, some clean rags, and barrel patches. Start by giving the bore a good wetting with solvent. Let it soak for a few minutes and then scrub it clean with the rod and brush. Run the brush completely through the bore before reversing direction. Repeat about ten times. This will remove streaks of lead and powder deposited in the barrel. Start from the breech if your rifle is a bolt-action. This will eliminate possible damage at the end of the muzzle, which could result in loss of accuracy. If your rifle is not a bolt-action, you'll have to clean from the muzzle end, but be careful. Be sure your rod and brush are clean; a good barrel can be ruined with a gritty cleaning rod.

After you finish the brushing operation, run a couple of clean patches through the bore. Then clean powder residue and grit or dirt from the various contours and slots of other metal parts with the toothbrush. Follow by wiping with a solvent-wetted rag, then wipe off all parts with a dry rag. Now rub a light coat of oil over everything and run an oily patch through the bore.

At this point your cleaned rifle is ready for storage, and this is the point at which a great mistake can be made: don't store a rifle in a gun case because gun cases often create and hold condensation which can cause rust and corrosion. One dramatic episode taught me how fast such storage can ruin a rifle.

Some local crook decided he wanted a good deer rifle. He decided my house would be the place to get one for free, so he broke in while my family and I were away on a winter vacation. In addition to stealing the rifle he stole a gun case in which he stored the rifle during anticipation of the following fall's hunting season. Small-time burglars usually get caught, as this one did. The police nailed him on another charge in late summer, searched his residence, and found my rifle. (I had reported the serial number when it was stolen.) The metal parts were almost completely covered with rust.

Store your guns in a dry, well-ventilated place such as a gun cabinet or part of a closet. Don't store them in the open where dust can accumulate on them. Guns in racks on open walls make great exhibitions, but guns stored in this manner collect dust in a hurry.

THE BOX YOUR NEW GUN COMES IN

A new gun today may be well-traveled by the time it reaches the hands of its ultimate owner. Along the way from manufacturer to wholesaler to retailer to customer, it receives rough handling. Yet your gun must survive this journey in factory-fresh condition—unscratched, unmarred, un-damaged in any way. Otherwise it can't be sold. This is accomplished be-cause quality guns leave the factory packed and recessed in form-fitting styrofoam or cardboard constructions which do an amazingly effective job of protecting them from damage. Surrounding the gun inside its contour-hugging form is a heavy-duty cardboard box. This is further protected by a cardboard shipping sleeve. Unfortunately for some guns, this may be the best—and sometimes the last—protection they'll ever have.

The safest way for you to transport a gun is inside one of the hard, foam-lined modern carrying cases made specifically for this purpose. But the next-best method, and one that's free, is to use the original protective ship-ping box.

So, when you buy a new gun don't leave its box with your dealer. Ask for the original box, bring it home, and keep it. If, for some reason you ever wish to return your rifle to the factory, your shipping carton is right at hand. Did you ever try to improvise a package for shipping a gun? It's a tough job.

NOTES ON CLOTHING

All-wool underwear is best for cold-weather hunting, but I can't use it since woolen underwear irritates my skin. I prefer two-piece dual-layer cotton suits so I can change either or both halves as I choose. These in-sulated suits were developed during World War II. They offer plenty of warmth except during the very coldest weather. Another fine bet is wool mixed with cotton, nylon, dacron, or silk. This type of underwear is warmer than an all-cotton garment and is favored by hunters who are sen-sitive to wool.

For socks, wool is again best. Wool absorbs perspiration and it has the ability to "breathe." Wear nylon socks underneath the wool if you have sensitive skin. All hunting socks should have thick cushioned feet. Such socks are more comfortable and offer added protection against the cold ground. Many hunters make the mistake of buying their socks too short. Short socks have a tendency to work down and bunch on the feet—an exas-perating situation. Knee-length socks are best for comfort and for turning down over short boots.

I can get all sorts of arguments over my choice of hunting pants. Person-ally, I don't like many of the pants that are designed for hunters. They don't fit well and they have too many useless giant pockets and other en-cumberments, which is why they don't fit well. Many of these pants are reinforced with rubber in the knees and seat. Well, I prefer my pants to perform their basic function. I can't see the logic in using them for gear carriers and rain suits. I wear plain trousers of hard-finished, water-repellent fabric. In extremely cold weather woolen pants are best, but most deer hunting is done in temperatures in which proper underwear provides plenty of leg warmth. Poplin or army cotton duck are pretty hard to beat for pants. These materials shed dew, briers, and branches and remain in fine shape. They also fit well without binding in the seat or chafing in the crotch. Remember to buy hunting pants large enough to fit easily over underwear. If they're too tight they'll bind in the cramped quarters of stands, or when you're kneeling and crawling.

There are two important things to look for in shirts: they should be full-cut and they should be light. A short-tailed shirt won't stay put where it belongs. Heavy shirts weigh you down. It's better to wear two light shirts than one heavy one. Two lightweight closely woven woolen shirts will be warmer than one heavy shirt because of the insulating layer of air between the fabrics. For my first shirt I prefer fine-grade, thickly napped cotton flannel that resembles chamois cloth. Such a shirt is softer and more comfortable than wool, though not quite as warm. Another advantage of wearing two shirts is that if the day warms you can take one off. With a single heavy shirt you're stuck with all-day discomfort.

I buy outsized quilted underwear shirts for an oddball reason that I find very practical. These modern insulated suits are extra-warm, ultralight, and have knit cuffs to hold in body heat. For very cold weather I use the upper part of one of these suits as an extra shirt worn over my other shirts. In effect, I use it as a jacket instead of underwear. If the day gets warm, it's far easier to slip out of my insulated shirt if it's on the outside instead of the inside of my other clothing. The same thing holds if I enter a warm room or cabin.

In cold weather I wear a snowmobile suit or a long-cut coat that keeps my hips warm. A down-filled coat is hard to beat, as is the modern design that mixes wool, polyester, and acetate. Such coats trap millions of air cells which hold body heat. Be sure your coat is water-repellent and includes a hood. When buying a coat insulated with down or synthetic materials, always check the manufacturer's tag giving you the temperature rating. Thus you can get a coat that ideally matches your hunting conditions.

The last items of clothing a deer hunter may need are gloves and mittens. If the weather is mild I prefer the ordinary, cheap cotton working gloves since they fit tight and don't interfere with gun handling. In colder weather the modern gloves combining thin capeskin with foam insulation and nylon linings are the best bets I've found. For very cold weather it's hard to beat leather mittens worn over woolen liners.

I feel that my selection of clothing offers the ultimate for the deer hunter's needs. Unless I'm on a stand in a snowmobile suit my outfit is without bulk, permits free body movements, is light in weight, keeps me dry, and fits me properly.

8

Techniques for Seeing Deer

Warren Holmes and I were pass-shooting ducks on a knoll in North Dakota. Scattered clumps of brush varying from house-size to several acres dotted the prairie around us. During a lull in the shooting my companion pointed to a small patch of thickets 300 yards away.

"Big buck," he said.

I stared at those thickets till my eyes watered. I couldn't see anything that even resembled a deer. I shook my head and said, "Warren, I think you're seeing things."

"Well, darn it," he answered, "he's standing right there next to the north edge. There, he's moving out. Surely you can spot him now."

I finally did see the deer, but not until his body began taking shape as a silhouette against the golden prairie. Even then it was difficult to spot his antlers till he turned his head to look at us.

Warren has worn glasses since childhood. I've never worn them and we're both in our late forties. My eyes are better than his, but he has made me feel like a fool on several occasions when he had to point out game to me.

One time in Wyoming we were hunting mule deer. Our host was a rancher who had hunted deer in the West for many years. His idea of hunting is to drive back-country trails in a pickup while looking for game. He is used to the system and used to the terrain, but Warren often spotted deer before he did. I recall one time we were driving slowly down through a gully.

"Hold it," Warren grunted. "Back up about 15 feet. I think I saw the top of a buck's head in those rocks 100 yards to our right."

Ken backed up and stopped. Warren had been correct. He pointed toward a precise spot and told us a small three-pointer was lying flat out while trying to hide. Neither Ken or I saw the animal till it decided to jump up and bolt.

"I'll be darned," our host said, "how'd you ever spot that little buck?"

Later in the day Warren decided he'd have a better vantage point if he rode in the truck's bed instead of its cab. Several times Ken and I were surprised by his sudden pounding on the roof. It was Warren's signal that he'd spotted more deer.

That evening Ken told Warren that he was astonished with his game-seeing abilities, particularly because Warren had little experience hunting in the West. He asked what the secret was.

"Well, I guess a deer is a deer," my partner began. "Even though I don't have much knowledge of mule deer I've hunted whitetails all my life. Most hunters make the mistake of expecting to see a whole deer. Most often you'll see only parts of a motionless animal. I seem to have a natural knack for recognizing cover where deer may be. I search that cover with my eyes, and I look for colors or shapes that could be parts of a deer. I often see a pair of legs, a flickering ear or parts of antlers before I can make out the animal itself."

You might hastily conclude that the photo on the left has no deer in it. But a careful study of the photo on the right will help you locate a buck in both pictures. Successful hunters study suspicious areas and forms.

Larry Price, a guide with whom I've hunted in Colorado, also has a great facility to see deer. He explained his ability in another way.

"Most hunters fail to see deer in heavy cover unless the animals are moving," he told me. "Movement is easy to see so I don't worry about missing it. I concentrate on looking for unnatural objects that aren't moving. When you think about it you'll realize that most objects in the woods are vertical. Sure there are blowdowns, logs, and rocks that are horizontal, but everything that's growing is vertical. Deer bodies are not. So I pay special attention to horizontal objects, and I really scrutinize anything that approaches a deer's size or color."

Wayne Fitzwater, a Montana game warden, once told me that experience is the most important factor in seeing game. We sat on the edge of a mountain ledge one evening and watched mule deer by the dozens come out of forests surrounding a logged-off area across a canyon. He claimed it isn't much of a problem to see game if you've had enough hunting experience to hunt where game is likely to be.

I'll have more to say about his theory shortly. But first I want to mention that Wayne's system had to be more complicated because he was pointing out bucks that were several hundred yards away. Not only that, he was seeing the animals as they were just beginning to walk out of the timber. Often I couldn't tell deer from stumps until they were well into the clearing.

That night in camp we discussed the art of seeing game, and Wayne mentioned something that I'd never thought about before. He just passed it off as matter-of-fact, but I believe it's an important principle most hunters are unaware of.

"Many hunters miss seeing detail because they take a wide-angle view of everything," he began. "That's because a panoramic view is naturally most interesting. The trick is to spend only half your time with the wide-angle view, the other half should be spent looking for detail. You were having trouble telling deer from stumps because you were trying to see everything at once. After you concentrated on a particular deer it suddenly didn't look like a stump at all. That's because you narrowed down your field of view. You saw a lot of stumps that looked like deer, but after you focused your attention you didn't see a deer that looked like a stump. It's just a matter of training your eyes to see detail."

How important is the art of seeing game? It's all-important for deer hunters because modern deer depend far less upon running to safety than the bucks of yesteryear. Today's bucks know their odds of staying alive are much better if they hide instead of run. Deer still panic and run, but they are apt to run for shorter distances, then hide sooner and longer.

When I started hunting mule deer years ago in the western states I was astonished to see so many deer in pastures, in fields along roads, and in plain sight in woodland clearings. That fact was brought home to me during a 1973 hunt with Ray Lyons, an outfitter in Collbran, Colorado.

When scanning for bedded bucks, hunters expect to see a prominently displayed head as shown in the top photo. But the savvy hunter will be alert to the tip of an ear or part of an antler. Had the buck in the bottom photo been a doe, it probably would have gone unnoticed.

There are seven whitetails in this photo. The casual hunter would probably spot only the doe at left. The key to success is in looking for parts of deer. The illustration on the next page will help you locate all seven deer.

We drove down out of the mountains one evening when a blizzard was brewing. In fields along the valley road we saw quite a few deer, often several of them feeding in groups. I mentioned to Ray that I'd spotted no deer along the same route during the several previous days we'd been driving it.

"They're feeding early because a storm's coming," he said. "There are plenty of deer down in these valleys but they normally don't come out of hiding till dark. Years ago you used to see deer all over the place, even during hunting season. They're much more secretive now and they're wizards at hiding. You have to look a lot harder to see deer today."

That statement comes from a man who has been a full-time guide and outfitter for nearly forty years. It's some of the best advice a modern deer hunter can get.

As for seeing whitetails, I believe Warren Holmes' convictions are about as solid as any. His score for the past eighteen years is eighteen bucks. He took all of them in a heavily hunted area of Michigan, a state where the deer-hunter success ratio is only about 11 percent. How can he score so consistently when nearly 90 percent of the hunters around him fail to go home with venison? Well, he hunts hard and he hunts only from stands, but it's likely that much of his success stems from his knack for seeing deer. One time he said to me, "The best shot in the world isn't going to eat deer liver unless he can see a deer to shoot at."

One of Warren's favorite topics is deer size. He points out that almost all hunters delude themselves into expecting the average whitetail to be much larger and taller than it really is. Tell a hunter that a big buck seldom stands taller than 40 inches at his shoulder and you'll have a doubting

hunter, but you'll be telling the truth. Warren claims that if a hunter thinks "small" he'll see more deer.

As I point out in other parts of this book, I think the odds are pretty well stacked against many deer hunters who go after their whitetail bucks by using the stillhunting technique. But I know one guy, now an old man, who used to be fairly successful with the system before his area became crowded with hunters. Years ago when I began to get serious about deer hunting I'd often visit with this fellow and ask him about the tricks of the trade. I've never forgotten one comment he made, and it's better advice now than it was then.

"I'd tell any hunter to use his eyes more than his feet," he began. "Most hunters are in too much of a hurry to see what's over the next hill. The plain fact is that once you're in good deer country your buck is just as likely to be in the thicket next to you as he is to be in one three miles away. You won't get a shot at him unless you see him before he sees you. You have to focus all your attention on the most suspicious things you see. That's the way to spot deer. Successful stillhunting is about 90 percent looking."

I'll admit that my ability to see deer is not too good, but it's far better than it was twenty years ago. Last fall I downed a mule deer buck that was almost invisible. He was standing motionless in a stand of timber so thick you could barely see the snow background behind the trees. When I first spotted him, all I noticed was a patch of gray that was out of place against the white snow and pale-green aspen trunks. Seconds later I picked out part of a rack of antlers, then I noted another patch of gray that was part of the buck's shoulder. That offered me a vital area to shoot at, and it was a big enough target since the range was short. My slug broke the deer's back and he dropped on the spot. I'm just about positive I'd never have seen that deer unless I'd known what to look for.

Is the deer in the left-hand photo a doe or a buck? Patience reveals that it's a buck—for a good shot.

Everything I've mentioned so far points out that much of the skill used in seeing deer is a skill that can be learned. I believe that most successful deer hunters develop much of this skill without being aware of it. In acquiring an extensive outdoor background a man automatically learns to interpret what he sees. As warden Wayne Fitzwater told me, an experienced hunter learns to recognize good deer country which, in turn, presents the possibility of seeing more deer. He learns to analyze where deer travel, feed, and bed; he literally thinks like a deer. In short, a man with lots of hunting experience knows where to look. The most successful veteran hunters also know *how* to look.

The most obvious way to get a better view of what you're looking at is to inspect a questionable object with binoculars or your rifle scope. Glassing for deer is especially important in western states where you're likely to see animals at greater distances than in the heavily forested East, Midwest, and South. Several guides have told me that average deer hunters have great difficulty putting their glasses or scopes on partially hidden deer even after they have located them with the unaided eye.

The reason is that most hunters seldom use their binoculars or scopes except during the few days each year that they are actually hunting. They aren't familiar enough with their equipment to use it efficiently. This is one fault I don't have because I'm a nut on using binoculars year-round.

My office windows face out on a large inland lake. I delight in studying migrating ducks in fall and spring, fishermen in summer and winter, and birds and squirrels and other interesting objects just about anytime. Scarcely a day goes by in which I don't use my binoculars several times. I'm as familiar with using those glasses as I am with touching a match to my pipe.

Bedded where light and shadow provide good camouflage, this buck would probably go unnoticed from a distance unless the hunter studied the scene with binoculars or a riflescope. Optics can be as important as the rifle.

Whitetails often bed where deadfalls or rocks conceal most of their outline. A flicked ear or a head movement may be your only tip-off unless you've drawn a sharp focus on the right spot.

This familiarity often has enabled me to see game that would have gone unnoticed. I go along with the guides who claim that the average hunter would do himself a big favor by learning to use optics efficiently. A deer antler that appears to be a branch in the distance can be identified for just what it is with the use of glasses. I could list many such examples.

If you can hunt upwind, try to move eastward in the early morning and westward in late afternoon. This will help silhouette deer against the brightest area in the sky.

Deer hunters of years ago didn't bother much with scopes or binoculars because they were relatively bulky and inefficient. Modern optics are far superior, and they represent one of the most important advances ever made in deer-hunting equipment. For today's deer hunter a good binocular can be just about as important as his rifle.

A problem among Eastern hunters who go after mule deer in the West for the first time is that they don't look for deer in the right places. Most whitetails seen from stands or during drives are likely to be spotted 50 to

75 yards away. In the more open country where mule deer are hunted, it's common to see potential targets several hundred yards away. Also, whitetails are much more likely to hide than muleys. A whitetail may not bolt until you're practically on top of him, a mule deer will seldom let you approach closer than 100 yards.

Hunters with whitetail backgrounds often go on their first mule deer hunt and continue to use the short-range vision they used back home. They miss seeing deer that may be in plain view across a canyon, down in a draw, or up on a ridge. The cure is to get local advice on where to look when hunting a new area for the first time.

A couple of years ago one of my Michigan friends joined five other fellows and drove to the Colorado Rockies for a mule-deer hunt. They had never hunted the area, they had no experience with mule deer, they had no guide, and they didn't bother to ask for local advice. They camped for six days, saw few deer, and scored on only one small buck.

In contrast, I booked a hunt in approximately the same area with a reputable outfitter. There were four hunters in my group, and we nailed four big bucks in only 2½ days of hunting. The difference was that our outfitter put us in the right spots and told us where to look for deer.

One of the main reasons hunters don't see deer is that the animals see or hear them first. Mule deer, more so than whitetails, are likely to spook and run when confronted by man. It's common sense to expect to see deer farther ahead if you're walking on crusted snow or very dry ground than if you're walking on wet or soft ground. You'll also make less noise if you eliminate noisemakers like keys or change in your pockets, canteens or binoculars banging against rifle stocks, or crinkly clothing and rain gear. The human voice is especially startling to deer. When hunting with companions it's best to save talkfests until after the day's hunting is finished.

The time of day can be a very important factor in seeing deer. One time in the prairie portion of Wyoming, I wondered why my guide started the day by stillhunting directly toward the brightening sky in the east. My unasked question was answered in a hurry when a three-point buck got up from his bed near the top of a rise 250 yards ahead of us. I'll never forget the coal-black silhouette the animal made against the dawn sky. Even his antlers were outlined in perfect detail. One of my companions shot the buck. When we reached the kill site I commented that the deer must have been stupid to let a hunter in plain sight shoot him.

"No, we weren't in plain sight," the guide answered. "Look back down to where we were when he stood up. It's still in shadows down there. He couldn't see us nearly so well as we could see him. If a man can hunt upwind he should go east in early morning and west in late evening. He'll see a lot more deer that way. On clear days, with the sun up, it's best to hunt with the sun behind you because it will shine on the deer. That's when the flick of an ear or flash of an antler really shows up."

Many hunters fail to consider the weather's effects on game movement. In this photo, bucks have retreated into a hollow to escape heavy winds.

The smart hunter knows where to look for the animals in various kinds of weather. On warm days, deer seek shade. On cold days, bucks often bed on slopes or ridges facing southern exposures where sunshine filters through the cover. Deer don't like windy places. When a strong wind is blowing it's best to look for them on the lee side of hills and ridges or in lowland pockets of cover.

The most dramatic experiences that have shown me how weather affects deer happened within a few miles of where I'm writing these lines. Deer live all around my place in mixed woodlands of hardwoods, birch, brush, and conifers. These forests are fairly thick, except where they give way to huge areas of sand dunes along the Lake Michigan shoreline. The dunes are mostly rolling hills of sand with low areas harboring scattered pockets of pine.

You could roam those dunes for days during spring, summer, and early fall and you'd be lucky to see a deer track, let alone a deer. But as fall wears on, the herds begin moving into the dunes. When heavy snowfall hits, they converge on the area. Take a trip through there in winter on a snowmobile and you'll see deer all over the place.

It's likely that deer movements in your area are affected to some degree by weather, too. I can't tell you how your local deer react to changing weather conditions because even the same species react differently in various parts of the country. But if you'll take the time to study your local situation and talk to local experts, you'll probably gain additional knowledge that will enable you to see more deer.

I believe it's possible for a man to train himself year-round to see game better. For example, I get a kick out of watching squirrels in the clearings and trees around my bird feeders. Sometimes they approach with caution, hiding against a tree trunk, flattening out on a limb, or jumping into a bush and freezing motionless for minutes. You learn something about the motions and movements of game by watching any wild animal or bird. I'm not saying you could train yourself to see deer by watching birds and squirrels in a big-city park, but I do believe that the more movements of wildlife you watch, the more you'll train your game eye to see those movements. Also, you'll be training yourself to understand what you see, and the benefits of that type of education can add up fast.

9
Why Stands Beat the Odds

East-central Montana has one of the highest deer-hunter success ratios anywhere, and I figured I'd score easily there when I scheduled a whitetail hunt with Dave Wedum, an information officer for the Montana Fish and Game Department.

Dave, who was an outfitter and guide before he joined the department, has been involved with Montana's fishing and hunting for more than thirty years. Because he figured our success was practically a sure thing, he didn't bother scouting the area we were going to hunt. What happened during our trip is a good example of the inherent advantages of hunting deer from a stand.

The weather during the first three days of our hunt was dry and still. That's the worst type of weather for still-hunting, the technique we were using because we were unfamiliar with the area. We saw some whitetails, but most were running through thickets. The only standing deer we spotted were far out of reasonable rifle range, and they were watching every move we made. In short, stillhunting just wouldn't work because the animals heard our movements and became alerted long before we were aware of their presence.

"I just can't figure where they are," said Dave. "Our surveys show there are lots of whitetails in these foothills. They must be bunched somewhere. We'll have to keep hunting new country until we find them."

That night the weather changed. When we awoke the next morning there was three inches of snow on the ground. Dave was all smiles.

"A stroke of luck," he said. "Today we're going to walk these hills until we find a lot of fresh deer sign in the snow, then you can go on a stand."

It turned out that we had spent the previous days hunting too high in the foothills. For some reason the animals were down closer to the valleys. We discovered our mistake after following fresh deer tracks leading into low-lying thickets. We found one sidehill laced with so many tracks and fresh droppings it resembled a well-used cattle pasture.

We selected a natural stand in a pile of brush and stumps that had been left by timber cutters. It was near the center of a block-wide clearing. The rubble offered a good view of the tracked-down runway that ran across the far edge of the opening. And, of great importance, I was positioned downwind from the runway.

I moved some of the brush to form a screen in front of my sitting spot. I scooped up a few handfuls of snow and scattered it over the brush I'd moved. When I was satisfied that my stand appeared natural I sat down and waited.

It was the shortest wait I ever made on a stand. I learned later that Dave had hiked down to the bottom of the sidehill a half-mile below me, then began working toward my position with a sweeping zigzag route back and forth across the incline. He began moving deer almost immediately.

I hadn't been sitting more than five minutes when three does appeared on the runway. They stopped in the clearing, looked straight at me, saw nothing alarming and continued on uphill. Minutes later a spike buck traveled the same route. He didn't look around at all. He just walked casually up the trail.

He scarcely had melted into the thickets when more deer appeared along the same route. There were half a dozen animals in the group. One was a three-point buck. I decided to try for him.

I thought I was well concealed, but when I leaned into my rifle every one of those whitetails turned their heads to stare at that brushpile. They didn't see enough to make them bolt. They didn't do that until my .243 Winchester Model 70 roared. Through my Redfield 3-9x scope I saw my buck drop.

That adventure happened years ago, but it illustrates several important principles of why hunting from a stand can be so successful. Let's analyze them.

Dave and I wasted three days stillhunting in weather conditions not conducive to it. From a stand, however, all weather conditions are fine because you're not moving. A buck's eyes and ears are conditioned to sound and movement; he can be fooled completely by something that does not move or make noise.

One reason I scored was that my partner jumped that buck and got him moving along an established runway. In heavily hunted country you don't

From a stand overlooking a known deer runway, the author collected a buck when his hunting partner made a zigzag drive up a timbered side hill. This forced the herd to retreat along their accustomed route.

have to depend on a partner or partners to move deer past your stand. Other hunters will do it unknowingly. This is the main reason hunting from a stand is so productive in areas where many hunters are in the woods. They are bound to move deer, and in effect are moving them for you even though they're strangers.

It's simple logic that as the number of deer hunters increases the more the deer will be forced to move, and the more they move the better the odds for the hunter on a stand.

The trail-watching hunter is the only one who can beat a deer at his own game. Any moving hunter is matching his ears and eyes against an animal whose senses are far superior. Not only is the hunter on a stand silent, but he can control his scent (by locating downwind of runways) and he can limit his vision to the area where action is most likely to occur. Also, he is most likely to get standing shots because he is hidden and quiet. All of these principles played a part in enabling me to score on the three-pointer.

Why were those deer in the thickets of low-level sidehills instead of the higher elevations where Dave expected to find them? It had to have something to do with browse conditions at that time of year. The hunter who

WIND

scouts his local area won't waste time as Dave and I did. The local hunter has the advantage of knowing where the deer are and understanding their movement patterns. Being a successful stand hunter calls for good reconnaissance.

SCOUTING

Deer often change location from season to season as browse and weather conditions change. Reconnaissance work done in summer may lead to an area loaded with deer, but they may not be there during the fall hunting season. Deer that fed in crop fields have to find a new dinner table when the crops are harvested. A field that was fallow during summer may offer a food bonanza when it's winter wheat begins sprouting in fall. Summer runways that led through leafy bushes may be abandoned when the leaves drop in fall because the concealment is gone. A woodland that attracted deer last year because of an outstanding mast crop may not produce nuts this year. If the food is absent you'll find no deer.

The point is that you should do your scouting for stand locations as close to the opening of deer season as possible, or during the season. Deer react differently when they're being hunted. I'll explain the importance in a moment.

One of the best—and most enjoyable—ways of scouting is to combine it with other activities. When I hunt grouse and woodcock in my local area of Michigan each October I'm always looking for deer sign. I have a friend

In heavily hunted country, you can depend upon other hunters to un-wittingly keep deer moving for you. The key is to take up a stand along an established runway, making sure the wind won't carry your scent to approaching deer.

who took up squirrel hunting in farm woodlots mostly because he was in those woodlots anyway looking for signs of corn-fed bucks.

Another guy I know killed a big buck last fall in a swamp near a river. There were so many deer in there that he took two friends back to the area and they killed bucks, too. He found his hotspot runway while walking the river's bank when he was fishing for steelhead. Still another friend jumped a herd of whitetails while he was out picking fall mushrooms. He scouted the area, picked a spot for a stand, and then went home with venison when deer season opened.

There is one all-important tip to keep in mind when scouting for runways: it's best to do your scouting a day or two after a heavy rain. If you do this you'll know that all the deer tracks you find will be fresh. There's no sense picking a stand site along a runway that isn't being used.

Deer may feel secure enough in the "edge" along farmfields until the first day of hunting season. When hunters suddenly descend on the area, the deer often head for heavier cover. With this knowledge, you can choose a stand offering likely shooting each opening day.

The best sites are near feeding areas, bedding areas, scrape areas, watering areas, the trails connecting these areas, and the trails used as escape routes. Locating a stand anyplace else probably will be a waste of time.

Some veterans claim the first thing to look for is a feeding area. This is sometimes true in mule deer country where the animals often feed in herds on ranchlands in early morning and late evening, but whitetails often feed in cover. There are important reasons why looking for well-used runways is the best bet in whitetail woods.

Whitetails don't roam as far between feeding and bedding areas as mule deer do. Mule deer roam the open country as a matter of habit. They'll often feed in low-lying valleys and bed down in high buttes or rimrock, and they may take different routes to their destinations from day to day. Whitetails don't have these habits. They often bed down just over a hill from a feeding area. Their runways are used more consistently and are well-worn and easier to find. Whitetails always have a movement pattern that you can discover by studying runways.

From my experience, it's a lot easier to find a whitetail's runway than it is to find his feeding area. The key point here is that once you find his runway you can find his feeding, watering, and bedding locations simply by backtracking on his trails. That's a relatively simple job because a whitetail's home area seldom covers more than one square mile, which is the key to deciding where to hunt.

The one thing a runway can't tell you is whether the deer using it are bucks or does. There's no sense selecting a stand site in an area not used by bucks. The best way to discover that some of the tracks on a trail belong to bucks is to get a good look at the animals. This is best accomplished by scouting just before deer season opens.

Antler rubs along a deer trail are proof the trail is being used by one or more bucks. Rubbing is done primarily before and during the rut, and it involves both antler cleaning and mock battles.

Another good trick is to look for rub marks in the brush along runways. Rub marks are made when bucks clean and polish their antlers on sturdy saplings. A rub mark looks as if someone had cut a foot or two of bark off a tree with a dull knife. Most are made about two feet above the ground on saplings of an inch or less is diameter. The important point is that fresh rub marks are positive evidence that one or more bucks are using the area.

Fresh scrapes offer similar evidence, but you'll find them only during the rutting season. A scrape is a calling card a buck leaves for does in heat. A buck makes a scrape by pawing out a fan-shaped spot in the ground. It measures from a foot to several feet across, and it will be completely cleared of leaves, twigs, grass, and other debris. The buck's calling card is actually his scent, which he leaves by urinating in his scrape.

A stand site by a scrape is effective because bucks usually return to their scrapes at least once a day to see if they have attracted ready-to-breed does. If your deer season is open during the rut you'll be smart to be constantly on the alert for buck scrapes.

LOCATING A STAND

If your choice of a stand site is to be near either a feeding or bedding area there are several factors to consider.

Whitetails leave their beds and move toward a feeding site sometime during the last hour before night. They travel slowly, scheduling their arrival to coincide with dusk. All during this time shooting light worsens. On the other hand, they'll leave feeding areas on a schedule enabling them to reach bedding locations shortly after dawn. During this trip, shooting light improves. You also should realize that stormy weather, often encountered during deer-hunting seasons, prolongs daylight movement of whitetails. In short, a stand near a bedding area offers more shooting light potential than does a stand near a feeding area.

Always remember that a deer's most basic instinct is to travel upwind. The clever buck depends on his nose to tell him of danger ahead. For this reason whitetails have alternate runways leading to feeding and bedding areas. Your stand must always be downwind of any well-used trail, but be sure your site is near a trail the deer will be using during the time you are hunting.

Being downwind from the route deer are likely to travel may not be enough in itself. Vertical air drifts—thermal currents—also are a factor. They carry your scent in the same way as the prevailing wind except they carry it up or down instead of horizontally. Cold air falls because it's heavy. Lighter air, which is warmer tends to rise.

At dawn, as temperatures normally begin to rise, the thermal current flow is upward. A dawn stand should be above an area where you expect to see deer because you want your scent to be rising skyward, not downhill.

Stands take many forms, but essentially they are places where you wait and watch. The hunter here may be able to see the area well, but deer would be likely to see him before he could take a good shot.

Tree stands that consist of only a crotch in a tree are okay for short waits but are usually too uncomfortable for long trail-watching sessions. They can lead to shaky offhand shooting, that may result in hazardous loss of balance.

This hunter has pulled pine boughs around a foxhole on a ridge from which he has a good view all around. Whenever you plan to make stands that will alter the natural environment, be sure you check with landowners or managers for permission and then restore the area before you leave.

Along farmfield edge, stands made from corn stalks work well.

The opposite is true if you're planning a late-afternoon session in a stand. As evening approaches and the day becomes cooler, the thermal currents begin falling. The rule of thumb is that evening stands should be in low-lands, dawn stands should be up on hillsides.

This principle holds if you hunt in a relatively remote region, but in heavily hunted whitetail country the animals abandon their normal move-ment patterns. They become much more concerned with staying alive and evading the armies of hunters than worrying about where they are going to feed or bed.

It's my contention that locating a stand on potential escape routes is one of today's best bets for bagging deer. A lot of gunners kill deer because the animals happen to blunder upon them after being jumped by other hunt-ers. The guy who kills his buck in this fashion seldom analyzes why the deer happened to be where he was at that specific time. If the hunter did figure it out, he would come to the correct conclusion that the buck was running an escape route. I could mention dozens of examples of what I'm talking about, but a few particular incidents that stand out in my memory will illustrate my point.

In my local area whitetails are normally scattered all over a terrain of hardwoods; pine and cedar pockets; and mixtures of brush, clearings, and farm fields. But when rifles begin roaring on the opening morning of deer season, many of the animals begin moving to what might be termed safety zones.

Within a few miles of where I'm typing these lines there is an area con-sisting of a few thousand acres of very thick jackpine clumps intermingled with grassy clearings. The area is not used by deer during the summer, but they flock to the place when they become harassed by hunters. Not too many locals know this, but it is known by the hunters who have done enough of their scouting *during* previous deer seasons to discover the movement patterns of those whitetails.

These hunters locate on stands along the low-lying escape routes the deer use when moving from their normal fall range into the range they use when rifles begin booming. Such stands have nothing to do with feeding, watering, or bedding areas. Their sites are selected with a simple principle in mind: "If I were a deer, which route would offer me the most cover for getting from where I am to where I want to go." Stand hunters who utilize this theory are among of today's most successful hunters.

I have a friend who gets at least one shot at a buck almost every opening day. His stand is near the bottom of a ravine where a power-line opening crosses the beginning of a huge cedar swamp. The cedar swamp is within a mile of the end of a large area of farm fields and small clumps of brush. Whitetails wax fat in that area before hunting season. They feed in the farm fields and bed in the small pockets of brush. But as soon as hunting season opens, those small clumps of brush offer less hiding security than

The author here shows the best whitetail he has taken. This bruiser was downed from a stand in Saskatchewan.

some deer want. Then the deer head down the ravine leading into the cedar swamp, and they walk right in front of my friend's stand.

Several times during deer-hunting trips in the West I've had a rancher, guide, or outfitter make a statement something like this: "The deer in this area usually bed down in the thickets at the bottom of that canyon to our right. I'll hike down there and jump them. Chances are they'll run up the canyon and top out over there by those two tall pines. I'll give you an hour to walk over there and get settled on a stand, then I'll go downhill and see what I can kick out."

My most dramatic experience with this sort of deer behavior took place in Saskatchewan. In the southeastern part of the province whitetails are hunted with a technique locally termed "pushing the bush." Most of the cover in that area consists of small pockets of brush ranging from the size of a city block to several hundred acres. Stand hunters are positioned near one end of a brush patch, then drivers work through the cover from the opposite end in an attempt to drive deer to the standers.

During my hunts in the province I was impressed with the fact that my guides always told me to stand in precise areas. One time Glen Holloway, a local guide from Wapella, said to me. "Stand right here behind these trees."

Then he pointed across 100 yards of plowed field toward the end of a large patch of brush. "If there's any deer in there they'll come out right next to those two big rocks when I push the bush from the other side. They'll run the field and cross into that cover on your left.

"A deer knows the best route to safety," Glen explained. "Unless he's unusually alarmed he'll run the same route every time he's jumped as long as he doesn't have to run downwind. I'm so familiar with this area I know those routes almost as well as the deer. A guy who does a lot of scouting gets that kind of knowledge."

All of these examples point out the importance of knowing where deer are likely to be and where they're likely to go when they get into trouble. A stillhunter or a stalker would have practically no chance for a shot at these traveling animals. But the man on a stand has the odds in his favor.

CONCEALMENT

Although a hunter on a stand usually won't spook a deer by creating sound, he still has the animal's nose and eyes to contend with. As I've already mentioned, no wild deer will approach a person he can smell, and, though naturally curious, no deer will approach something he sees that looks suspicious.

The subject of concealment of a hunter on a stand can promote plenty of arguments. Down through the years many deer hunters have thought of a stand as no more than an old stump, a fallen log, or an outcropping of rock. You may find such objects on perfect stand sites, but they won't be perfect stands because you're underestimating a deer's eyesight. Few clever bucks will approach a hunter they can see even if the man is motionless.

Another factor is comfort. I've heard hundreds of hunters discount hunting from a stand because they "just don't have the patience to sit on a hard stump all day." This is nonsense. A deer certainly doesn't know or care if you're sitting on a hard stump or a soft lawn chair if he can't see you, and he won't see you if you are properly concealed. It follows that if you're properly concealed you might as well have some of the comforts of home. It also follows that if you have a few comforts you'll be able to stay on your stand longer, and that's all-important because it's the guy who stays put who shoots a deer.

Last summer my son Jack and I built a deer blind that a lot of veterans would laugh at. We put four corner posts in the ground, connected the posts with wire, and tied cedar and pine branches to the framework. We

The burlap screen around this tree stand breaks the wind and helps mask the hunter's silhouette. Tree stands offer a firearms safety bonus: Bullets thrown from them enter the ground near the target rather than careening great distances. Before building a tree stand, you should check state hunting laws to be sure such stands are legal and to determine whether there are height limitations.

The stand this hunter is climbing to is hardly visible in the photo. Yet it provides good visibility and is easy to mount. Here natural camouflage will help mask the hunter's movements. The author prefers a roomier stand than shown here, with poles or wire fastened all around for shooting rests.

Few deer would notice the hunter in the top photo. But the overhead view, bottom, reveals the reason why the birds are announcing an intruder.

used cedar and pine because the foliage from these two species doesn't fall when it dies. If we'd built the blind with branches from maple and hemlock it would have been a skeleton by deer season. It was quite an elaborate affair, big as a duck blind. Our stand didn't blend in well with the surroundings because it had a boxlike appearance, but it worked perfectly for several reasons.

First, it was located on a knoll above two crossing runways. A stand located on such a spot doubles your chances of seeing deer. Second, we built the blind long before deer season. The whitetails using those runways no doubt were suspicious of the structure for weeks after it was built, but as time passed and it produced no trouble the deer accepted it as harmless. Third, it offered perfect concealment because it was constructed of thick cover.

The opening morning of the deer season produced rain mixed with snow. But we were quite comfortable, sitting on soft lawn chairs. We were able to move around because our movements were concealed. We watched deer move past us long after many other hunters probably had become wet, chilled, hungry, and disgusted. Similar experiences through the years have cemented my belief that hunting from a stand doesn't have to be a dull and lonely experience. Anyone can sit longer if he is warm, comfortable and concealed well enough so he doesn't have to sit like a statue.

Years ago I used to hunt from deer blinds that were more conspicuous than the one I just mentioned. The area we hunted covered several square miles of sand dunes intermixed with pine forests. The deer in that region fed on dune grass and bedded in the thick conifers. They were vulnerable to rifles only when they traveled from one clump of forest to another, and the only vantage points from which they could be viewed clearly were the tops of bare dunes.

The problem, of course, was that if a hunter stood in the open on top of a sand dune he would be spotted by deer before they left the fringes of cover. So we built blinds on the dunes long before deer seasons opened.

We did our best to camouflage those blinds. First—and it's a good trick to consider wherever you can use it—we dug in. We dug foxholes in the sand to conceal the lower halves of our bodies. We lined the foxholes with upright weathered boards cut long enough to conceal the rest of our bodies to eye level while in sitting positions. Then we lined the rims of the blinds with pine branches.

The blinds were built high enough to break the wind, and big enough so a man could move around while showing a minimum of movement. They were built in wide-open places, were constructed mostly of unnatural materials, and were of unnatural contours. Did they work?

The first day I hunted from one of those blinds I saw twenty-eight deer, three of them bucks. The first buck was behind me. I didn't spot him till I stood up to stretch. We saw each other at the same time. He bolted back into cover before I could get my scope on him. The second buck offered a fair shot but I missed him. The third offered a good shot. I piled him up with one .243 slug. None of those twenty-eight deer were wary of that blind because they had passed it so many times without trouble before deer season that they didn't associate it with danger. That's one of the most important points a stand hunter should remember.

Hunting from specific locations can boost your odds in another way, too. You can mark a trail to your stand which can be followed by flashlight. This means you can eliminate the mistake many hunters make by arriving at their site too late and leaving too early. Deer begin traveling at the first hint of dawn. If you wait till it's light enough to walk to your stand without a flashlight you'll miss seeing a lot of deer. You should be on your stand long before dawn, and you shouldn't leave in the evening until all shooting light is gone.

I don't mean to imply that you should be on your stand all day. Most hunters just don't have the patience for that, and it isn't the best technique, anyway. Many expert stand hunters agree that six hours of waiting per day is about right. The sitting periods should consist of the first two hours of daybreak, the last two hours before darkness at night, and two hours at midday. The off-hours should be spent scouting for new or better stand sites. I've already mentioned why it is so important to scout when the hunting season is open.

Though deer normally are bedded at midday, these hours are producing ever more venison as the hunting army continues to increase in numbers. Most hunters take a break in late morning to return to cars or camps for lunch, and they return to hunting areas in early afternoon. This means there is much activity in the woods during midday hours, and this activity moves deer.

Another factor contributing to the success of midday standers is the growing use of gang-type drives. Going hunting early in the morning serves no useful purpose for drivers, so they normally don't get organized until after deer have bedded down. Since the purpose of a drive is to move bedded deer, the drivers also aren't active late in the day. This means that the man on a stand who hunts only during early and late daylight hours is missing a chance at deer moved by drivers. If you hunt where driving is popular you can up your chances by hunting from a stand when drivers are in action. I'll cover gang drives in the next chapter.

Having more than one stand has definite advantages. Most hunters who think about hunting from a stand have the idea of building one blind. However, it's a good idea to have several stands in the area you hunt. Then you can go to an ideal site regardless of wind direction, time of day, thermal currents, driving activity, or time you have available to hunt. An obvious example is a wind shift. Suppose you're in a spot downwind of a run-

THERMALS

In the absence of an apparent prevailing wind, it's good to remember that thermal (heat) currents travel uphill in the early morning and downhill in the late afternoon. This will help you locate your stand so that your scent isn't carried to the runways you want to watch.

way when the wind reverses itself. If you have a stand on the other side of the trail, you can move to the new site in moments.

Standers who don't have the inclination to build good blinds underestimate the value of concealment. A buck will usually materialize out of nearby thickets and be in plain sight before you suspect he's anywhere near you. At this point it's too late to think about concealment. He'll bolt and be gone before you get your rifle half way to your shoulder if you're not hidden. It's a shame to do everything else correctly, then miss getting your buck because you didn't take a few moments to properly conceal yourself.

If you don't build a blind in advance, the first thing to consider is light density. Locate in a shadowed area low to the ground so any movements you must make are less noticeable. Then take advantage of natural concealment such as windfalls, ground-hugging limbs, stumps, or clumps of brush. If there isn't any natural material where you want it, perhaps you can put some there. Dead branches will help to break up your outline. A good trick in areas where there are conifers is to cut off a few twigs and jab them into the ground.

The important point to remember about temporary concealment is that it must be as natural as possible. If you upset the landscape appreciably, a deer is sure to notice it. Any deer knows his home-territory objects as well as you know the furniture arrangement in your house. If you come home and see a chair out of place it stands out like a sore thumb. A deer will notice something out of place just as readily. It then becomes a potential source of danger.

One reason this principle is so important is that bucks normally follow does on runways. Your concealment must be so natural that all deer will freely use the trail without the slightest suspicion of your presence. Does and fawns must move along as if there isn't a hunter within 10 miles. If they don't, and they act wary, you'll never see the buck that may be following them.

This lesson—among several others—was driven home to me one time on a hunt in northern Wisconsin. My job was to take a stand ahead of the rest of my group while they organized a drive. I was told to locate near a creek.

. When I got on location I found several choices for stands. One was in a thick clump of blueberry bushes near the creek, but I passed it up because the ground was mucky in there. Instead, I picked a spot on a small knoll. The cover was meager but the vantage point offered an excellent view toward the woods my companions were to drive. At the appointed time they showed up. I hadn't seen a deer. After I told them that they hadn't moved any whitetails I got a real surprise.

"C'mon," said Lyle Laurvick, my host. "I want to show you something. Those woods were full of deer. We had 'em moving straight toward you."

We walked 100 yards along the edge of the woods, then cut in to where the drivers had come through. In moments Lyle pointed out a runway which was loaded with fresh deer tracks. We walked down the trail a few yards, then Lyle gestured toward a place where the deer had left the runway and headed into some hills.

"Right here is where they spotted you," he said. "You can't expect whitetails to walk by a man if they can see him. I'll bet the first mistake you made was that you were standing up. Never do that on a stand. Always sit down. Get as close to the ground as possible. That cuts your silhouette in half and it restricts your area of movement.

"Your second mistake was picking a stand site on that knoll. Not enough cover there for one thing, but you also made the common error of trying to see too much territory. The object isn't to see a lot of deer, it's to see one deer that doesn't see you. That's the only way you'll get a good shot. If you'd been in the thickets near the creek that herd would likely have walked right past you. You wouldn't have seen them till they got close, but they probably wouldn't have spotted you either. You've got to pick a stand on the hard-nosed basis that deer won't see you."

That lesson was emphasized later in the day when another member of our group nailed an eight-pointer ahead of a drive. He showed me his stand site. It was behind an old pine stump on a hillside.

"It's a good idea to get behind something when you're on a temporary stand," Don Johnson said. "Stumps, blowdowns, thick tree trunks, or rock piles all make natural hides. I also like to locate above a runway because deer don't expect danger from above. They seldom look up. Anyway, two does walked down the runway minutes before the buck showed. Those does had no idea I was behind the stump, so there was no way they could alert the buck."

Don touched on an all-important point when he mentioned that deer seldom look up. In states where tree stands are legal, they're the best bet by far. Earl Hoyt of St. Louis, Missouri, has some thoughts on why this principle is so valid. Earl is a nationally known manufacturer of quality archery equipment and is a veteran bowhunter.

"The first suggestion I'd make to the novice bow hunter is to hunt from a tree stand," said Hoyt. "I'd guess that 65-75 percent of bow-killed deer are taken from trees. They offer a lot of advantages. Deer are not bothered much by movements in trees. It's because they are used to seeing wind-blown branches moving and they just don't expect danger from above. Also, deer do not scent hunters in trees as well as hunters on the ground. Further, I've found that sound from tree blinds doesn't seem to have as much effect as sound from ground stands.

"Even so, I don't think the novice hunter is careful enough with his movements. He tends to look around while turning his head and body rapidly. He should make slow turns or rely on eye movements. This works well in a tree because a hunter can see through brush much easier if he's above it than on the same level with it."

Earl emphasized another factor that I've already mentioned, but it's important enough to be highlighted again.

"Another big mistake I see among archers is trying to hunt the whole state," he said. "One place this weekend, another place the next. Hunters should become totally familiar with their hunting location and know the habits of the area's deer. You can't select a good stand without knowing when and why deer are likely to move past it."

Tree blinds range from a crotch between limbs to deluxe, weatherproof and heated miniature cabins placed on top of A-frame piers. The latter are used in Texas, the former can be utilized anywhere tree stands are legal. The most common tree stand is a platform, mostly because a platform offers far more comfort and freedom of movement than does a crotch between limbs. It's usually reached by nailing climbing rungs to the tree's trunk.

The first thing to consider when building a tree stand is that the tree belongs to somebody. Defacing a tree without the landowner's permission is unpardonable. So is digging foxholes for blinds.

Once you have permission there are a few things to consider. Weathered boards will show up less than fresh-cut boards. Remember that lumber construction in a tree will creak as the tree sways. You can eliminate much of this creaking by building the platform as small as possible. It should be no larger than what you need for a comfortable seat. Creaks are also produced by hunter movement. You can deaden these sounds somewhat by placing an old piece of carpet on the platform.

The author's son Jack here poses with a good whitetail he took from a stand in the South Texas brush country.

An important consideration in tree stands—or all stands for that matter—is freedom of movement to shoot. After a stand is completed you should dry-fire your firearm through any expected shooting area. If it knocks against branches they should be cut away. A deer will bolt when he hears an unexpected noise whether or not he's looking up.

The same thought includes proper housekeeping. Never position your rifle where it can fall. Place thermos bottles and other gear in locations where they won't be knocked over. Clear away dead leaves or twigs from your sitting area. It takes only seconds to do these things, but they help insure against making unnatural noises.

There are other major keys to keeping quiet. The first factor is comfort. The more comfortable you are the longer you can sit still. For standers in cold-weather states I rate a modern snowmobile suit as tops. I buy mine in either bright red or bright yellow for safety reasons. Another good trick is to buy an oversize Blaze-Orange shooting vest. You can wear it over a snowmobile suit of any color (or any other clothing) and have more safety coloration than most deer hunters wear. Besides being warm, a good-quality snowmobile suit is windproof and rainproof. So are good quality snowmobile boots, the warmest footwear ever invented.

The problem with snowmobile suits and boots is that they're designed for sitting, not walking. If I have considerable distance to walk to a stand site I carry my suit in a rucksack, then I suit up when I'm ready to begin hunting. A rucksack is a good bet for all standers. You can use it to carry such things as binoculars, thermos jugs, lunch, rope, camera, and gloves or mittens. And, when it's empty, you can use it for a dry seat cushion.

There have been long arguments about whether a stander should smoke. Personally, I'm much more comfortable when I take an occasional pull on my pipe. My theory is that if a deer can smell my pipe smoke he can smell my body odor just as easily. The thing here is that any smart stander will be downwind of where deer will be likely to appear. If you're downwind of a buck he isn't going to smell you, whether you're smoking or not.

The main problem with smoking is noise and movement. Reaching for smoking material, tapping pipes or cigarettes, striking lights, and coughing are all unnatural noises in the woods. The odds are that the nonsmoker will see the most deer.

I suppose the noneater also would see more deer because he would eliminate the movements and noises that go with eating. But, here again, the man who is the most comfortable is the man who stays on stand the longest. You can cut down your eating noise by using soft foods and by wrapping your chow in a soft towel instead of the usual crinkly foil.

An important key to success on a stand is alertness. You should expect to see a deer at any moment. If you keep in an alert frame of mind you'll keep your smoking and eating movements to a minimum, and you'll make them slow and easy.

The techniques of hunting from a stand have been around a long time, but most deer hunters have never appreciated how effective they are today. That thought bounced around in the back of my mind for years. Two years ago I decided to find out if my assumption was correct.

I conducted a survey of game officials and veteran deer hunters in all of our forty-eight contiguous states and neighboring provinces of Canada. That survey showed that expert stand hunters are enormously successful. Refer back to Chapter 2 for details.

I've heard many stories of successful hunts made from stands, but the one I remember best came from Don Wooldridge of the Missouri Conservation Department.

"It happened in 1972," Don began. "Jim Keller, his Jefferson City neighbor Don Skaggs, and Don's son Chris, went hunting in Ozark County. The eleven-year-old climbed into a tree stand with his dad. He nailed a four-pointer right after dawn. The Skaggs dressed it out and drove it to a Gainsville locker plant.

"Upon returning Don and the boy again climbed into the tree. Before long a six-point buck ambled along the edge of some nearby cedars. The elder Skaggs downed the deer with one shot.

"Keller helped them dress it out," Wooldridge continued. "Then he decided to try his luck from the same stand. The Skaggs' car was hardly out of sight when Keller saw a nine-pointer sneaking along with his head low. Jim waited until the animal moved into an opening, then he killed it. All three of the fellows told me they saw numerous does in addition to the bucks."

You'll probably never find a deer hotspot that good, but the story illustrates what can happen when you hunt from a stand.

10

The Gang Drive

Years ago the old-fashioned gang drive was one of the best techniques for producing venison anywhere in whitetail country. It worked well in those days because when deer were jumped they ran for their lives. They ran straight away from the drivers and into the rifle sights of standers who were posted ahead of the drivers. In those times of less hunting pressure than we have today, deer were startled at the mere presence of a hunter. The naive critters bolted as soon as they realized men were in their area.

It's all a new ball game today. Modern bucks who flee for safety without thinking about the consequences wind up in freezers. Those that make it through their first hunting season have learned that the way to stay alive is not to run but to hide or sneak. That's precisely why the old-time gang drive—a line of hunters moving aimlessly through good deer woods—is seldom productive today. The keys to success of the modern drive are organization and leaving nothing to chance.

How determined to hide are today's bucks? I talked about the cleverness of deer earlier, but let me mention some more incidents that should serve to illustrate the cleverness of modern deer. Here's a story from a local friend, Jim Sutton.

"It was during pheasant season," Jim began. "My dad

Hunters on stands are often surprised by a nearly silent blur of motion as driven deer flee past. At other times frightened deer may make a noisy, brush-breaking approach. They may sneak away from the drivers toward the standers. Or they may double back through the ranks of the drivers. Gritty-nerved bucks often remain in their beds as drivers pass unaware.

and I watched about 15 shotgunners work out a valley of underbrush no more than 150 yards wide. They were only a few yards apart as they walked down through the thickets. When they moved on over a ridge a rooster flew in and landed behind them. Dad and I walked down and zig-zagged all over the area trying to flush that bird. Finally Dad came close to stepping on a big eight-point buck that bolted from almost under his feet. Some of those pheasant hunters must have passed within 20 feet of that deer. The thing that got me was that this took place over a month before deer season opened, yet that buck was so determined not to move that he didn't blow out of there till his last hope of not being seen was gone."

I have a personal story that's comparable. Last fall while grouse hunting I tumbled a bird I couldn't find. I put my cap on a bush at the spot where I thought the bird had gone down, then I searched in ever-widening circles around the cap. After I'd worked around that small area for about ten minutes a buck jumped up and roared out of there. I must have been within a few yards of him several times before he decided enough was enough.

Again, this incident happened long before deer season. How cagey do clever bucks get when rifles begin roaring? Here's another story, told to me by a retired newspaper writer:

"I had twelve deer that came to my orchard every day," he began. "I fed them apples. I knew those deer so well I had names for them. I knew their exact habits, especially in the evening when they came in for food. The night deer season opened they didn't show. I didn't see any of those whitetails again until about a week after the season closed. One night seven came back, the next night ten, the following night eleven. Only a fawn was missing, yet the surrounding woods had been full of hunters. Those deer simply hid out when the gunning began, and they didn't revert to normal movement patterns till the shooting was over."

Two years ago an archer friend of mine discovered a large herd of whitetails feeding on acorns along an oak ridge. He bow-hunted those deer for weeks. During that time he identified seven different bucks. When gun season opened he and six other riflemen stillhunted the same area. They never saw a single buck.

A Montana hunter told me that his uncle had hunted a specific snow-covered small area for four days. Finally he climbed a lightning-killed deadfall for a better view of his surroundings. He happened to glance into the thick brush immediately below him. He couldn't believe his eyes when he spotted a buck lying motionless in the thickets. He slowly inched his rifle to his shoulder and killed the animal in his bed. The astonishing thing about this story is that there wasn't a single deer track leading in or out through the six inches of two-day old snow on the ground around that small thicket. The buck hadn't moved for at least two days.

If these stories aren't enough to convince you that most modern deer won't run blindly in front of drivers, let me pass on some information from a man I consider a real expert on driving deer. I've mentioned Lyle Laurvick several places in this book, simply because he has had as much deer-hunting experience as anyone I know. How much experience? Well, I'll let him tell you about his hunting years and his driving techniques. Driving and hunting from stands ahead of drivers are the only systems he uses.

"Since I got out of the service after World War II, I've missed only a few days of our total Wisconsin deer seasons," he began. "You've hunted with my group, so I don't have to tell you we hunt from daylight to dark every day of the season or until each member of our group kills a deer. As soon as a man downs his buck he's automatically a gunless driver for the rest of the season.

"Working as a driver is hard labor if it's done right. That's why a lot of so-called drivers give up too soon. Some will work a drive for a couple of hours in the morning, then go from tavern to tavern. By the time they reach the sixth gin mill they're convinced there isn't a buck in the whole county, and they've got proof from all the would-be hunters in the last five bars they visited.

"Then there are the guys who do most of their driving in cars, not on foot. They cover 200 or more miles in good deer territory in a car, but only two or three miles in boots. They can't understand how they can cover all those miles and never see a deer. A good driver doesn't spend his daylight hours anyplace except back in the boonies where the deer are. But there's a lot more to it than hard work because modern deer are far more clever than their forebears.

"Years ago a given area could be driven and the deer of this place always went to that place, via this or that trail. That's why the driving technique used to be so successful, even when used by drivers with little skill. But no more. The hunter who lives in the past and refuses to change his driving tactics is bound to be lost in the shuffle because he can't break the new codes of our modern bucks.

"Many of the places we used to drive years ago still harbor good deer herds, and they still can be moved. The big difference is in the way they move and when they move. The buck of yesteryear used to break out across wide openings such as clearings, apple orchards or railroad rights-of-way in a headlong dash to escape drivers as soon as he was alerted to their presence. Today's buck won't jump unless he thinks he has to, and when he does he stays away from openings of any type. I've looked at thousands of fresh deer tracks that prove these points without question.

"Take a power-line opening in thick brush as an example. A running buck could clear such an opening in two leaps. Years ago, 90 percent of jumped bucks would take the gamble; today that figure is more like 10 percent. I couldn't begin to tell you the number of times I've followed the tracks of a jumped buck to an opening, then discovered that the cautious critter changed his route to parallel the opening instead of crossing it. This thinking is all-important when you consider the sites where you should put standers ahead of drivers. The standers who locate on the edge of openings—as was standard procedure years ago—seldom go home with venison today. It's best to locate near escape routes in thickets.

"There's another factor most drivers overlook. Many guys figure there are fewer bucks today than years ago because they don't see as many. In the old days 90 percent of the bucks ran as soon as they realized a man was headed toward them. Today 90 percent will lie still and hope the hunter will walk by. How do you lick this problem? The answer is several drivers working closely together while covering the driven area slowly and thoroughly. They've got to work out every thicket. The more men a buck has to cope with, the closer they are together, the slower they move, and the more thoroughly they work the cover, the more nervous the deer will get. The more nervous a buck gets, the more likely he is to move out."

When driven up a wooded ravine bordered by open ridges, clever bucks will usually hold to the ravine cover and head for an established escape route near the top. The stander should set up where the wind won't betray him.

WIND

Lyle is quick to temper that statement with another of his principles. He claims that a clever buck doesn't worry much about coping with a known danger, it's the unknown that makes him edgy. For instance, a buck won't worry much about one or two men invading his territory, particularly if the men are moving rapidly and making considerable travel noise. A clever deer knows he can avoid trouble by remaining hidden or sneaking around a man. However, when a group puts on a drive and the men move slowly and carefully, even a clever buck doesn't know what he's up against. He doesn't know how many hunters there are, what they're doing, where they're going, or whether they have already spotted him. That's when he's likely to jump, and it's the main reason well-organized gang drives can be successful.

Here are some more of Lyle's thoughts about how deer react to the known versus the unknown:

"Did you ever wonder why the whitetail harvest in most states is highest the first two days of each new season? I'm convinced that when the hordes of hunters first move into the woods and the rifles start roaring, many of the deer panic. They're caught by surprise. The ones that make mistakes get shot. The ones that survive figure out what's going on and they adapt by hiding or moving into remote areas.

"The principle is that if you can hunt a buck when he doesn't know what's going on you have him at a disadvantage, and that's when drivers can move him. This happens early in the season, but it also happens when the woods are damp or covered with a few inches of fluffy snow. If a buck can hear men moving he has little fear. His extremely sharp sense of hearing enables him to place himself where he'll be out of trouble. This is why so many modern deer sneak back through drives without ever being seen.

"But if you get conditions where men can walk quietly, especially if it's windy, deer often go wild because they realize danger can be upon them at any moment. It's the unknown that makes them commit errors and move out ahead of a drive. Our kill always goes up dramatically when new snow is on the ground. This is the best time to make a drive. Not only because the sounds of the drivers are reduced, but also because deer can be seen more easily against a snow background. In short, if a buck can't be sure where the drivers are and he can't be sure whether or not he'll be seen, he's much more likely to get on the move."

PLANNING PAYS OFF

Every successful driver I've talked with claims that good planning is the key to the successful modern drive. Haphazard driving of any ill-selected woodland won't work today for the reasons I've mentioned. The two most important considerations revolve around what areas to drive and how to drive them.

Throughout this chapter I've been talking principally about whitetails. These deer inhabit terrain most suitable for driving techniques and they're more apt to hide and sneak than mule deer. However, the tactics work with all deer found in woodlands regardless of species. Today's mule deer are developing the cleverness of whitetails as hunting pressure continues to increase. Muleys, more and more, are tending to seek safety in forests and to utilize the cunning of whitetails. Wherever you find mule deer in woodlands you'll find that they can be driven effectively.

The question of what areas to drive applies to all species of deer. Don't drive big woodlands where deer have too many escape options. You could put a couple of dozen drivers in a few square miles of forest and never see a deer, let alone get a shot at one. In big woodlands deer will keep doubling back and forth, always staying out of sight of drivers and seldom moving past standers. The trick is to drive toward areas deer are likely to use as escape routes.

An example is a wooded ravine bordered on both sides with open ridges. Since clever bucks won't want to top out in the open, they'll probably move up or down the ravine in a direction away from the drivers. When they reach the end of the depression they'll sneak out through the best cover available.

Consider in the above example how organization fits in. If the driving group is very familiar with the ravine, all the members have valuable

Some hunters mark "Xs" on their maps where standers have seen bucks. If a buck is killed, they draw a circle around the X. As deer seasons pass, the hunters have a graphic record of the most productive stands in the area.

knowledge of where the deer are likely to be hiding and where they're likely to go when jumped. All men in the group know where the standers will be and precisely how long it will take to make the drive. Everything is executed with military precision.

Drivers and standers can't execute such an operation without intimate knowledge of terrain, and this is why driving unfamiliar country is usually a waste of time today. You have to have all the advantages in your favor simply because modern bucks won't move unless they have to. And when they do move you have to have some indication of where they'll go and why they'll go there. There's no way you can have this knowledge when hunting unfamiliar terrain.

That's why—in every group of successful drivers I've hunted with—I always hear statements such as: "Tomorrow morning we'll make our first drive in Miller's Hollow if the wind holds north. After that we'll work Munson's Forty, then Blueberry Ridge." Such hunters have intimate knowledge of their hunting lands. They know exactly how to hunt those lands and, from past experience, that they know deer are likely to be there.

The first consideration is to select hunting country that can be driven efficiently. I just mentioned a ravine bordered with open ridges, but let's go to a simpler example.

Say we have forty acres of oak trees loaded with acorns and dotted with thickets of brush large enough for bedding areas. The oaks are surrounded on all sides by dense cedar swamps. Though the oaks and the thickets may harbor plenty of deer, there isn't a chance in the world of driving them efficiently because they can sneak out to safety in any direction.

Now let's assume we have an identical forty acres surrounded on two adjacent sides by wide-open fields. The other two adjacent sides border dense cedar swamps. In this case, because modern bucks seldom cross openings, we've cut down the whitetail's escape routes by 50 percent. A drive here would have a chance of success, but it would be slight because the deer still have too many options for getting away without being seen.

Since deer generally seek an escape route with cover, this tree stand was built with a good view of the brushy draw. The "X" in the drawing shows an alternate stand site for use if the wind were blowing from the tree stand toward the woodlot. Sometimes a drive through a woodlot known to contain deer will fail because the deer sneak unnoticed through the line of drivers. If this occurs, a second drive can be staged from the same starting line, with one or more drivers dropping behind the others to watch.

WIND

Now let's take another identical forty acres surrounded on three sides by open fields. The fourth side is bounded by scattered cedars, except for a narrow draw running downhill from the oaks into dense cedars. The draw is lined with relatively thick brush. Here we have an ideal situation. If the forty acres are driven from the side opposite the draw, any deer that are moved have only a single logical choice for escape. Their best route by far is through the thickets in the draw. Consequently, the best sites for standers are along the edge of the draw.

This example is somewhat simplified, but it illustrates the type of thinking that should go into the selection of driving areas. The key to success is to consider any areas used by deer, but to select only those areas bounded on at least two sides by openings which cautious deer won't cross. Such openings could be fields, highways, power lines, rivers, lakes, mucky marshes or any type of clearing. Barriers such as cliffs or steep hillsides serve the same purpose. Deer, when driven *slowly*, will almost always move ahead along the path of least resistance so long as it offers adequate cover.

The next thing is not to select too big a tract of woodland. The key consideration here is how many drivers will be in action. Ten drivers could adequately cover a woodland twice the size of one adequately covered by five men. (Laws of your state may affect the options you have on numbers of drivers. Several states limit the number of hunters who can operate as a group.) The type of woodland makes a big difference, too. A woodlot 200 yards wide and consisting of scattered ground cover might be driven efficiently by three men. The same three men could not efficiently drive a thick cedar swamp 200 yards wide. A clever buck probably wouldn't jump in thick cedars even if the drivers were only 25 yards apart because he knows his odds on staying alive in thick cover are best if he hides or sneaks around the drivers.

We also have wind-direction problems. Let's go back to the forty acres of oaks surrounded by openings except for the thicket-lined draw. If the wind happens to be blowing from the draw to the oaks there's no sense in making a drive because deer would scent standers along the draw. They'd turn back and take their chances with sneaking through the line of drivers.

At this point it's easy to understand why anything less than the best planning won't work with a drive. Today's successful drivers know exactly how they're going to drive an area and when they'll go into action. Again, this type of knowledge comes only from experience.

When I talk about experience with terrain I don't mean just the physical characteristics of woodland. I also mean experience with hunting success. For example, you could hunt two areas of the same size and physical characteristics and discover that one often harbored deer while the other seldom produced any animals. Why? There could be many reasons, but experience gained through hunting the two areas soon tells the hunters that it's a waste of time driving the nonproductive area.

There are problems with weather, too. Some areas may hold deer early in the season but not late in the season. In northern states, whitetails often change locations when the woods become covered with snow. In all areas deer are prone to change locations in direct proportion to how much hunting pressure they're subjected to. That's why knowledgeable drivers don't waste their time driving some specific areas until the hunting season is well along. They know that deer don't move into those given areas till they're forced into them by gun pressure. Such areas are almost always sections of the thickest cover available.

So, knowing where to put on a drive all boils down to experience. If you can't join an experienced group of drivers you'll have to form your own group, and you'll wear out a lot of boot leather gaining the experience of knowing where and where not to put on drives. Choosing potentially good driving areas and then driving them is the only way you'll gain the experience of knowing which areas hold deer and which escape routes the deer are likely to use.

SHARING THE WORK

If you form your own group there are some thoughts to keep in mind. Deer hunting does not have the same objectives for all men. The guy who likes to hunt from a stand will not make a good driver because he's basically a loner. He wants a serious and quiet hunt by himself. Other men can't stand to sit on stands; they thrive on the get-togetherness and good times of groups. They're the kind you want if—and it's a big if—they're the types who take their hunting seriously. You can't put on efficient drives unless all members can be counted on to participate in each scheduled hunt. The fellows with little desire don't make good drivers.

However, one advantage to forming a driving group is that the members may include some novices and men of various ages or physical abilities. The novice can be told what to do and where to go by experienced members, and in that way he gains his own knowledge of deer hunting. He'll learn the tricks of the trade a lot faster by hunting as a member of a group than he will by stillhunting or trail-watching on his own. Driving also gives the out-of-shape or older members a chance to hunt efficiently. Since standers are always required ahead of the drivers, there's always a place for the weaker members. Many good stands are often reached by walking short distances from roads.

On the other hand, the drivers themselves may have to engage in very hard work. Some drivers—especially the end members on a sweep drive (which we'll discuss shortly)—may have to travel fast to keep up. Driving through swamps and tangles can be especially rugged. So it's good to have young members in your group, guys with the stamina to plow through the tough stuff and enjoy every minute of it.

In spite of such considerations it's best to be fair in sharing the work load. If all members of a driving group are in reasonably equal physical condition, the rule of thumb is that all members spend half their time driving and half standing.

DRIVE SAVVY

All drives should use the contour of the land to the best advantage. Just as the flow of water is narrowed as it goes through a funnel, so should the escape options of deer be narrowed as the drive progresses. A pie-shaped piece of woodland should be driven from the wide end toward the narrow end. A ravine or canyon, which is normally narrower at its top than bottom, should be driven uphill.

But such considerations should take into account the direction of the wind. As I mentioned earlier, don't drive upwind toward standers because deer will never approach a man they can smell. At first thought it would seem that drivers should move with the wind because deer will scent them and move ahead. But I question this accepted procedure. We've discussed why deer are more apt to get edgy and move when faced with the unknown rather than the known danger. With a crosswind, the animals won't be able to smell either the drivers or the standers. Hence we introduce an unknown factor when deer can hear drivers but can't smell them.

Again, this is the type of reasoning that goes into an organized drive. Experienced leaders of successful drives take such things into consideration before they decide where each day's drives will take place. An east wind may be perfect for driving a given area, while a south wind in the same area may make a drive totally inefficient.

Another key to an organized drive is timing. Many things are involved here. Standers must be on their sites before the drive begins or all effort may be wasted. The obvious example is when deer are moved past stand sites before the watchers reach them. Without complete knowledge of the terrain to be driven, the drivers can't know where the standers will be or how long it will take them to get there. One factor in this chain of events happens when the drive is finished. If a driver doesn't know where the standers are—the point at which the drive ends—he may filter through them and proceed beyond the group. This can lead to great delay in beginning the next drive. It's just another example of why efficient drives require systematic organization.

This is as good a place as any to point out that there is no optimum number of drivers or distance between drivers. However, too large a group gets unwieldy and promotes the chances of mistakes in timing. I think ten or twelve hunters (where legal) is maximum for good control. As to distance between drivers, it all depends on terrain. In dense cover 20 yards is not to close, in open woods 200 yards could be about right. Spacing should be decided on the basis of how close drivers should be to each other to prevent deer from sneaking back through their line unseen.

Timing becomes most important when the drivers begin their part of the operation. The hurried and noisy drives of years ago won't work today for two important reasons. The noisy driver—the fool who shouts, blows horns, or beats on pans—is giving deer the exact information they want. Noise pinpoints a man's location and progress, which is all the information a whitetail needs to sneak away or hide. A hurried driver gives the animals the same options. Also, in a slow-moving drive, deer are apt to be little frightened. They'll tend to move ahead at a slow pace. This gives standers the best shooting opportunities.

Most novices assume that a line of drivers should be just that: a straight line of men moving forward. But today's experts feel that the line of men should more closely represent a U or V. The forward parts, or ends, of such formations tend to intercept deer which try sneaking around the ends of drives. Incidentally, some veterans shape their stander lines in inverted U's or V's. This planning enables a military-type "pincher" effect as the drivers move toward the standers. It helps prevent deer from sneaking around either drivers or standers, an option they have continuously if drivers and standers are formed in straight lines. Also, deer detest being surrounded. When they're confronted with this situation they'll keep moving while trying to find an outlet.

In order for the drivers to maintain a U formation, each driver must maintain the same rate of travel. Unless each man can see his right and left companions, and this is often impossible in thick brush, the formation is in danger of falling apart. Some experts time their drives based on past experience. They know that it should take, say, forty minutes to reach standers from the time the drive begins. If a man knows his terrain he knows his landmarks, and consequently he knows where he should be at any time during the forty minutes. In such drives the watch is an all-important tool.

Keying driver positions to natural sounds is another stunt used by drivers who can't see each other. Natural sounds in the woods include calls of birds. Some drivers keep in proper position by whistling bird calls to their companions.

One time I was on a stand in an area that I didn't realize was being driven. I eventually became aware of the occasional caws of crows. Imagine my surprise when I heard a crow caw right in front of me, then saw a man step out of the brush where I assumed the crow was. Until I saw the man I had no idea there was another human within miles of me. Such a sight is startling. I imagine the same discovery would be startling to a buck, and it would probably get him moving, which is the object of any drive.

Drivers should move ahead with the speed of a leisurely walk. Deer will use their normal escape routes if they know they don't have to hurry. Push them too fast and their reactions become unpredictable. Push them slowly and they'll likely come out in the natural places where your standers are located.

I've had many experiences proving my statement that deer will mosey along in normal fashion if they aren't pushed hard. One time several does moved slowly past my stand. They browsed and acted unconcerned in every way, except they'd look back over their back tracks occasionally. Eventually they moved out of sight.

A short time later two hunters came into view, following the deer tracks. They appeared to be ready to shoot at any instant. They obviously believed they were just behind the deer and that they would spot them soon. Those deer knew exactly where the hunters were, and they assumed they were safe as long as they traveled just fast enough to stay far enough ahead of the men to stay out of sight.

Though this chapter has nothing to do with stillhunting, I want to mention here that such experiences have convinced me that tracking deer, whether in snow or not, has little merit today. Most modern deer are simply too clever and cautious to get waylaid by the tracking hunter, unless he's an expert.

Another variation of the old-time straight-line drive, modified to fit modern conditions, is known in some areas as the "sweep" drive. A sweep drive sweeps around a pivot man (stander), who locates in cover on a point of land or on a hill where he has a good view. The drivers closest to the pivot man have to move very slowly because they don't cover much distance as the drive sweeps around, but the men on the far side of the line have to leg it fairly fast to keep up. Those are the positions for your young and sturdy fellows. The sweep drive is the only one requiring any drivers to walk rapidly.

The reasoning behind a sweep drive is twofold. In some areas deer have become so used to the old-time straight-line drives that it has become second nature for them to sneak around the end man. In a sweep drive, the pivot man never moves and he has a top vantage point. He'll see most deer that try sneaking around his end of the line. And, since the far men on the driving line are moving a definite arcing route, they tend to confuse deer. The animals don't know which direction is straight away from the line of drivers, so they tend to stay ahead of the men instead of trying to sneak back through the line.

In the sweep drive, the pivot man is also the stander. Drivers closer to him move slowly. Those on the far end usually have to step out swiftly to keep their end from bowing back and, thus, letting deer slip around them.

WIND

However, as the years pass, more and more bucks are discovering that the best way to outwit drivers is to sneak back through their ranks. Once they accomplish this feat, and once their initial fear is gone, they'll revert to traveling established game trails to get to where they want to go.

Knowing this, many expert drivers check the beginning sections of their driven area after the drive is over. When they find fresh tracks of deer that had sneaked through the drive they note the routes the animals used to escape. Then, the next time the area is driven, the "dropout" technique is used. As the drive progresses a couple of men will drop out along the escape trails and take up stands as the other drivers continue forward. Many of today's bigger bucks, who assumed they had long ago figured out how to outwit any drive, wind up as deerburger when this modern stunt is pulled on them.

Years ago I wanted no part of drives because I figured they were dangerous. It seemed logical to assume that as a line of drivers moved toward a line of standers there could be bullets coming both ways. But as the years passed, and I hunted with driving groups who knew what they were doing, I found that they never had accidents. Why?

Organization again is the key word. When drivers know exactly where standers are going to be there's practically no chance a stander will be shot accidentally. More important, most deer killed during a modern drive are downed by the standers, not the drivers. No deer on the move is going to let a driver get too close to him. That means that by the time a buck goes by a stander he'll be far out ahead of drivers, particularly in more open country. In thick woods he'll still be far enough ahead of the drivers to insure a wall of trees behind him.

Even so, I wouldn't go deer hunting at all today unless I was wearing plenty of Blaze-Orange outer clothing. So many studies have shown that fluorescent blaze orange cuts down hunting accidents that it's stupid not to wear it. As I've said in another chapter, deer are color blind, so there's no chance that the brilliant orange will spook them. In short, a well-organized drive conducted by hunters wearing some Blaze-Orange clothing is a pretty safe way to hunt.

MAPS

Good topographic (topo) maps are key tools for driving groups. They should always be used to orient group members as to location of stand sites, driving routes and meeting spots. But much of their value comes before members gain a lot of experience with a hunting area.

A topo map gives a good indication of the shape of the land and what's on that land. As such it can be used as a planning board. It will show you which patches of woodland are of good size for driving operations. You can select a few such areas, then check the map further to determine which of those areas are bounded by the most openings or natural barriers which deer don't like to cross.

An example would be a section of woodland bounded on one side by a river and on the other by steep slopes or high hills. Perhaps you can find an area on the map where a sharp bend in the river comes within 100 yards or so of a point of high hills. Such a "narrows" is a natural for stand sites. Once good stand sites are chosen it's easy to determine where the drive should begin and what routes the drivers should travel. It's largely a matter of deciding how long you want the drive to last and how much area you want to cover.

As a new area is hunted over a period of years, you no longer need the map to acquaint you with the physical aspects of the terrain, but it can still provide you with great information if you use it to coordinate additional details.

For instance, it's a good idea to mark X's on the map where standers saw bucks. If a buck is killed, draw a small circle around the X. As the deer seasons pass you'll have graphic information showing which stand sites were most productive. Analysis of the terrain features at those sites often offers clues as to why they're good. Such information can be helpful in selecting stand sites in new driving areas.

There are many other advantages inherent in the use of maps. I'll discuss them all in Chapter 24 "Maps Can Work Wonders." In that chapter I'll tell you which maps are best, where you can get them, and more about how you should use them.

11

The Two-man Drive

There are several important reasons the two-man drive can be one of today's best bets for collecting venison. First, the odds per hunter always favor the small drive over the gang-type drive. Large drives seldom pay off in more than one or two bucks, for up to ten or twelve hunters. One buck per ten men is only a 10 percent success ratio. One buck for two men is a 50 percent ratio. The comparison becomes more meaningful when you consider that gang drives take much more time than small drives.

Deer also react differently when faced with one driver than when faced with a team of up to a dozen men. Whether a buck is a mule deer or a whitetail his reaction is to sneak or hide when confronted with a gang. But when faced with a single man he sometimes feels that safety is easy to come by with a simple dash for freedom. Sometimes a modern buck will be curious about what the man is doing and what he's going to do.

Because of this trait a buck will often circle a lone hunter, get downwind from him, and then follow him by scent. Today's bucks often pull this trick. They know that when they keep track of a single hunter's location they're in no danger. This trait can turn the tables on bucks when hunters employ a two-man drive. I'll explain the tactics later in this chapter, but I want to emphasize here that the system won't work for gang drivers. The principle is that deer always want nothing to do with gangs, but they're often curious about the goings-on of lone hunters.

Another advantage of the two-man drive is that the planning of the military-type tactics and organization necessary for a successful gang drive are not required. A small drive is easy to put into operation with a minimum of planning, and it's ideal for those hunters who dislike trail watching or mingling with large groups.

Perhaps the top advantage of the two-man drive is that it often works best in areas never hunted by gangs. I'll mention a couple of examples that should serve to illustrate.

One time Bob Wolff and I were ruffed grouse hunting on 120 acres of second-growth woodlands. We were working along the edge of the woods which bordered an open field. Two grouse bombed out in front of Bob. He nailed one, the other flew out over the field and landed in a patch of brush no larger than an average house. The brush patch appeared as an island out in the wheat stubble.

"Well now," said Bob. "That bird made a hell of a mistake. We'll just walk out there and flush him again."

We walked the 70 yards to the brush, then separated to pull a circling maneuver. All of a sudden I heard a crashing of branches from Bob's direction, then a big eight-point buck bolted past me, not 10 yards away. He crossed the open field and ran into the main woodlands. If it had been deer season I would have had a fine shooting opportunity.

I've experienced similar incidents and I've been told about many others. They prove that some of today's cleverest bucks often bed in the smaller pieces of cover relatively close to much larger woodlands. Why?

Because those little hideaways are overlooked by most deer hunters. Deer get used to outwitting hunters in cover that looks like deer country. Country that looks as if it should harbor deer gets hunted. Habitat that appears to be the last choice a buck would accept for bedding security never gets hunted. Clever bucks learn this lesson. These are the bucks that are setups for the two-man drive.

The trick is never to overlook the little islands of trees or thickets close to the larger woodlands that are known to harbor deer. A buck doesn't live in these little patches of cover, he just beds there. He feeds and travels with other deer in normal range, but when the others bed down in natural areas he returns to his own little hideaway. This is why the hotspots are close to normal deer woods. Our buck doesn't want to get too far away from established feeding areas, but most of all he wants the security of bigger woods should a hunter accidentally stumble upon him. He wants to be able to bolt to the bigger woodland in seconds. Keep this principle in mind: The little pieces of cover 50 to 100 yards from big woods have potential; if they're over 100 yards from the safety of big woods it's not likely that clever bucks will use them.

The two-man circle drive may move a deer past the stander. But since the stander may not know where the driver is, the stander should try to set up in an elevated location to ensure that his bullets don't hit the driver.

Other small areas that are great for two-man drives are those places that are difficult for gang drivers to hunt, and that's precisely why they hold deer. A river boasting small islands of thickets is a top example. Gang drivers may work both sides of a river many times during deer season, but they'll never work the islands if they can't wade to them. Such a situation is ideal for a couple of men in a boat. They simply travel from island to island and put on their two-man drives. The system is deadly. Another good bet is a narrow draw leading to a big woodland.

Once many years ago I was walking the bank of a small creek while jump-shooting wood ducks. The section I worked meandered from a bridge over a dirt road down through farm fields to a big woodland bordering a large lake. Near the bridge the thickets along the banks of the creek consisted of scattered willows. Downstream about 100 yards from the woodland the creekside cover broadened into a circular island of cover about 50 yards in diameter. This patch of thickets contained willows, birch and cedars.

When I moved into the island of cover three wood ducks flushed off the creek ahead of me. After my first shot roared I heard a sudden commotion. My initial thought was that my gunfire had put more ducks into flight; then it registered that the new noises came from a patch of solid ground to my left. I glanced that way and saw a fine buck streaking for the big woodland near the lake.

I jumped that buck from the same spot two more times while duck hunting. I figured I had him dead to rights when deer season opened, but when I went in there with a rifle he was gone. It's likely he had had enough interruption with my duck hunting and had found a new bedding area. In any event, my experiences with that little chunk of cover illustrates a couple of principles.

First, that general area—a band of woodlands bordered on one side by the lake and on the other side by farm fields—offered a natural area for a gang drive. But no gang of drivers would even consider working the cover along the creek because, except for the small island of thickets, the brush is only a few yards wide. So that buck bedded where he did because he figured he could stay out of trouble there.

Second, his cover was so ideal that he hated to give it up. He did so only after I had jumped him three times. That's a good indication of how

145

appealing to bucks these tiny pockets of thickets near big woodlands can be.

Now we get to the all-important point of why a two-man drive can be so effective. Though I jumped that buck three times I never did get more than a fleeting glimpse of him. Not once did he offer a good shooting opportunity. But each time he dashed away he took the same route: straight toward the closest edge of the big woodland bordering the lake.

Take the same situation, assuming that deer season is open and I have a partner with me. My partner locates on a stand between the small-cover area and the big woodland. Then I walk into the small patch of cover and jump the buck. Unless something very unusual occurs, that buck is going to just about run over my partner as he makes his break for freedom. It isn't quite that simple, as we shall see, but the example serves to show how effective the two-man drive can be.

The small drive certainly isn't limited to hunting tiny pockets of cover. Let's go back to the curiosity trait I mentioned at the beginning of this chapter, the trait that often compels a buck to circle a lone hunter, or a hunter that he thinks is alone. Of course a buck won't do this in a small-cover area. He'll make his dash. But in big woods, he'll prefer not to run far. Let's use another example to show what can happen.

Say one hunter sneaks slowly and quietly 100 yards into a big woodland bordering a field, then takes a stand. When he's in position his partner starts from the edge of the field and walks a 200-yard-wide circle around the man on stand. If the walking hunter jumps a buck the chances are he won't get more than a fleeting glimpse of it. But, if the buck decides to circle the walking hunter to get his scent, he may move right past the man on stand. This trick can be worked anywhere in whitetail or mule deer woods.

Great care should be taken not to make noise when you're executing the circle drive because the drive takes place in a limited area. When two hunters arrive at a woodland they shouldn't converse, slam car doors, or make any other racket that a buck within hearing range can pick up. When a clever buck gets any indication he's dealing with more than one hunter he'll decide to hide or to sneak into another area. In either event the circle drive won't work.

Most hunters using the circle-drive technique alternate between walking and standing. They may make one drive in a small area, or walk many adjacent circles in a large woodland.

Another system that takes advantage of bucks that circle behind a lone hunter might be termed the "straggler drive." In this instance, the lead man moves slowly, and with considerable commotion, into the wind. The straggler man follows quietly behind him. The distance between the two men will vary according to the denseness of the terrain, but 75 to 100 yards is about average.

The staggered drive exploits the wind and a buck's trick of sneaking behind a hunter to catch his scent and keep an eye on him. If both hunters move into the wind, the second hunter often gets good opportunities.

Deer jumped by the front man are likely to move off to his side, then swing and circle behind him to pick up his scent. If all goes well, this maneuver may give the following man an excellent shooting opportunity. Keep in mind that both hunters must move into the prevailing wind. If they were hunting downwind, a circling buck would pick up the scent of the following man before presenting a shooting opportunity. Once again, as soon as a clever buck learns he's dealing with more than one hunter all bets are off.

The type of two-man drive I'm most partial to is the type I use in the farm country around my home. In this case the hunt isn't limited to two men; there could be three or four although two men can pull it off handily.

The key to success is farmer contact. They're the guys who live and work in farm-buck country year around. They see deer, they know where

WIND

Knowing the runways and likely bedding areas in small farm woodlots is essential in anticipating deer movement.

they feed and where they roam. The thing they don't know, unless they're deer hunters themselves, is the precise routes the deer use while moving between feeding, watering and bedding areas. It takes scouting to determine these runway locations.

The man who takes the time to develop friendships with farmers can gain a wealth of information. He'll hear such things as: "Last year there was only one buck on my place. This year there's at least two, and one's a real bruiser. Mostly I see them around my south forty. I think they're working the acorns in there."

What does such a tidbit of information offer? First it tells you there are two bucks in a relatively small area, and it tells you where the area is. It also gives you a clue as to where the deer are feeding and bedding. A man could scout big woods for days to determine the same facts a farmer can give you in minutes. That's one of the great advantages of hunting farm country, whether or not you elect to hunt with driving methods.

Anyway, with such information you can walk down to the south forty and do some scouting work. It shouldn't take long to finish as deer don't have too many runway options in farm country. I look first for well-used trails leading across roads. Deer almost always have to cross roads in agricultural areas simply because there are so many of them. Runways leading to road crossings will take advantage of best natural cover. Brushy fencelines, valleys, unplowed swampland, fingers of thickets, and edges of woods that dead-end at roads are typical good bets. The trick is to find runways utilizing such cover, then backtrack on them to find feeding or bedding areas.

When you find a bedding area you'll know where your deer are likely to be during daylight driving times. Now you have all the dope you need to put on a drive. You select the runway the deer are most likely to use when pushed from the bedding area, put a stander on it or near it, then drive the woods. Pick the farm-country woodlots that are small enough for one man to drive effectively while working a zigzag course. Those are the ones that are ideally suited for the two-man drive.

I'll mention some of the typical hotspots in my area. They may give you clues as to what to look for.

Close to where I'm writing these lines there are four square miles of typical northern Michigan farm country consisting of grain fields, potholes, small tracts of timber, brushy fencelines, wooded hills, and brushy ravines. The entire area harbors deer. Where they feed and where they bed each year depends on crop production and whether the mast-producing trees produce bumper amounts of nuts. In any event, the deer are in the four-square-mile area every year but they'll use different runways, depending on annual conditions.

Last year one farmer put in eighty acres of winter wheat. The wheat field edged gravel roads on the south and north sides. The east side was bounded with a paved road. The west side was bordered with a 100-yard-wide strip of timber and thick underbrush. The timber thinned close to the north side road, but a narrow ravine of brush ran to the road, then led into a larger patch of timber across the road. This woodland ended at a lake.

A friend of mine got word from the farmer that deer were using his winter wheat. My buddy analyzed the situation. He guessed that the whitetails were bedding in the strip of timber on the west side of the field because it offered good security close to the food supply. He concluded that when those deer wanted water they would head north through the ravine leading into the timber that ended at the lake. He drove down to where that ravine was cut by the gravel road on the north, parked his car, and looked for fresh tracks. He smiled to himself when he noted the well-used runways coming up out of the ravine on both sides of the road.

"Okay," he told me later, "I figured that if those deer were pushed from the south they'd have to run north along the ravine runway toward the woods bordering the lake. That's just what happened. When daylight came on I had my partner Gordy work into the bedding area from the south end. The first deer that came out was a spike buck. He trotted right in front of me. I'm no trophy hunter; I nailed him in his tracks."

Right here I'd like to point out a principle involved in this incident. My friend would have had little chance if he'd tried stillhunting that buck in his bedding area. He might have jumped him, but at best he wouldn't have had a good shot because of thick cover. As it turned out, his partner who jumped the buck didn't even know he jumped him. He wasn't aware that he had moved a deer until he heard my friend's rifle roar. That's how effective the two-man drive can be in farm country. One man jumps the target, the second takes a stand along the route the target is most likely to use as an escape runway. These runways are limited in farm country, and that's the reason why they're relatively easy to find.

Not far from where my friend killed that spike buck there are two pie-shaped areas of bottomland too boggy to plow. Each area contains about 20 acres of weeds and thick alders. Their narrow ends are joined by 20 yards of trees, mostly small birch and maples. Deer use the bottomlands as bedding areas. Depending on wind direction, one can be driven toward the other. When jumped, deer normally route through the 20-yard width of small trees joining the two areas. The escape route can easily be covered by one stander, and each bottomland can easily be driven by one driver working a zigzag pattern.

A somewhat similar area contains a long, narrow swampland that dead-ends at a point of hardwoods. The point of timber is about 50 feet wide at the head of the swamp, but it rapidly broadens as the trees continue uphill to merge with about 80 acres of woodland. On all sides of the woodland are crop fields. Deer moving from the swamp into the woodland—or vice versa—have established a runway leading through the point of woods. This runway resembles a cattle trail leading to a barn. Even the most in-experienced of deer hunters would have little trouble locating such a well-used runway.

All of these terrain situations I've mentioned have one point in common: each contains a fairly large area (for farm country) of cover which deer require for bedding, and each is reached or left by a narrow escape route. They're naturals for the two-man drive because the cover areas are small enough to be driven by one man, and the escape areas are narrow enough to be covered by one stander. Find such farm-country areas, try to determine which routes deer should logically use for moving from one cover area to another, and then scout these routes until you find well-used runways. Hunters who do this and then employ the two-man drive are likely to stock their freezers with venison. Driving the farm country is deadly because deer have so few escape options.

A cardinal rule of any driving operation is that the most successful drives are those on which the hunters can best predict what the deer will do when pressed by drivers. In big woods deer have the options of running, hiding, or sneaking. In farm woodlots, which usually are quite small, deer will usually run when driven. Perfect the two-man drive technique in farm country and you'll be on to one of today's best bets for frying deer liver.

Not only is the system an excellent way to hunt, but it also has other things going for it. One feature that appeals to me is that the two-man drive in rural areas is not time-consuming. Your car will take you exceptionally close to your hunting locale, and you can often complete a drive in an hour or less. My teen-age son and I can execute a couple of drives after he gets out of school in the afternoon. Some of my deer-hunting friends put on drives before going to church on Sunday mornings.

Mule-deer country, especially the areas showing sparsely wooded canyons and draws of small to medium size, are excellent bets for the two-man drive. I once learned a neat system in Wyoming from a rancher who frequently had nobody to hunt with except his son.

"In this area we have a lot of draws that top out on level rims," he told me. "Many of these draws are in series, and they might be only 50 to 100 yards apart. We begin our hunting by having one man take a stand at the top of a draw. The second man works up from the bottom. If the drive is unsuccessful we'll walk half the distance along the rim to the next draw. Then one man walks downhill to the bottom, crosses over to the bottom of the draw and takes a stand. The man on top walks over to the top of the draw and drives it to its bottom.

"With this technique we hunt lots of draws and share the climbing work. The guy doing the driving almost never gets a shot because the deer sneak out ahead of him. It's the two-man effort that produces meat."

Although I've talked mostly about drives involving two men, I want to mention again that three or four men can pull the same stunts. All I'm emphasizing is that the systems can't be worked by a lone man. In cover areas larger than those I've described, it's often necessary to have two or three drivers. But I wouldn't consider tackling woodlands or outlets to such woodlands requiring more than three drivers and one stander. Give a deer too many escape options and you can't control his movement directions. Except for use of the circle and straggler drive techniques, it's best to tackle big woods with gang drives.

One last point should be considered when employing the two-man drive: the driver should never follow a straight line. Deer in small cover areas don't like to jump and dash unless they feel they have to. I've mentioned that single drivers should walk zigzag courses, but they should do so with definite intent. The idea is to penetrate the thickets, walk out the edges, and explore each area where a deer is likely to be. A driver using such tactics makes a deer nervous because he doesn't know what the man is up to. As soon as a small-cover-area deer decides the jig is up, he'll make his dash for safety. It's the brush-beating driver who moves deer on the small drive.

12

The Art of
Stillhunting

The intriguing thing about stillhunting is that the action often is explosive. Of all the deer I've killed, some of the bucks I remember best hit the ground while I was stillhunting. I recall these incidents so well because the action erupted suddenly. Such activity puts a strain on a guy's nervous system.

You always remember the first deer you kill because it's such a highlight in your life, but in my case I remember the situation more than the killing shot. I didn't know much about deer hunting during those boyhood times. On the day in question I was pussyfooting around my local Michigan woodlands trying to imagine I was making like an Indian.

I walked across some oak-lined hills and then dropped down into a ravine that had a creek coursing its bottom. To my right, 20 yards downstream, a small clump of cedars fanned out on both sides of the creek. The clump looked like a good place for deer to hide, so I turned toward it. As I made my move those cedars seemed to explode with bounding and running deer. There must have been a dozen whitetails bursting out of there. One small forkhorn buck made the mistake of running right at me. The range was almost point-blank when I pulled the trigger, and I guess that's why I didn't miss. My first buck hit the ground dead and skidded into some blueberry bushes only yards away.

I believe most of those whitetails had been watching me from the time I began walking down into the ravine. When I made a sudden change in direction and turned toward their hiding spot they decided it was time to leave. The buck I shot must have become confused. He ran the wrong way when the rest of the herd erupted.

I've walked into many similar situations in the years since. The stillhunter must sneak in among deer, and this calls for all the skill, stealth, and caution a man can muster. The very nature of the game implies that you'll occasionally come upon deer that are unaware of you until you get very close. More often you'll come upon deer that are very much aware of your presence, but these animals choose to try hiding till they no longer can stand the tension of a nearby human. In any event, the shocking thrill of deer exploding from cover at close range is almost always an adventure reserved for the stillhunter.

It sometimes happens to stalkers, less often to drivers, and still less frequently to standers. A stalker may pussyfoot onto a deer while sneaking up on another. A driver seldom experiences the explosive dashing of deer because he doesn't travel silently enough to get close without altering them. A stander is stationary except for the travel required to get to his stand, so his opportunities for jumping deer are greatly diminished.

Stillhunting is probably the least understood of all the deer-hunting techniques. To begin with, the term is a misnomer. It would seem to imply that a man hunts by remaining still. In some states in the Southeast this definition is still in vogue. If a man in that area tells you he got his buck while stillhunting he probably means he shot the animal while sitting still on a stand.

The basic concept of stillhunting is moving slowly and as quietly as possible while looking for deer you suspect to be in the area. In contrast, stalking means moving slowly and quietly as possible while trying to sneak within shooting range of a buck you have already spotted. Stillhunting can change into stalking on a second's notice when you suddenly spot a buck that's unaware of your presence, but stalking never changes to stillhunting unless the stalker blows his chance and has to resort to finding another buck.

Stillhunting properly done in thick cover is a half-dozen slow steps and then a stop to look and listen. During the stops you should look to your right and scan on a distant plane in an arc to your left. Then drop your line of view a few yards and scan on the same plane from left to right. Drop the sight plane again and continue inspecting the terrain ahead back and forth. The idea is to check out every piece of cover from the horizon to a few yards in front of you. What you're trying to do is see deer before they see you, or to see them before they become nervous enough to jump and move out. Seeing these animals takes the special skills I covered in Chapter 8.

If you travel more than a mile an hour you're not stillhunting properly;

you're going for a walk. Some experts say you can't stillhunt at more than
half a mile per hour and expect to see the details your eyes must interpret
to spot motionless deer. They also claim that if you move at a faster pace
you're bound to make too much noise to sneak in on a target. Which brings
up another aspect of the misnomer of stillhunting.

The word "still" means remaining in one place or free from sound. Since
a stillhunter is moving, however so slowly, he's bound to make some
sounds. You should take it for granted that deer usually hear you because
their keen ears pick up every approaching sound. There is no such thing as
a completely noiseless approach. And herein lies one of the most important secrets of stillhunting.

The key is that game itself isn't noiseless. A deer moving down a runway
makes sounds, but they're natural sounds if another deer hears them because he expects to hear them on game trails. The same deer would not expect to hear off-trail sounds. especially if they were loud and persistent. So
the sounds of movement can be natural or unnatural, and deer positively
know the difference.

The significance of this is that a stillhunter should work upwind on natural deer runways, and he should travel slowly. A deer moving along a runway stops frequently to look and listen, to browse a bit and to attend to
natural functions. This is one reason why it's so important for the
stillhunter to move slowly, it's the only way the few sounds he can't avoid
making will come off as natural sounds.

It's best not to head directly across country without any regard for game
trails. As soon as you do this the sounds you create become unnatural and
have no counterpart in the wilds. On-trail noise is in order; off-trail noise is
not. Your job is to duplicate in your movements both the sound and the
pace of a deer; that's the best way to get in close.

The second reason for moving slowly is that you must have the time to
carefully scan the terrain ahead, as I've discussed. The general rule is to
take only enough slow steps to give yourself a new perspective of your surroundings, then stop and study them again in detail. It's usually impossible
to discover a partially hidden deer unless you take the time to inspect
every suspicious item as it comes into view. Don't forget that a deer hears
better than you do and is probably aware of the sounds you can't avoid
making long before he sees you.

But deer also expect to *see* movement on runways. The slight swaying of
a bush or limb is not alarming to them. If you're hidden enough so that a
deer can't tell you from another deer he'll pay little attention to the movements and sounds you make. Your advantage is that you're concentrating
on seeing part of a deer, but your unalerted buck is not expecting to see
part of a man. So stay hidden as much as possible. The only way to do this
is to move slowly behind thickets or other types of natural terrain. Do your
looking from behind a particularly thick bush or a tree. The faster you

move the more your body comes into view from any specific point where a deer may be. By moving slowly and studying every part of the land ahead, you have the best odds on seeing a buck before he sees you. And even if he does see you first, he normally won't move out till he sees enough to be sure you're an enemy. By moving slowly and sticking to cover I have several times made out deer standing and watching me. If I had been walking normally they would have run long before, but because of my very slow approach they were not at all sure of what I was.

In the West, where the country is more open than in the East, it's a tremendous help to do most of your studying of the terrain with binoculars. Good optics will show a piece of an antler or a section of deer body in brush far quicker than the naked eye. In this part of the country it's almost impossible to spot game before it sees you unless you glass more than you move. The almost constant use of binoculars will tire your eyes, but it's worth the effort. Adopt the policy of moving as quietly as you can for 10 yards or so, then stop and glass every detail of the land ahead. This sounds tedious, but when you master the technique you'll be amazed at the number of deer you'll pick up in your optics.

Another advantage of stopping so often is that you get a chance to use your ears. If you're dead still you have the opportunity of hearing deer that would otherwise sneak away without disclosing their presence. I recall a Montana incident that proves the point.

A hunting partner had jumped a big whitetail buck in thick brush. The deer melted into the thickets so rapidly Russ had no chance for a shot. Moments later he noticed the buck running up and across a rocky slope more than 500 yards away. The deer continued up into the foothills until he came to a shelf of aspen and pine. The shelf of forest covered only about 120 acres, and it was surrounded on all sides by more rocky slopes. Russ watched the area for half an hour, didn't see the buck come out of the timber, and concluded that the animal had bedded down.

When my partner and I got together for our lunch break he told me about the situation. We decided to stillhunt into the wooded area from opposite crosswind directions. That way, if neither of us spotted the buck, one of us was almost bound to jump him. In that event the deer might offer a shot to the other man when he tried making his escape.

It almost worked. I was following my stillhunting procedure of walking a few steps and then stopping to inspect the area ahead. After one particularly long stop—I thought I had spotted the buck's white throat patch among some deadfalls. But detailed study through my binoculars revealed only a white rock. I was ready to step ahead again when I heard something above and behind me. I whirled and spotted not only the buck but also four or five does. They were above the timber, only 150 yards away, and running in the open. I had a perfect shooting opportunity except for the fact that that crafty old buck ran in such a way he kept the does between himself and me. There was no way I could risk a shot. I stared open-mouthed as the deer ran around the side of a ridge and disappeared.

In any event, if I hadn't been standing still I never would have heard those deer. It's my strong belief that many stillhunters miss hearing deer move out—especially sneaking deer—because they're too busy moving. When you move slowly and stop often you can depend on your ears as well as your eyes.

There's no sense in stillhunting an area that doesn't harbor the animals. A good bet is to scout for recently used bedding areas. When you hunt a bedding area you should try to determine which trail deer would use in reaching it. For example, no unalarmed deer will travel downwind. If you approach a bedding area along a downwind trail, a buck will immediately become alerted to the unnatural sounds and movements that wouldn't concern him if you were traveling a trail in an upwind direction. The basic rule is always to stillhunt with the wind in your face or partially in your face.

Consider the weather, too. On windy days deer will lie upon the lee or most protected side of a bedding area. If a day is very cold but sunny you can expect to find the animals on southern exposure ridges or slopes. If the weather is hot they'll prefer thickets offering shade. Just remember that a wise buck can come into a bedding area from almost any direction. Try to determine what might have attracted him to take a specific route, then stick to the same trail. This is the type of thinking that takes the success of your hunt out of the "luck category" because you're depending on good basic hunting knowledge. Thinking out strategy always makes a hunt more interesting from start to finish.

The main advantage the stillhunter has is that he often has an element of surprise. Today's deer, much more so than their ancestors of years ago, are likely to try a sneak getaway when they're caught unawares. Here again is why those long and frequent stops of the knowledgeable stillhunter can be so productive. If you spend most of your time looking you're much more likely to catch one of these sneaking bucks in the middle of his act. It's also good to keep in mind that a deer can materialize out of the brush 50 feet away and be in plain sight before you know he's anywhere around. If you happen to be moving rather than looking at the time, he can be gone just as fast as he appeared and you may never know he was there.

One time during a hunt in South Dakota's Black Hills I was stillhunting along the edge of a creek when I decided to cross to its other side via a fallen log. The operation didn't take more than about 1½ minutes, but during that time a fine buck got up just in front of me and sneaked away unseen. How do I know? Because some guy was on a stand 150 yards away and he watched the whole sequence. It shook him up so badly he rushed over and blurted, "Why didn't you shoot that buck?"

When I told him I hadn't seen the deer he took me to the spot where the whitetail had jumped up. Then he pointed out the fresh tracks leading away. So much for the importance of restricting your movements. Spend 90 percent of your time looking and only 10 percent pussyfooting along trails.

The unfortunate thing about stillhunting is that it won't work in heavily hunted country. You need solitude. In an area where there are many hunters there just isn't the room to practice sneaking tactics because there's too much human interference with normal movement patterns of deer. Stillhunting also doesn't work well in most of the heavily forested sections of the country east of the Mississippi.

In dense woodlands it's too difficult to move quietly and almost impossible to see very far ahead. If you hunt under such conditions it's almost always better to take a stand. The more open country of the West and Southwest is where stillhunting works best. And you can get results in isolated areas of the East where cutover lands mix with clearings that are lightly hunted. Some areas of the Great Lakes have sand dunes and jackpine clumps boasting soft floors of pine needles. That's stillhunting country, too—if it's back in the boonies and lightly hunted. I mention this to point out that if you don't hunt in terrain that's suited to stillhunting there's no sense in trying it. On the other hand, if stillhunting possibilities are open to you, here are some further tips that should make your ventures more successful.

Many deer hunters have the mistaken idea that stillhunting must be practiced only by lone hunters. This thought is based on the principle that one man will make only half the noise of two men. Well, this principle isn't necessarily true. I came across some enlightening and conflicting information a few years ago when I was working with Linn Thomason of Tulsa, Oklahoma, on a magazine story.

"Two men can actually make less noise than one," Thomason told me. "The first trick is to use hand signals to eliminate all talking or whispering. The main thing is for one man to move ahead about 100 feet, concentrating entirely on traveling silently. His attention is riveted on not stepping on sticks or dry leaves or brushing against branches. The stationary man watches for game while his partner travels. Then the lead man watches while his partner moves up. The system is time-consuming, but it combines the twin advantages of practically noiseless travel with having one set of eyes and ears that are always alert for game. With this technique two men can hunt more efficiently than one.

"Another trick my partner and I use is to stillhunt about 150 yards apart," Linn continued. "One man walks in a valley while the other travels parallel on a ridge. The high man stays about 150 yards behind his partner. The principle is that air rises as a new day warms, and thermal currents carry the scent of the low man up the ridges. Deer like to bed below ridge tops. They'll pick up the scent of the low man while generally failing to

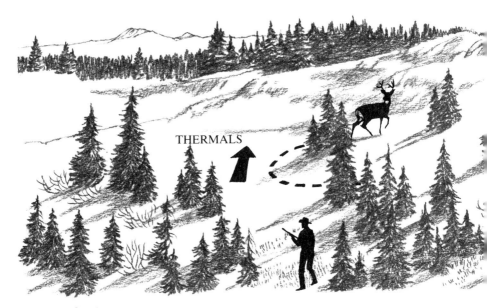

THERMALS

Here, the first man stillhunts along the valley floor ahead of his partner, who moves through cover near the ridgetop. Thermals carry the first hunter's scent to a buck bedded on the slopes and rouse him to move opposite the route of the first hunter—and into view of the second hunter.

detect his partner. It's typical of big game to determine the direction of travel of the lower hunter and then sneak back along the ridge in the opposite direction. The hope is that the animal will be seen by the high hunter who is stillhunting along at the same pace as his partner. The high man must keep concealed as much as possible, and above all he must not expose his outline to the open sky. The clever buck, especially when he's sneaking away, will be constantly on the lookout for danger ahead."

Somebody once told me that he wouldn't think of stillhunting without first covering his rifle with flat paint of camouflage colors. This guy claimed the glint of light from polished barrels and stocks has spooked many a deer from stillhunters who did everything else correctly. If you do a lot of stillhunting this tip sounds like a good one.

Although I've emphasized the importance of hunting along established game trails, there are times when you almost have to stillhunt cross country. Such times include working from where you park your vehicle to where you want to go in a prime hunting area, hunting for feeding or trav-

THERMALS

eling deer, and scouting out new areas. During such times you should be especially alert when approaching open areas, meadows, and the tops or ridges and hills. Make sure there's no game in sight before you show yourself at the edge of any opening. Stop just short of the crests of ridges and hills and peer over them so you don't sky-line yourself. A good trick is to sneak along just below the crests, then move up every so often to peer over. Use the same system when hunting along the edges of clearings, openings and swales. Stay inside the edges of cover where you won't be seen during most of your travel. Limit your inspections of open terrain to momentary trips to the bushes or trees which will offer the best concealment at the very edge of cover. Staying in brush is the best way to conceal your movements during travel, and being in brush helps to dampen noise and contain human scent.

In other places in this book I've mentioned Doug Burris, Jr., the Texan who killed the world-record mule-deer buck in 1972. Doug is a stillhunter who has phenomenal success with the techniques I just mentioned. He has the mounted heads of three mule-deer bucks hanging over his fireplace. The middle one is the world record, yet at first glance it doesn't appear much more massive than the other two. In short, Burris is a master at taking big bucks. He attributes his success to stillhunting, the only system he uses. But he points out that his stillhunting doesn't consist of steady stop-and-go travel. Here's what he told me:

"My system is actually a combination of stillhunting and working from stands. The Colorado oak-brush areas where I do my mule deer hunting are tailor-made for the technique. They offer broken terrain in the forms of canyons and fingers running off the canyons to mesas or plateaus. I like to stillhunt the plateaus and fingers of canyons coming off them. I've learned that deer work these fingers, get down into the very bottoms of them, then range back and forth through the canyons and up to the mesas and plateaus.

"This means the deer are often moving at the same time I am, so when I'm stillhunting I'm apt to spot deer ahead or across canyons and draws. If I take a stand on a good vantage point I may have deer working toward me. So I stillhunt awhile, then sit awhile, and just keep going like that from dawn to dusk. The problem is that mule deer may use one area today and vacate it tomorrow. So I pick an area and hunt it out. If there are deer in there I stick with it. If there aren't, I move over to the next area. Stillhunting is the best way of making sure I'm hunting an area holding deer, but if I know the animals are moving, I don't hesitate to take a stand."

Another important point for the stillhunter to consider is that the more he blends into the cover he's working the less apt he is to be seen. This principle takes on added importance if the day is bright. Always keep to the shadows as much as possible.

If you're after mule deer always remember that they love elevation; it's their personal kind of protection. But it can be their downfall because they don't expect danger from above. It's a habit of muleys to bed two-thirds or more of the way up a ridge from feeding or watering areas. So if you still-hunt a bit higher you're far less likely to be seen than if you hunt lower where deer can look down on you.

Hunting high is the ideal way to turn a stillhunt into a stalk in a hurry. It happens when the hunter suddenly spots a bedded buck that's unaware of danger. There are many ways in which stillhunting and stalking are closely related, but the best way I can clarify them is to get into the subject of stalking, which is covered in the next chapter.

13

Develop Your Stalking Skills

It is possible for a knowledgeable hunter equipped with the proper modern rifle and cartridge to drop a deer in its tracks at ranges of 500 yards or so. There are a few long-range rifle nuts owning target-type rifles equipped with high-power scopes who have killed bucks a half-mile away. Such shooting leaves much to luck because of poor sighting pictures, but ballistically it can be done.

Now consider that the crafty Indians of pre-firearm eras killed their deer with primitive archery equipment which was almost impossible to shoot with any degree of accuracy. Yet they produced venison for their families year-round by their uncanny ability to get in close to deer. There is no better way to point out that the combination of accurate shooting ability and knowledge of stalking skills can be deadlier today than it ever was.

I pointed out in earlier chapters why hunting from a stand is usually surer and easier, but stalking may be for you if you simply don't have the temperament to sit on a stand for long periods and would much rather be on the move. And success from a stand can often involve a certain amount of luck which may not be appealing to the hunter who wants to score by the exertion of individual ability. The successful stalker makes his own luck. If he fails he usually has only himself to blame. Top this off with the fact that, of the various methods of hunting, stalking sustains interest and excitement the longest.

In mule deer country especially, and when the area hunting pressure is low, you may have to stalk or stillhunt because of the lack of other hunters to keep the deer moving.

If you hunt in a mule-deer state, particularly in an area where hunting pressure is low, use of the stalking or stillhunting techniques may be necessary because there aren't enough other hunters to keep deer moving. Mule-deer country is also most appropriate for stalkers since deer are often seen in the distance. Such considerations aren't so readily applicable in whitetail terrain, but times do arise when the success of your hunt may *depend* on your stalking ability.

Throughout much of this book I point out that the modern deer hunter enjoys many advantages the old-timers never dreamed of. In this chapter I want to make a dramatic exception. Let me emphasize that the successful stalker or stillhunter must learn how to hunt *first*, then he can go on with bettering his shooting ability and taking advantage of modern gear. Always remember that before you can kill your buck by stalking you have to approach close enough to get within a certain range. This takes specialized skill of a type the Indians and old-timers had to a far greater degree than does the average deer hunter of today. They specialized in stalking because they *had* to get close. We don't have to get quite so close today. This, again, is why the knowledge of the old-timers combined with the superiority of modern rifles can make stalking so efficient.

A basic rule in stalking is that it's often necessary to get as close as possible to the ground. The man who is willing to get down on his belly and crawl through mud, muck, and brush is going to get far more shooting opportunities than the man who is concerned about comfort or what the stalk is doing to his fancy hunting clothes. The old-timers wore no fancy clothes and they didn't waste a single thought on their appearance; they put up with discomforts that would make many a modern hunter wince. They knew that getting down in the dirt, getting scratched by briers, crawling over rocks, and getting wet could be parts of the game.

In most stalking situations you must move ahead without disturbing the outlines of the terrain between you and your buck. The crown of a cap, a moving shoulder, or even a pair of prominent buttocks can ruin a stalk. In normal stalking you have to get natural terrain features that are higher and wider than you between yourself and the deer, and you have to keep them there. This often means you have to take advantage of various cover features one piece at a time. You have to pick out a bush, tree, rock, or whatever; utilize it to move ahead to a certain spot, then determine another piece of cover that will best shield you for the next part of your advance.

This type of stealth takes time. The old-timers didn't get excited and they never rushed things. I've often thought that one reason they were so successful at stalking and stillhunting was that they didn't have to worry about getting home at 5 o'clock to take the wife out for cocktails, getting to the office Monday morning, meeting the boys for bowling, or any one of dozens of other modern reasons for hurrying up. They stayed in the woods on the theory that impatience invariably scares game. That's still the truth.

Taking your time can mean such things as avoiding the habit of looking up to see your deer too often while you're moving ahead. Instead you should keep your eyes on the ground and have the patience to look for and avoid every twig, stick, or stone that could produce the slightest rustle. Don't look up until you're close behind a concealing piece of cover.

Taking advantage of the wind also takes time. After the game is located you must make your way to a point downwind—or at least crosswind—of the animal before you can attempt a successful stalk. Such an approach eliminates your scent and deadens the sounds of your movements. And once you begin closing in on your deer you should lie motionless when a calm comes on. Wind doesn't blow steadily; it comes and goes with increasing and decreasing velocity. You should move ahead during the increases, which helps drown some noises you are sure to make. Stop as the breeze dies out.

During these stops take the time to note the characteristics of your deer. If it's feeding, get the time intervals (usually about five seconds) between when it lowers its head and when it looks up to scan the landscape. Notice which directions the deer observes most while looking for potential danger. If it spends an unusual amount of time looking in your direction you should go to the bother of figuring out an alternate approach route. In any event, don't try moving ahead through scant cover till your deer's head is down or he's looking in another direction. If he should suddenly look up or turn his head toward you while you're moving, your only option is to "freeze" instantly. Sometimes you'll get away with it. A deer isn't suspicious of an unidentifiable motionless object, but a clever buck invariably will become alert at the first sign of movement.

When I made my first tries at stalking deer years ago, I was never successful. I was ready to give up the technique and I said so to a veteran hunter who killed a buck every year. His comments gave me the determination to keep trying.

"Look at it this way," he began. "If a stalking cat can catch birds you can shoot a deer. The cat doesn't have the benefit of a firearm so it has to get close enough to the sparrow to pounce on him. The bird has wings which enable him to escape easily in a split second if he becomes aware of the cat, yet he gets caught. You have a firearm and your buck doesn't have wings, so you don't have to be nearly as proficient as a cat at stalking. Stalking is an art that's instinctive in cats. Man has to learn it and it takes time. Whenever you have the opportunity to watch a cat sneaking in on a bird you should watch him very carefully. You'll learn a lot, especially how much time the critter uses to make every move perfectly. Knowing when to move and when not to is something no person can tell you. You have to develop a feel for it and, again, this takes time."

The most important principle in stalking is to see your deer before he sees you. When you accomplish this you have a decided advantage because you can focus all your attention on where the animal is and how to close in on him. The buck, on the other hand, has his mind on something else and is expecting danger only in a general way.

The best times to take advantage of this factor are early morning and late evening when deer are moving about and feeding. After a deer has bedded down his attention is no longer absorbed with getting food. Now, even if you should spot a bedded buck before he sees you, you have to compete with all his senses, which have been tuned to hearing, seeing, or smelling an intruder. Not only are deer easy to spot when they're moving about, there's also the chance they may move toward you and make your stalking job easier. Further, you can get away with making some small noises during the early and late hours. When deer are on the move they expect slight disturbances in the woodlands from the movements of other game. But once the woods are quiet you'll be at a disadvantage with every movement you make.

The best way to cut down your odds of alerting deer is to be in a hotspot area before the animals begin moving during early and late hours. In the morning the stalker should be in his hunting area before the stars begin to fade. Take a flashlight to help guide you in, then sit down and wait for the first hint of dawn before you begin pussyfooting about, looking for a buck.

Most modern hunters start the afternoon hunt too early and end it too early. Today's deer, particularly whitetails, do not move out of cover as early in the evening as they did years ago. Now you'll seldom see a deer till just before dark. There's not much sense of getting into the area you want to stalk until the sun is close to setting. When you do start hunting don't give up till the last minute of shooting time passes. The later you hunt in the evening the more deer you'll see. You may not have time to stalk some of them, but there's no chance in the world of stalking a buck you haven't spotted.

One of the greatest errors would-be stalkers make is going too fast and too far while looking for a buck. The hunter who barrels through the brush has almost no chance to spot a deer before the animal becomes aware of him. The trick is to scout for good deer country long before the hunt, then soft-shoe through it while spending about 90 percent of your time looking and 10 percent walking. Step on solid rocks or firm ground, never put your weight on anything that may snap or crackle. Any deer hears better than he sees, and he's sure to be instantly alerted to any unnatural sound. The beginning hunter often sees these deer because they may wait to make sure the noises are produced by a hunter and not something harmless before they bound away, but he never gets a chance to stalk them. This is why some beginners will say, "Those deer never knew I was there till I got within 50 yards of them. Next time I'll get closer." Nothing could be further from the truth. Deer are well aware of bumbling hunters.

I want to emphasize again that one of the most important keys to successful stalking is good scouting. If the stalker knows where deer are likely to be he won't have to make much noise or do much walking while trying to spot them. It follows that the stalker who has continued success has a thorough knowledge of deer. He knows their habits and how they can be expected to react in various situations.

For example, the expert stalker knows what reactions to watch for in the buck he's closing in on. If the animal throws up his head and stares, he's alerted to something. Obviously you should stop and freeze at this point, but just as important, you should interpret what happens next. If your buck moves his head from side to side he's attempting to see his problem. This usually means he hasn't spotted you yet and probably won't run until he does. You shouldn't attempt a risky shot at this point because if you don't move for several moments the deer may resume his normal routine.

Sometimes such a buck will resort to foot-stamping. This is a sign that he's curious and uncertain and attempting to make a possible enemy reveal himself. He isn't about to run off at this point. When he lowers his head or changes the direction of his gaze he has decided no danger is near. Now you can resume your stalk. If you're up against a whitetail, watch his flag.

When deer check for danger, they cup their ears and look in various directions while listening. The deer shown here are not frightened yet because the stalking photographer has frozen in his tracks. But a careless movement would send these youngsters into flight.

When the buck gives his tail a switch from side to side he has made up his mind all is well.

However, you'd best get ready to shoot if your whitetail's tail rises and straightens out. This is a sure sign he's alarmed and ready to run. Knowledgeable hunters watch a buck's ears, too. When he becomes suspicious that danger may be near he'll cup his ears toward you, straining to catch any noise that may be out of place. He isn't about to bolt yet, but watch out if he folds his ears back and tucks them under his antlers. This signal means he's about to depart in a rush. Why does he fold his ears back? Because he doesn't want them vulnerable to the sting of brush as he crashes through cover. When you see your buck's ears go back you're going to have to shoot in a hurry or not at all.

When you mention stalking or stillhunting to most hunters, you immediately create the mental picture of a man pussyfooting along while trying to eliminate noise produced by his feet. The smart hunter knows that the clothes he wears also have a great deal to do with the noises he produces. You should wear clothes that are quiet when you come into contact with briers or brush. Any of the canvas hunting clothes are extremely noisy. They scratch with unnatural loudness in the woods. So do hard-material hats, high rubber boots and plastic rain gear.

Wool is the softest material you can select for general clothing. Leather boots get the nod for footwear, but wear your trouser legs over the outside of your boots to further deaden sound. I'm a nut on Blaze Orange for safety's sake, so I wear a Blaze Orange vest and cap when I'm stalking. These items have become available in soft materials during recent years.

Regardless of the type of boots you prefer, be sure they're soft-soled with foam rubber or crepe. Quiet boots are a must for quiet movement. If you hunt in dry country don't underestimate the advantage of taking off your boots during the last and most crucial part of a stalk. You can move much more quietly in stocking feet than in the best pair of boots ever made.

Human scent is another problem that must be reckoned with. The obvious way to lick it is to stalk into the wind or quartering into it. But sometimes you'll get conditions of wind shift or no wind at all; that's when other tricks of licking the scent problem pay off. Tobacco smoke is particularly offensive to deer. Take two guys with equal stalking ability and you can bet that if one doesn't smoke he'll come home with more game. It's as simple as that because you can't get smoke odors out of your clothing without a thorough washing. Campfire smoke presents the same problem, as does the exhaust smoke of automobiles, outboard motors, or other machinery.

One solution is to utilize a set of "stalking clothes" that are never worn except while hunting. At other times (such as traveling to hunting country or relaxing after the hunt) these clothes can be kept in a heavy plastic bag where no man-produced odors can get to them. A trick some of the old-timers used was to rub moderate amounts of pine or sage oil onto their hunting clothes to mask human odor. For an in-the-field substitute, use a handful of pine or sage needles.

Don't figure you can achieve the same objective by using the modern "deer scents" on your person or clothes. They may mask your scent and they may not alarm deer, but they definitely will produce the one situation the stalker must avoid. A deer scent will attract the attention of your buck and he'll focus his senses directly upon your immediate area. This is exactly what you don't want.

A common conception of the old-timer is that of an old woods rat who didn't take kindly to bathing and who wore the same clothes for weeks at a time. The old-time stalkers and stillhunters who were serious about their hunts were an entirely different breed. They bathed (with particular emphasis on thoroughly washing their hair) before every hunt. And they wore clean hunting clothes. The clothes may have been worn and ragged about the edges, but you can bet those old boys wanted them clean and completely washed of human odor. I remember talking with one of these guys years ago who washed his hands and face with some kind of scent-masking solution that he made himself. I've long since forgotten what the ingredients were, but I've always remembered the implication of that washing rite before the hunt. The old-timers had great respect for the cleverness of deer, far more so than does the average modern deer hunter. Perhaps that's one reason they were able to get so close to their bucks. But some of the new-generation hunters hold onto the old traditions, too.

Whenever a discussion comes up on the importance of controlling human scent I always recall the thoughts of Harry E. Troxell III, a young Colorado bowhunter I once worked with on a story for *Outdoor Life*. Troxell's advice highlights how important the control of scent really is.

"My camping equipment surprises many hunters," Troxell told me. "My gear is selected on the theory that the quickest way to spook game is to advertise your presence with human scent. I camp cold. In other words, I never light a fire for cooking or warmth. I pack in canned meats, fruit, and other ready-to-eat items. Cold camping not only eliminates scent but it also eliminates the disturbances of woodchopping, cooking, and other camp chores. A bowman has to get close to his quarry and that's almost impossible if his clothes carry the odors of smoke or cooked food.

"Getting within sure bow range is especially difficult if the game already has been alerted by the distant sounds of human activity. Though I can often drive close to my hunting areas, I seldom consider doing it because of the noise. I'll drive into a general area, then backpack into the section I want to hunt. Cold camping may be uncomfortable, but it's a definite help in getting close to game."

The next time you think you're being careful about controlling scent and noise factors you'll do well to remember Troxell's advice.

One thing that can ruin a stalk is the activity of other creatures of the wild. I refer to certain birds and small animals which, after becoming aware of your presence, may sing out with their particular vocal alarm which will be understood by all game animals. The alarm caw of a crow is more than enough to tell a buck that there's danger nearby. Other offenders that lend a helping hand to deer include red squirrels, blue jays, kingfishers and magpies. Should any of these pests show up while you're making a stalk you'd best freeze or lie low till they have gone elsewhere. This may take considerable time, and it's one more example of why the efficient stalker is never in a hurry.

There's one stalking technique that may work for you, but which never has for me. It's based on the knowledge that a deer's eyes, like those of a horse or a cow, are set at such an angle in its head that it cannot see anything not directly under its nose while its head is down for browsing. This is why a browsing deer raises its head every few seconds to look around and assure itself that all is well.

Further, the theory goes that you don't need any stalking cover at all if your approach movements are made only when the buck has his head down. The implication is that a deer cannot distinguish between a stationary object such as a bush or tree and a stationary man even if the last time the animal looked up the bush, tree or man wasn't there. Supposedly, a deer also does not have the mentality to realize that a stationary tree or man is getting closer and larger each time the animal looks up.

The secret of this stalk is in timing the sequences of how long the buck has his head down before he looks up again. Normally, this is about five seconds. The stalker gets into position behind the last available cover and then makes, say, a four-second dash toward the quarry as soon as the deer lowers its head. Then he freezes in a predetermined position, usually holding his rifle in front of his body, muzzle pointing at 45 degrees to the sky and finger on safety. The idea is that you must present the same contour to the buck every time he looks up.

The theory stipulates that if you make your moves soundlessly and only when the buck has his head down, you can get close enough to hit him with a rock. Maybe so, but I've found that making quick dashes in average deer country can't be made soundlessly. At least I haven't been able to make them without alerting my bucks before I got within good shooting range. Every time I've tried this stunt my quarry has heard me coming. Perhaps it would work well in grassy fields or on sandy terrain. However, the theory has its supporters among many knowledgeable deer hunters, and it's claimed that the Indians were masters at making this technique work. Maybe I'm just not enough of an Indian.

In any event, the system is almost limited to the stalking of a single deer. When two or three or more are browsing together, you have the situation where each individual deer looks up at different times. It would take a wizard to time all those movements.

Any stalker using any system will often encounter conditions when it's impossible to make a successful hunt no matter how skilled he may be. During extremely dry weather when everything underfoot snaps or rustles there's no way you're going to get close to an unalerted deer unless you're able to hunt into winds of gale force. Crusted snow is also an exceptional noise maker. A thin, frozen crust on the ground is another. Skim ice produced by freezing rain is worse yet. On such days you'll be far better off to take a stand somewhere, sit still, and hope a buck will come to you.

On the other hand, rain or snow softens the land and also produces sound baffles. The stalker or stillhunter welcomes a gentle rain as the greatest assist he can get. Not only does rain make the going much quieter, but it also produces natural pattering noises that help cover the hunter's approach. I mention these facts to point out that the best deer hunters don't live by any single system. The successful veterans have learned to master several techniques, and they may use two or three during a single day's hunt. Stalking is no cure-all, but mastering its principles can be most desirable when proper weather conditions present themselves.

One last word on stalking: if you blunder during a stalk, don't let your startled buck stampede you into shooting unless you have a good chance for a killing hit. Once you touch off a rifle in deer country you alert every other deer in the area. Your chance of making another stalk in the same section immediately goes down the drain. If you don't shoot you may be able to walk over the next ridge or hill and spot another buck that is at ease.

14

Use the Secrets of Archers

The most intriguing thing about hunting deer with archery tackle is the advantage of hunting under ideal conditions. Far fewer hunters are in the field than during firearms seasons and the game is less wary. In many states, bow seasons begin in early fall and last through early winter. This means you can hunt at your leisure, hunt the way you want, and have little fear that other hunters will spoil your chances.

Archers are afield during the most beautiful part of fall. They seldom have problems getting permission to hunt exactly when and where they want to hunt. Land-owners know that archers are dedicated sportsmen who enjoy the odds against scoring with a bow, and they know the bowman is no menace to their property, livestock, or well-being. All of these attractions make bowhunting a highly rewarding outdoor experience.

Another intriguing thing about this sport is that some bowmen are extremely successful at harvesting deer. Take Frank Tolivar of St. Charles, Missouri. Recently he took a whitetail on the state's Danville Wildlife Area. It was the seventeenth deer he'd taken with archery tackle in seventeen years. That's a far better score than most riflemen come up with. I've heard similar stories about archers who have scored three, five, and eight years in a row. Some do even better. Bill Denkins, a Dexter, Missouri tool-and-die maker, took ten deer in five years. During each of those years he took one deer on an archery permit and another on a gun permit. Many of the better bowmen score once every two years, and that's still a better record than the average rifleman can claim.

Even more surprising are the statistics I wrote about in Chapter 2. There I pointed out that in some eastern states gun hunters come up with success ratios of less than 10 percent while bowhunters in nine states west of the Mississippi River score 10 percent or better. This highlights the fact that a great many archers are successful when they hunt in the right places and use the right techniques. Many of us don't realize that the secrets of bowhunters should be even more deadly when utilized by firearms hunters because the gun hunter doesn't have to get nearly as close to his quarry. In a moment I'll get into those secrets that will benefit you most, but first let's take a quick look at bowhunting in general.

Today's 1.5 million archers are a far cry from the few hundred of yester-year. Missouri's case history is an interesting example of how the sport has changed. Here's Dean Murphy, an avid bowhunter and Assistant Chief of the Conservation Department's Game Division, with his view of that change:

"In the old days the few bowhunters we had were clannish. They used to gather in big camps. Perhaps twenty-five or thirty hunters would camp for a week while they scoured the woods. Occasionally they would organize and drive out a ridge or a hollow. That's rarely done anymore.

"Today most archers hunt alone. They hunt close to home in familiar territory. They hunt early and late in the day, before or after work, and they hunt animals whose habits they have studied. Those who change their hunting places every hunt are the least successful. Bowhunting is time-consuming. An archer has a great love for just getting out in the woods. He understands his limitations. He's going to have his greatest success by hunting an area he has scouted well. He must know where the deer are and he must be familiar with their movement patterns. In many instances he's going to be hunting a particular animal in a particular spot."

Murphy's statements emphasize that bowhunters don't go about their sport in a slipshod way; the successful ones have to be perfectionists. So it follows that you'll do yourself a favor if you pick the brains of every archer you know who eats venison he downed with arrows. I've been doing that for years. Here are the most important things I've discovered.

SHOOTING PRACTICE

Serious archers are fanatics about practice shooting. They point out that all the hunting skill in the world won't help a bit if a guy can't put his arrow where he wants it to go when a shooting opportunity arises. They don't just go out in the back yard and shoot a few arrows once in a while.

They visualize themselves on an actual hunt and practice accordingly. If they hunt from tree stands, they practice shooting from an elevated position. For ground shots they practice from standing, sitting, and kneeling positions.

They even practice hitting targets in dim lights as well as in bad weather. Every conceivable hunting situation is duplicated in their practicing. Bowhunters know that deer are seen in a wide variety of locations in the woods, so they put plenty of the same type of variety into their warm-up shooting. They try to get used to deceptive types of terrain by shooting across wooded ravines and up and down hills. And when they miss they spend a lot of time figuring out what they did wrong and how the situation can be corrected.

All this sounds like a lot of work, but it's precisely why some archers are so deadly. The average rifleman wouldn't think of devoting one-tenth as much effort to shooting practice. Most firearms deer hunters don't practice shooting at all, and that's why so many bucks are missed. Take a tip from the archers and become as familiar with your firearm as you can.

HUNTING SKILL

However, archers are quick to point out that shooting skill rates a distant second to hunting skill. If you spend much time with bowmen you'll frequently hear a statement like this: "Put a champion tournament archer in the hunting field on his own and I don't care how sharp his shooting is, if he doesn't know how to hunt he won't have much chance."

The hunting skill most important to the archer is the skill of getting close to deer. According to statistics compiled by the National Field Archery Association, the average bow-killed deer is shot at a range of less than thirty-five yards. These statistics vary slightly from year to year but almost always fall between thirty and thirty-five yards. So an important rule for the archer is that if he can't get close to a deer he isn't going to make a kill. In order to get close he must study the habits of deer so he knows what to expect from his quarry. This means logging many hours on the hunting grounds, and it's another fact that can be proven statistically.

A recent North Dakota study showed that the average bowhunter requires 3½ years to down his first deer. The study pointed out that until a bowhunter has spent about four years in the field learning the habits of deer, he seldom has enough experience to get shooting opportunities.

The top bowhunters I've talked with all say you should be honestly critical when you analyze your hunting technique. The trick is to review each hunt carefully. Each time you get a shot at a buck you should determine the factors that were responsible for the opportunity. If you didn't get a shot, try to figure out why. Lack of success could involve reasons ranging from few deer in an area to hunting at the wrong time in the wrong place.

Most successful bowhunters are devoted practice shooters. They imagine themselves on actual hunts and practice accordingly.

Most unsuccessful rifle hunters shrug off their unsuccessful hunts with the notion that they just weren't lucky. Archers know that the only luck they're going to have is that which they make for themselves. So they analyze what happens during their hunts with the idea of sticking to the most successful hunting systems. This is probably why it takes the average bowhunter years to get his first buck, but from that point on, many of these guys go on to score every year because they've studied and practiced hunting techniques until they've become expert hunters. The firearms hunter who doesn't bother with all this has a chance to be lucky and kill a buck once in a while, but he isn't going to down very many.

One eastern bowhunter I know credits a lot of his hunting knowledge to his many summer days spent woodchuck shooting. "Months before the deer season opens I'm getting valuable practice in the techniques of moving quietly, taking advantage of cover, waiting patiently on stands, and shooting under the pressure that's lacking when aiming at inanimate targets," he told me.

"An archer may be deadly on paper targets, but you can't expect shots at game to be so favorable. Shooting at chucks hones my skill. I also like to hunt during bad weather because it gives me a chance to test my gear and clothes in conditions I often run into during deer season. When I'm after a buck I want to know that my gear and shooting ability are ready to meet the test. An archer doesn't get many shooting opportunities; he has to be prepared to take advantage of each one when it comes along."

That's top advice. Gun hunters can do the same thing by going after rabbits and squirrels with .22 rifles long before deer seasons open. Though this guy didn't mention scouting new country, many archers claim that pre-hunt tune-ups are always great for making sure their favorite deer-hunting area will be productive this year. In other parts of this book I've pointed out that you should never take it for granted that last year's hotspot will repeat this fall. Small-game hunting will not only sharpen your skills, but it can be invaluable when it's combined with scouting for deer hotspots.

All of this takes on even more importance when you consider the advice of one of the most respected bowhunters I know. This fellow gets his kicks by traveling from his Midwest home to Wyoming for his annual away-from-home hunts.

"When I start a one-week hunt away from home, I don't expect to shoot a broadhead at game during at least the first two days," he said. "It takes that long to find where the deer are, where they're feeding and bedding, and where I should take a stand."

This man is an expert hunter and he can do the job in two days. Many of us can't, and this is why pre-hunt scouting is so important. It's no chore when you can mix in the fun of small-game hunting. Just keep in mind that most successful archers get that way by knowing how to shoot and knowing how and where they're going to try for their bucks. Many gun hunters don't bother taking advantage of these improved odds, and that's why they end up saying they're just unlucky.

One of my local cohorts is a dual-weapon hunter; he enjoys hunting deer with both rifle and bow during respective firearms and archery seasons. He emphasizes that one of the main differences between the two types of hunting is in the importance of wind direction and thermal currents. In short, the problems of scent.

"Before I started bowhunting I applied only mild attention to wind direction," he told me. "My first principle was to hunt an area I knew the deer were using. It usually paid off, even though many of my shots were at long range. Then, when I began bowhunting, I noted I still saw plenty of deer. But most of the animals were far beyond the accurate range of arrows. It finally dawned on me that my inability to take full advantage of wind direction could easily be the reason for my failures.

"The closer a deer comes to my stand the more critical wind direction becomes because my scent is becoming ever stronger. The tricks of breeze variation may make my scent escape a deer's attention at 200 yards, which is effective rifle range, but under the same conditions he may become well aware of me at 50 yards, which is beyond the most effective bow range. So my first rule is to build two or more blinds in the area I want to hunt. Then I can hunt with the breeze in my face regardless of wind direction. My next rule is that any unusual scents spook deer. I never use after-shave lotions or body deodorants before going hunting. I don't smoke at any time, so that's no problem. The average gun hunter pays far too little attention to the problems of scent, the bowman knows he has to constantly check the wind."

Amen.

This same fellow has another tip that's almost a religious tenet with successful bowhunters:

WORK PAYS OFF

"If you want a deer you have to plan to work. You can't just go out in the woods, sit down someplace, and hope a deer will come to you. That's what many gun hunters do and they sometimes get lucky. But an archer doesn't get a shot unless he's cleverer than his quarry. You absolutely have to spend a lot of time figuring out how you're going to outwit your deer, and that takes work. I figure I average only one bow shot per eleven hunting trips. Each of those trips may average only a few hours, but they all take planning. In addition to hunting time, I have to allow time for getting in and out of the woods. Time for scouting and building blinds and all the other incidentals are parts of successful hunting, and it's all work. You have to condition and discipline yourself in patience and perseverance."

MINIMIZING MOVEMENT

Bowhunters soon learn the importance of making all moves to shoot in slow motion. Raising a bow and drawing an arrow involves quite a bit of movement that must be accomplished at extreme close range. Anytime you're within 35 yards of a deer, you can bet the animal will notice fast movement unless it is looking away from you or has its head down. The archer also realizes that a close-in deer is likely to hear fast movement. So he makes his draw in a very slow and even manner. If the gun hunter keeps this tip in mind he'll spook fewer deer.

CLOTHING AND CAMO

All knowledgeable archers take camouflage very seriously. They don't go along with the popular theory that deer don't see well. They know from experience that this notion isn't true. They admit deer are color blind, but they're well aware that a clever buck will quickly spot movement of something that contrasts in shape with its surroundings. It's impossible for an archer to remain absolutely still, even before he draws his bow, so he does his best to camouflage his movements.

The wise archer camouflages his entire body, bow, arrows, and all his accessories. Camouflage make-up cremes are used on his hands and face. Regular camouflage clothing, bow and quiver covers, and headnets are standard equipment. Some fellows even camouflage their arrows. They'll concede that brightly colored arrows assist in confirming a hit or miss and that they are easier to find in case of misses but they insist that the bowman who uses camouflaged arrows will get the most shots.

All of this can't be applied to many firearms hunters because they're required by law to wear a certain amount of Blaze Orange, red, yellow, or white outer clothing. But it still makes sense to be sure that the rest of your clothing matches your hunting surroundings in terms of general color. Even if you can't hide your entire body you can hide part of it. The experience of archers certainly proves that the more you hide yourself the more shooting opportunities you'll get. One way to hide yourself is to stay away from solid colors. A plaid wool shirt, say with black and green squares of about an inch and a half, will offer far more camouflage than the same style of shirt in solid green. The idea is to wear clothes that have irregular patterns.

Another bowhunter's trick regarding clothing will work just as well for firearms hunters. In the early years of archery deer hunting there was no such thing as waterproof camouflage clothing. So bowhunters improvised in rainy weather by wearing lightweight waterproof parkas under their camouflage suits. This way they stayed dry and yet retained their deceptive coloration. Some hunters went to the same system to deaden sounds produced by the waterproof fabrics that crackled with every movement. It's still a good trick. In wet conditions any hunter can wear an outer layer of wool or cotton over noisy rain gear. The sodden material may be a bit heavy but it will muffle sound and, if chosen for its irregular pattern, will coffer some of the advantages of a camouflage suit.

HOW TO GET STARTED

I'm convinced that the beginning bowhunter often has a better chance of eventually becoming a skilled hunter than does the beginning firearms hunter simply because bowhunting has a ring of mystery to it. To kill a deer Robin Hood style seems to be almost an impossible feat to the guy who has never tried it, so when he does decide to take up the sport the first thing he looks for is advice.

Because he knows nothing about archery tackle he doesn't buy his bow from a discount store that sells everything from batteries to groceries. The clerk in the sporting-goods department of this kind of store usually has no archery-hunting experience. The thinking newcomer knows this fact. So he goes to a dealer who has a good reputation as an archery specialist and who is interested in repeat business. This way the beginner gets off to a good start with suitable equipment.

Much also depends on the newcomer's introduction to the sport. If he has a place to shoot, friends to shoot with, and someone with experience to help him learn how to hunt, he'll probably develop high enthusiasm. This is probably why there is so much interest in archery clubs. Again, the beginning bowhunter has the feeling he is getting into a mystery of some sort so he looks for the best help he can get. Many beginning firearms hunters don't bother with such preparation. They probably figure that if hundreds of thousands of deer are shot every fall it can't be too much of a trick to shoot one for themselves. So they buy a gun most anywhere and take to the woods with the idea of quickly harvesting some cheap and easy-to-get meat. This is a surefire way to get skunked.

The moral is that if you want to be a successful deer hunter you must hunt with proper equipment of suitable quality and you must know what you're doing whether you go with gun or bow. If you feel you're lacking in expertise take a tip from the bowhunter: Seek some advice on how to correct your problems. These problems are numerous, but expert deer hunters have most of the answers. One expert can help you a lot; two will help you a lot more. If a man could talk to hundreds of experts he'd come up with an enormous wealth of information. That's what I did, and the information I got is in this book.

DEER MOVEMENT PATTERNS

At the beginning of this chapter I quoted avid bowhunter Dean Murphy as saying: "A successful archer must be familiar with the movement patterns of deer. In many instances he's going to be hunting a particular buck in a particular spot."

Through the years I've been impressed with the great number of times I've heard similar statements. Take the case of Tony Schatz of Mandan, North Dakota. While doing some preseason scouting recently, Schatz spotted one of the biggest whitetail bucks he'd ever seen. Being a veteran bowhunter he decided to concentrate on taking this prime trophy. During the next three months he spent every moment of his free time in tree stands in the big buck's home range. Several times he passed up fine shooting opportunities at smaller bucks.

Schatz's chance of a lifetime came just before the state's archery season closed in December. That evening the enormous buck finally came close enough to afford a good shot. Tony's well-placed arrow did its job. Schatz had scored on the biggest buck taken in North Dakota with a bow that year. Its antlers measured high enough in Pope and Young Club competition to make the top ten in North America.

The point is that it's not unusual for an archer to locate a particularly fine trophy when he's scouting and then to discover as much as possible about the buck's habits. The trick is to learn where the deer beds, feeds and waters, and what trails he uses and when he uses them. By concentrating on learning the life-style of one particular animal, the archer eventually determines how best to waylay him. The firearms hunter could do the same thing if he wanted to put forth the effort. So once again we get down to the fact that successful bowhunters get that way because they're willing to work hard enough to achieve results. The tip to remember is that all these guys have traits of desire, determination, and strong concentration. And they have extensive knowledge of the quarry and its habits.

15
Unusual Hunting Methods

In other parts of this book I point out that tracking is usually a waste of time because modern deer have learned to rely heavily on watching their back tracks. Today it's almost impossible to catch a buck off guard by tracking him. When I tell my local friend Bob Wolff that tracking is a waste of time, he smiles and says: "It's a useless technique for you and most other hunters but it works fine for me."

Why? Because Bob is still in his thirties, he doesn't smoke or drink, he does fifty or more pushups and situps each day, and he lifts weights. He is a physical-conditioning nut. He walks his deer down simply because he can outlast his quarry. He thinks nothing of tracking a deer through snow for ten miles or more.

"The trick is to jump a buck, then I know I'm not tracking a doe," Bob says. "From there on in it's pure physical endurance. For several miles I don't waste any time thinking about getting a shot. The buck will be watching his back track, trying to put distance between us, staying to thick stuff and sneaking away from other hunters. During this time I just keep the pressure on him, keep him moving.

"I'll stay with him for maybe five miles before the buck begins to wonder about me specifically. There comes a point when he gets to wondering why I've pursued him faster, harder, and longer than any other hunter who has ever tracked him. That's when curiosity sets in. He wants to get a look at his adversary. By now he's also getting tired. He wants to rest longer between runs. So he lets me get closer before he jumps and his dashes keep getting shorter. The more I wear him out the less concerned he becomes with me because I have yet to shoot at him. I think some of these bucks finally decide that I'm more of a nuisance than a threat. When they get to thinking that way they get careless. Sooner or later they jump up and stand and stare for a moment before dashing off, or when they do dash they'll choose an opening instead of tearing through thick stuff.

"It's usually only a matter of time before I get a good shot. Sometimes I've tracked bucks all day and had to quit when darkness fell. I pick up the tracks of these animals the next morning and keep going and keep the pressure on. A guy can walk a deer down, but he has to be in better shape than the deer to do it. The technique I use would put most guys in the hospital long before they're close to getting a shooting opportunity."

CALLS

Other unusual techniques take little energy or no energy at all. For instance, modern varmint hunters using predator calls have discovered that deer often get very alarmed when they assume a predator is on the prowl nearby. The artificial scream of a dying rabbit seems to be a signal—particularly to whitetails—that it's best to get away from the predator doing the killing. So, to flush whitetails from dense cover, take a stand on a hill or other vantage point and blow a predator call at full volume. You may have deer running out of the cover in all directions. I once had a guide pull this stunt. A fine whitetail buck almost ran over me in his hurried attempt to vacate the area.

Mule deer don't seem to be so alarmed by predator calls. Sometimes they'll jump up and move out, sometimes they'll be attracted to the call out of curiosity, and sometimes muley bucks will move in on a caller with downright fight in their eyes. If you suspect deer are in your area and you can't get them to move out of dense cover, try blowing a loud series of dying-rabbit screams through a predator call. The results may be astonishing.

USING A BOAT

Another modern trick that can cut down on the use of energy is to try for your buck by boat, especially if you're after a whitetail in heavily hunted country, particularly if you're hunting farm country or edge cover. In such terrain deer are used to man and dogs year-round. Here's how all this ties together:

Most deer hunters don't wear hip boots or waders or use boats during normal hunting activities. In heavily hunted country, clever deer have learned to take to the water as one of the most effective ways to escape gunners. It's a trick that works to perfection because a deer is a great swimmer. A man has no choice but to give up on a buck if the animal chooses to escape by swimming to safety. Deer use the same technique to escape free-running dogs that harass them. Most farm dogs can swim but they're seldom water breeds and dislike taking to water.

Even deer that are not run by dogs or subjected to heavy hunting pressure soon learn there are certain sanctuaries where they're never bothered. In some areas the cleverest bucks never get shot at because they move to safety zones as soon as they hear the first rifle go off on the first day of each new season. Many times these safety zones are islands in rivers or lakes that the animals can reach only by swimming. If you know of such islands in your deer-hunting locale, you'll be wise to use a boat to check them out.

Using a boat for float-hunting down rivers or streams is another unusual technique. The theory behind this trick is that deer, especially whitetails, usually head for the thickest cover they can find as soon as hunters swarm into the woods. Often the densest thickets are found bordering rivers and streams. Deer know that such cover offers ideal hiding spots, and they also know they can hear a hunter coming from long distances because it's impossible to traverse such terrain quietly. These animals assume they can't be seen, and that they can sneak away long before a noisy hunter gets close.

The same hunter won't make one bit of noise if he drifts silently along such streamside cover in a canoe or small boat. I've floated so close to whitetails that I've been startled half out of my wits by deer that jumped up within a few yards of my boat. Deer don't expect trouble from water areas, that's why use of a boat can be so effective.

A knowledgeable deer-hunting friend of mine in North Dakota uses a boat for a different reason.

"Our state law says you can't use a vehicle off established roads and trails during deer season," he told me. "This means a lot of rugged back country doesn't get hunted by the man on foot because it's too far removed from vehicle routes. But, thanks to our huge reservoirs, I can reach a lot of top deer country by boat. I load up my outboard with camping gear and take off for days. It's an uncommon occurrence to see another hunter way back in the wild terrain I get to by boat. And, of course, deer aren't as spooky in remote country as they are in areas loaded with hunters."

Jack Connor, a late outdoor writer from Minnesota, used to tell me of the great deer hunts he enjoyed while based in a houseboat in the far northern part of Minnesota, a large trackless area composed of more water than land. Connor used a small outboard to reach neighboring islands harboring deer that had seldom seen a human being. I planned on making one of those hunts, but Jack passed on before we could work everything out.

These examples point out that a boat can often be a deer hunter's best friend even though water and venison would seem to have little in common. The potential for this hunting in one way or another exists wherever there is a river or waterway deep enough to float a boat.

Keep in mind that a boat can be more than a mode of transportation; it can also be a tactical convenience. For example, a friend of mine and his buddy use a canoe to go after deer by floating rivers, but the serious hunting doesn't start till they reach particular areas harboring typical S-curves. Take another look at that "S" and note that it contains two peninsulas which are joined by narrow necks of land. One hunter posts himself on stand near a neck, the other continues floating to the tip of the peninsula where he beaches the canoe and then makes a drive toward his companion. Here we have a ready-made drive area bordered on three sides by water. The technique is a deadly maneuver. The beauty of it all is that many S-curves can be driven in a short time by use of the canoe. Without the craft it would take hours to walk into the remote areas.

Islands can be worked in much the same manner. One man is deposited on one end of the island and waits there on stand. The second man motors or paddles to the opposite end and begins a drive. A variation is for both hunters to stillhunt toward the center of the island, hoping to sandwich deer in between.

Hunters in the northern Great Lakes region are often faced with chains of lakes and swampy or boggy ground. It's difficult to get around on foot in such country, but a small outboard can put a hunter or a party of hunters most anyplace in minutes. Consider also that dragging a deer through marsh is almost impossible. Here again, a boat can be a great time-and-work saver. Hauling out a deer by boat is a simple chore.

"HORN" RATTLING

There's one unusual deer-hunting method that still has me stumped. It's termed "horn" rattling. A few years ago when the subject first was written about in outdoor magazines, it really intrigued me. I figured rattling should work with deer in about the same way a duck call works with ducks. In other words, it's far easier to make the quarry come to you than for you to go to the quarry. So I got some antlers I had lying around in the garage and tried rattling bucks out of local cedar swamps. I tried the trick for several years and, so far as I know, I never had one buck show the slightest interest in my rattling. I gave up and decided that the authors who wrote the rattling stuff I'd read were hunting unusual deer or else they were taking very considerable liberty with the truth.

Hunters in the Southwest call-up bucks by simulating the sounds of bucks fighting. To make the sounds, callers manipulate rattling antlers in each hand. Bucks in the area may make a blustery charge or sneak timidly toward the sound to investigate.

That was my approach to the subject until three years ago when I made a Colorado hunt with Ken Callaway of Houston, Texas. Ken films, directs, and produces a very popular nationwide TV show, "Outdoors with Ken Callaway." Anyway, during our hunt we somehow got onto the subject of rattling. Ken was astonished that I doubted the success of the system.

"Some of the best film I've ever made is of rattling up whitetail bucks in Texas," he told me. "I've got scenes of bucks coming in so fast they just about ran over the guys doing the rattling. There's no question that the technique is deadly."

After I saw that film I had to agree 100 percent with Ken. Since that time I've clipped and saved everything I've found in the outdoor magazines concerning antler rattling for deer. Every one of those articles dealt with rattling in Texas, and one also mentioned success in New Mexico and southeastern Colorado. Every mention of the subject that I've come across had its setting in the Southwest.

Why is this? I have no idea. I simply can't understand why Texas whitetails will fall all over themselves reacting to antlers being rattled and whitetails in other areas could care less. Could it be that experts in Texas have been at the game so long they have perfected a system that is far more complicated than they say it is? If this is true, then does it follow that an expert from Texas could rattle up a buck in any part of the nation? The facts don't seem to justify this possibility.

Perhaps the system works in Texas simply because that state has so many deer. In other words, perhaps the more deer you have to work with the more likely that any given hunting system will produce venison. In any event, many a Texas rattler is positive that rattling will work anywhere there are deer and whether they are muleys or whitetails. From my experience this attitude is wrong, but here are the basics in case you're interested in trying the technique.

There is a definite time limit on rattling, I'm told. The only time a buck will respond to other bucks fighting is during the rut. When a buck is looking for a doe to breed he'd just as soon steal one from bucks that are fighting over a demure little female. So, presumably when he hears a couple of his cousins knocking their heads and antlers together, he moves in with the idea of making off with the doe the battlers are fighting over.

Another theory is that a buck will head for a fight in much the same way that schoolboys can't resist the temptation to crowd in and watch a couple of their classmates whale the daylights out of each other. Still another theory has it that some bucks are always spoiling for a fight during the rut. These mean ones just want to crash the party and get in on the action. Anyway, the experts point out that antler rattling won't work except during the rut.

The obvious first step is that you have to rattle within hearing distance of a buck. It follows that a clear, cool, and windless day is perfect because sound carries well in still air. I'm told that on such a day the sounds of clashing antlers can be heard up to half a mile away. So, in still weather, move about a half-mile between rattling attempts. In windy weather you shouldn't move more than a couple hundred yards between attempts.

Some rattlers add a lot of mystery to the sport by saying that antlers used for rattling must be special. They say the horns must be kept "alive" with such processes as soaking in oil, rubdowns with tallow, or baking in ovens at prescribed temperatures. Others say such treatment is nonsense. One Texan told me that some of the best rattling he'd ever done was accomplished with an old set of bleached-out antlers he'd found on the ground. Another fellow told me he used rattling antlers that his father had used before him, and that they had never been processed in any way.

The consensus seems to be that any pair of antlers will work. All a hunter has to do is slam, knock, and twist them together to produce sounds comparable to a couple of fighting bucks. Realism is added by occasionally breaking a few limbs and twigs of brush with the antlers. Pounding or stomping the ground with the butts of the antlers adds more realism. These added commotions are supposed to simulate hoofs striking the ground and bodies breaking brush during the heat of the battle. When two big bucks really go at it their fighting sets up a spine-tingling racket.

I'm told by rattling experts that there are two kinds of bucks: the chargers and the sneakers. A charger comes blundering in without thought of danger. A sneaker is cautious, approaches behind cover of brush, and is reluctant to step into the open. You'll have to be well hidden to get a shot at a sneaker.

So all you have to do to rattle up a deer is have a set of antlers and be in the right place at the right time. The problem for most of us is that the only right place seems to be the Southwest, particularly Texas.

If you're wondering how I can give advice on rattling without ever having been successful at it, I can only tell you this: I got so enthused about the subject I made a deer hunt with Ken Callaway in the south Texas brush country in December of 1975. We tried rattling, but Ken predicted it wouldn't work because the rut wasn't on. It didn't work, but I got a lot of advice from Texas experts so I'm just passing it on.

MORE ON CALLS

Attracting or luring deer with mouth-blown calls is another controversial subject. Most of the deer hunters I've talked with who have tried calling have had poor results. They seem to feel that calling is still in the experimental stage, but that some day somebody might very well perfect a deer call that really works. The reasoning here is that deer have exceptional hearing and are exceptionally curious, so why shouldn't they move in on a sound that attracts them?

Murry and Winston Burnham, two Texas-based call makers, have become famous because of their game-calling ability. The call they developed and market for calling in deer is loud and sounds like an anguished squeal. The Burnhams have letters from purchasers of their calls who claim great success with calling. Perhaps calling is in the same category as rattling antlers in that if you're in the right place at the right time and know what you're doing you might be successful.

There are two things about calling that I know for sure: in some states deer calls are illegal, and in all my deer-hunting travels in many states I have yet to meet a hunter who used a deer call. From my experience the top experts use the more surefire techniques to get their venison.

STORM FRONTS

One method that involves no mystery at all is to hunt the storm fronts. The only reason I classify it as an unusual method is that so few hunters utilize it. Even many experts are unaware of its significance. I well remember the first time I became aware of the fact that there is concentrated deer movement before a storm moves in.

It was the third year I hunted from the same stand. In many hunts from this stand I had never seen more than three to five whitetails per day, but usually one of the animals would be a buck. That's why I kept hunting from the site. On the day in question I saw six deer during the first hour after dawn. One was a spike buck, but I didn't try for him because I sensed that deer were going to be moving all over the place.

Later I let a forkhorn go by. Still later I shot a nice six-pointer. This buck was the twenty-first deer I saw that day.

When I walked to my stand before dawn that morning the stars were winking brightly in a clear and windless sky. The sunrise was so beautiful I wished I had my camera. The day became so warm I had to peel off some outer clothes. It was only when I was field-dressing my buck did I note a switch in the weather. And when it switched, it really switched. Wrinkled gray clouds shut out the sun. The temperature dropped from 50 degrees before dawn to less than 30. This fact was abundantly clear because when the rain came on it froze as it hit the ground. By the time I got home that night there was two inches of fresh snow on the ground.

The point of all this is that deer—and all other wild animals—have a built-in "sixth sense" when it comes to knowing that a storm is brewing. Before any bad storm deer will move about and feed heavily to prepare for the time ahead when they will be relatively confined to cover areas. And again, right after a storm, deer will come out to stuff their empty stomachs. They'll keep right on feeding throughout the day if it takes that long to fill up. Then, during following days, they'll go back to their basic pattern of feeding at night and bedding during daylight hours.

The significance of this is that the only time deer will move about unnaturally under their own free will is during daytime hours just before and just after unusual storms. This fact didn't mean much to the old-timers because years ago man's ability to forecast weather scientifically was practically nil. Today weather forecasting is a generally reliable science. The deer hunter who watches weather forecasts and is able to go hunting just before and just after bad storms is going to see far more deer than the guy who hunts in nice weather.

Keep in mind, too, that a deer engrossed in laying on the food before a storm, or making up for lost time after a storm, is less cautious. Not only is he on the move and more apt to be seen, but once he is spotted he is far more vulnerable than under normal conditions because he's not concentrating on danger. The more severe the incoming storm the more vulnerable deer become. And the longer a bad storm lasts the more vulnerable deer are the day after the weather quiets down.

16

Hitting Them
the Modern Way

I'll begin this chapter by mentioning several incidents which should set the stage for telling what I've learned about deer rifles and shooting deer during the last thirty-three years.

I was fifteen years old when I made my first deer hunt in our local Michigan woodlands. Since my dad had passed on several years earlier I had no one to tell me about deer hunting or deer rifles. Dad's old .32 Remington Woodsmaster automatic had been gathering dust for many seasons. I took it to a local gunsmith who checked its condition and told me how to operate it. The rifle was equipped with a peep sight, which seemed as good as any to me.

Snow covered our deer woods the first day of that long-ago season. I picked up the fresh track of a big whitetail and began following it. Soon it mingled with tracks of other deer. After a couple of hours of sneaking along those tracks I came onto deer droppings so fresh they were still steaming. Buck fever had begun to come over me much earlier and now it built to a peak.

I remember getting down on my hands and knees and literally crawling through the snow toward a small clump of jackpines 100 yards ahead. About the time I decided the whitetails had moved on that little clump of pines began exploding deer. They burst out in several directions.

Most of the deer were running, but one small forkhorn buck stopped after a couple of leaps and stood staring at me. He was broadside, about 70 yards away, and he offered as good a shot as one ever gets at a deer.

I flipped the safety on that old Remington and began shooting. I fired the semiautomatic rifle as fast as it would operate, but I have no idea where the bullets went. The buck ran off untouched.

A few years later, after I'd missed a couple more bucks, I decided my .32 Remington with its peep sight wasn't much of a deer rifle. My mind was made up that I'd do better if I had a better and more up-to-date firearm. I was old enough then to believe all the stuff I had read about brush-busting bullets, advantages of various rifle actions, and so forth. At the time I didn't have enough deer-hunting experience to know if what I read was true, but I was convinced that anybody who hunted deer with a .32 Remington with a peep sight was hunting at a disadvantage.

I know now that conviction isn't entirely correct. As the years passed I began to get the sneaking suspicion that any rifle can be a good deer rifle if the man who is using it is a good deer hunter. This suspicion took on weight during many seasons, but I especially remember a whitetail hunt I once made in Montana.

One of the hunters in my group was a local citizen who turned up with—of all things—a .32 Remington Woodsmaster with a peep sight. The rifle looked so identical to the one I used to have I wondered if it could be the same one. It wasn't. It turned out that this old-timer had owned the rifle for about thirty years. He wouldn't tell me how many deer he'd shot with it for fear of being quoted, but he did tell me of something that's good advice.

"It ain't the rifle that makes the killing shot," he began. "It's the man behind the rifle. I know exactly what this Remington will do, and I know how to make her do it. A guy's a good shot or he ain't. The best modern rifle won't kill a deer for a man unless he knows how to use it. That's the thought you writers ought to promote instead of wasting so much ink on ballistics and such."

There's a lot of truth in that opinion, but it has to be qualified. Recently I was discussing the statement with one of today's leading gun writers. He summed up the qualification very neatly. "I've run into a lot of those old-timers who are excellent shots with old rifles," he told me. "These guys don't keep up with modern advances in guns, ammunition and scopes. They have no reason to. They nail their bucks every year with their old rifles because they've had the hunting and shooting experience necessary to do the job.

"The thing is, today's average deer hunter just doesn't get the chance to use his rifle except during deer season. The only way he can up his odds is to use the equipment that's best suited for the type of hunting he's going to do. Today's rifles and scopes enable the modern hunter to down deer the old-timers would have had no chance at regardless of their hunting skill or familiarity with their guns. You get an old-timer who will cooperate with you and try modern equipment and you'll really see his eyes light up."

I was part of such an incident ten years ago in Wyoming, though the hunt involved antelope rather than deer. My partner and I were camped with a fold-out camper along a cottonwood creekbottom. One evening the rancher who owned the property drove up to see how our hunt was going. It so happened there was a small herd of antelope grazing along a hillside above us. They were nearly 400 yards away. Neither of the two small bucks in the herd wore horns that interested my partner or myself. However, they interested the rancher very much.

"That's prime eating up there," he said. "Wish I had my rifle, I'd sneak up there and pop one of those bucks."

"No need to be sorry," I said. "Take my rifle and try dropping the buck you want. You can shoot from right here, you don't have to sneak closer. Just lay the rifle across the hood of your truck, put the scope's crosshairs just above the animal's shoulder, and squeeze off a shot."

The guy looked at me to see if I was kidding, decided I wasn't, and then asked, "What caliber is that rifle?"

"It's a .243," I said. "it's sighted in to hit dead on at 250 yards. The slug will drop several inches at your range, that's why I'm telling you to hold high. But it will get there and do the job. Try for one of those bucks. You might be surprised at what happens."

So he did. At the crack of my rifle the rancher's antelope went down as if his legs had been kicked out from under him. The animal didn't move an inch after he hit the ground.

"That's damned hard to believe," the man said with awe. "I wouldn't have the least idea of where to hold my rifle on a target that far away."

When we analyze this incident we arrive at a conclusion which seems contrary to the statement made by the Montana hunter with the old .32 Remington who said, "The best modern rifle won't kill a deer for a man unless he knows how to use it."

Well, my answer to that is simple. Though the Wyoming rancher wasn't familiar with my rifle he was more than familiar with his own firearms. He used his rifle more or less year around for shooting coyotes, and he had used it for many years while hunting mule deer and antelope. He knew how to get a sight picture, he knew how to squeeze off a shot, and he wasn't much concerned with buck fever. In short, he knew plenty about how to use a rifle. All he had to be told was where to hold and then he sent his bullet home with no problem.

Now we come to the premise I've been building up to. Though there's no substitute for deer-hunting experience when it comes to knowing how to shoot a deer, at no time in history have modern rifles, ammunition, scopes and equipment been so reliable as they are now. The so-so deer hunter of today is going to eat a lot more venison than his counterpart of years ago because he has the opportunity of hitting his buck the modern way with modern equipment. Let's develop this thought a bit further.

Years ago the Model 94 .30/30 was a famous deer rifle. Winchester has sold more than 3 million of them, practically all to deer hunters, since the rifle was introduced in 1894. Twenty-five or more years ago when you saw another deer hunter in the woods he probably would be carrying a .30/30. How many of those rifles do you see in today's woods? Not many, and here's why:

The muzzle velocity of 170-grain factory loads for my .30/30 is 2,220 feet per second, and their energy at 100 yards is 1350 foot pounds. The muzzle velocity of 100-grain factory loads for my .243 is 2960 feet per second, and the energy at 100 yards is 1620 foot pounds. Obviously the .243 slug, and others comparable to it, steps out faster and hits with more shocking power.

Sight-in a .30/30 to hit at point of aim at 100 yards. If you have to shoot at a deer 300 yards away your bullet will drop 29.6 inches from point of aim. My .243 slug will drop only 12.2 inches. Again it's obvious that, given the same shooting opportunity, the man firing the .243 or a comparable modern caliber is much less likely to miss than the man with the .30/30 if both men have the same shooting skill.

Going a step further we can say that the old-timer with a .30/30 would have no business shooting at a deer 300 yards away because his iron sights and beer-belly bullet trajectory would give him a very bad combination of sight picture and bullet-placement estimation. The same guy shooting my .243 would have a most reasonable shot because he would be shooting a flat-trajectory bullet and he could turn my variable scope up to 9x and be presented with a very good sight picture. Also, if shooting light happened to be poor, iron sights would be difficult to line up. A scope gathers light, so it offers a far better sight picture and will allow a hunter to shoot earlier in the morning and later in the evening, especially on the dull days which are common in deer country everywhere. This is crucial in whitetail woods because deer begin moving at the first hint of dawn, and again at dusk.

MORE ON SCOPES

If the foregoing isn't enough to convince you that the modern hunter is foolish to go into deer woods without a scoped rifle, consider another important point. Most whitetails are shot in thick brush, which means the hunter must shoot through openings in the brush so his bullet won't be deflected before it gets to his buck. A scope, because of its magnification, often makes it possible for a hunter to pick a clear path for his bullet. Iron sights of any type lack this advantage.

Also, a scope has more of a built-in fail-safe system for accurate shooting than does an iron-sight setup. With iron sights you have to line up two different sighting points at different distances from the eye. With a scope you have only one sighting point, normally the intersection of the crosshairs.

I believe that many shooters, especially inexperienced deer hunters, tend to line iron sights on a deer's vital section and then look up as they pull the trigger. This tendency results in shooting high and is due partly to buck fever and partly to the fact that it's difficult to keep two sights lined up, especially on a moving deer. You can't fall victim to this problem with a scope because you must have the crosshairs (or post) on the buck to get a sight picture. If you look up for any reason that sight picture is gone immediately. So, with a scope, you either have a good sight picture or none at all. This is not true with iron sights. Also, a scope is superior on running shots because you can try to keep the horizontal crosshair along the deer's body. It's a sighting reference line that you don't get with iron sights.

The biggest problem with using a scope is its comparatively narrow field of view. The average hunter thinks he should close his left eye as he mounts his rifle for the shot so that he can pick up his target through the lens with his right eye. This is *all wrong*.

You should get into the habit of keeping both eyes open as you shoulder your rifle. Use the same technique you use with a shotgun. In this way you can see both the deer and his surroundings with both eyes until you get roughly on target. This eliminates the problem many scope users have when they suddenly see a deer against the wide landscape, then have trouble finding him through the scope. This happens because the field of view from natural eyesight becomes abruptly narrowed.

You should get roughly on target with both eyes open before you close the left eye and lay the crosshairs exactly where you want them for the shot. The reverse is correct for left-handed riflemen. The both-eyes-open technique will greatly help the sight-picture problem that many unknowing scope users complain about.

Most hunters who have trouble finding game through a scope bring it on themselves because they never look through their scopes except during deer season. Practice makes perfect in anything we do, so it's just common sense to practice with your scope during the off season. The both-eyes-open technique can be used for dry-firing practice any time and anywhere. You could take a few moments right now to pick up your rifle and do a little scoping practice through a window in your home. Do this several times a year and you'll become familiar enough with your equipment to find an instant sight picture.

A good trick I've always promoted is to get plenty of practice with a scoped .22 rifle. I use one for small-game hunting before deer season and for plinking year-round. When you get to the point where you get pretty good with the .22 you won't have any problem finding game with the larger scopes used on deer rifles. Any shooting practice with any type of scope helps lick the sight-picture problem.

What scope is best? There's no specific answer, but much depends on where you hunt. If you hunt in densely wooded whitetail country where brush is thick and shots are short you'll want a scope with a wide field of view. Most modern scopes have a very wide field of view, which is the main reason they have become so popular in recent years. The scopes of years ago had such narrow fields of view that most old-timers figured they were nearly worthless. They were right, but that's all changed now.

An average modern scope of 2½x will present a view circle of 42 to 44 feet at 100 yards. A 4x covers 30 to 34 feet. As the power increases the view-circle coverage decreases. Short-range whitetail hunters will limit their ability for quick shooting in thickets if they go beyond 4x.

However, if the same hunters mix their deer gunning with occasional trips west to mule-deer states where shots are often long, they'll be limited with their 2½-to-4x scopes because of lack of target definition at long range. One answer for these men is a variable scope which will adjust from, say, 2 to 7x or 3 to 9x. I have scopes on my deer rifles in both categories, so I'm set to hunt whitetails in the East or mule deer in the West with no problems concerning scope power.

There's one problem with scopes that seems to be a holdover from the old days. During those times it was common practice to come in out of the cold and stack rifles in the corners of cabins or tents. perhaps near blazing-hot wood stoves. This habit caused no problem because the rapid change from cold to hot temperature had little effect on iron sights. It's a different story when glass optics and mounts are involved. Too-rapid temperature changes can expand or contract scope mounts and stocks, and cause them to shift sufficiently to change the point of aim.

My most telling experience of this sort of thing occurred during a hunt for mule deer in the West. We were in a tent camp during a blizzard. The temperature plummeted. We stayed in camp for a day and a half, and my rifle happened to be placed near a hot stove. The next day I was on a stand when a fine mule-deer buck trotted up and stopped in front of me. I lined up on his lung area and touched one off. He piled up on the spot.

I was very proud of that shot until I examined the carcass. I couldn't believe my eyes when I found that my slug had broken the buck's back. The situation confounded me till I realized that my scope had to be lined off my point of aim. I test fired the rifle later and found that it shot high and to the right. And that was a mystery because it had shot exactly on target when I tried it the day before the hunt. The rifle hadn't been dropped or abused in any way. I finally came to the conclusion that the rapid temperature change was the culprit.

Since that day I've been careful not to make the same mistake. If I'm hunting my local area I store my rifle away from heat runs in my house or in my locked car after I have sighted it in. If I'm on a trip I store it in the coolest and safest place available. (Fogging, either on the inside or outside of a scope, can be caused by rapid temperature changes, too. Storing my rifle in the coolest place available also licks this problem.) And, if I'm on a trip, I always resight my rifle after I reach my destination. Often this can't be accomplished before I reach the hunting area, but I'd much rather risk spooking game than shooting at a fine buck with a rifle that doesn't shoot where I think I'm aiming it.

When scopes first became popular with deer hunters a few years ago there was the tendency to feel that they were fragile and could easily be knocked out of line, particularly in vehicles and airplanes. Such concern is understandable, but most scopes and mounts manufactured today are far more rugged than the early models. With normal care you won't have to worry much about your scope's vulnerability.

You'll be a lot better off worrying more about the condition of the optics. The average automobile driver wouldn't think of driving with a dirty windshield, yet few hunters seem concerned with the fact that a scope's lenses can easily become dusty, water-spotted, dirty, finger-marked, or oil-smeared. Trying to aim through such neglected lenses dramatically increases the odds of missed shots. If you don't have protective caps for the ends of your scope you should buy a pair. Keep caps on your scope at all times except when actually hunting. While in the field I keep a few sheets of camera-lens tissue in my wallet. It takes only a moment to clean my scope's optics whenever they become dusty or dirty. Camera-lens tissues can be purchased at any photo shop, and they won't scratch a lens as will your dry shirttail or handkerchief.

WHERE TO HIT THEM

Regardless of what caliber rifle or sighting setup you use the object of the game is always to put your bullet where it will make a clean kill. Since bullet placement is the critical factor it logically follows that the biggest vital area of a deer will be the easiest to hit. The lung area is very vulnerable since lungs are filled with blood vessels and protected by only a thin rib cage. Hit a deer in the lungs with any expanding bullet of suitable caliber and he's yours. He may go a few feet or yards, but he's going to go down in the immediate area and he's going to stay down.

As long as there are deer hunters there will be arguments about this premise. Many veterans say a deer shot in the heart, brain, neck, or spine will drop in his tracks. This is true in most cases, but my contention is that the guy who can hit these small areas consistently has the shooting ability to make the Olympics. Shooting at deer under normal hunting conditions is too tough a job to permit hitting the smaller vital areas with any degree of success.

During my thirty-three years in the deer woods I've seen so many bucks shot in the guts, back quarters, or legs that I long ago concluded that many hunters don't have the shooting ability to consistently hit a deer, period,

Since the lungs make up the largest vital area and since deer that are lung-shot with modern expanding bullets are goners, your aiming for the lungs will give you the optimum record of kills over the years. Shooting offhand at 100 yards, few good riflemen can hold a one-foot group anyway. Even from a rest, a perfectly squeezed longer shot may miss the mark because of misjudged distance. A shot for the lungs that ranges high may hit the spine; forward, it may smash the shoulder; low, it may enter the heart—all capable of downing deer quick. Odds are with the lung shooter every time.

let alone in a specific area. Even among good rifle shots there are few who can keep all their offhand shots in a one-foot circle at 100 yards or a two-foot circle at 200 yards. So what sense is there in the advice of many so-called experts who promote heart, head, spine, or neck shots? The average guy simply can't hit targets that small under hunting conditions. I lost a couple of bucks years ago because I gambled on shots I should not have tried.

Just before the 1958 deer season my family and I moved into our new home. I had a beautiful den with a wall perfect for hanging a head-and-neck mount of a trophy buck. I had a couple of buck mounts but neither seemed to do justice to that new den wall. I decided I was going to try for a really fine Michigan whitetail.

The first day of that deer season I passed up an average six-pointer. A week later I got my chance at a bigger buck. I was on a stand near a narrows in a small lake. Deer often used that narrows as a swimway when they were pushed by drivers. This particular buck swam across from the north side of the lake. I was on the south side. After looking at him through my binoculars I was sure his rack had four points on one side and five on the other. A fine specimen for my den. I decided to try for him as soon as he stepped into the point of woods 70 yards in front of me.

But he didn't come ashore where I expected him to. Instead he swam closer to me and stepped into the woods only 30 yards away. I decided to try for a spine (backbone) shot because I knew I wouldn't ruin much meat, the head, or the cape. For some strange reason I figured the shot would be easy because the buck was broadside and standing still, and I was aiming from the relatively stable sitting position. So I touched one off.

That fine buck blasted out of there under full power with his flag high. I took another desperation shot but I knew I'd goofed. My first bullet must have gone over his back by not more than an inch. When I realized this and the fact that the same amount of sighting error would have produced a kill had I aimed for the lung area, I was beside myself with disgust. As it turned out I didn't get a head mount or venison that year.

One time I was still hunting along the edge of a small pond in northern Wisconsin. A new fall of fluffy snow was on the ground. It was so soft that my movements were practically silent. Because of the ideal stillhunting conditions I practically walked on top of a spikehorn buck. He was drinking out of the pond, unaware of me, and I spotted him as I came around a bank. He was no more than 30 yards away. I thought I had a perfect opportunity for a heart shot.

When I fired, the buck wheeled and bolted into thick cover. I didn't have time to squeeze off a second time, but during the instant it took for the whitetail to disappear I noticed he was dragging his left front leg. I knew in a flash my bullet had gone a bit low and to the left and had broken the deer's foreleg. I mentally kicked myself all over that creek bottom for not having shot for the lung area where the near miss would have been a fatal hit. As it turned out another hunter got the wounded buck after I'd tracked him for an hour, so I didn't feel as bad as I would have if I'd been convinced I'd left a wounded animal in the woods.

Why do so many hunters discount the deadliness of the lung shot? A good question, and I can only guess at the answer. It seems to me that a good many riflemen feel that if a high-powered slug hits bone it will blow up something and create sudden and violent shocking force. This may be okay if you're after dangerous big game but it doesn't hold true when you're after deer. If you put a properly expanding slug of good construction and weight into a deer's lungs, it's a physical impossibility for him to go far because an expanding bullet will produce profuse hemorrhaging and the animal has to drown in his own blood in moments. It's as simple as that.

MORE NOTES ON CARTRIDGES AND RIFLES

Note that I said "a properly expanding slug" in the last paragraph. The implication here is that if a bullet doesn't open up well it won't do maximum damage upon entering the lung area. This is why some over-gunned hunters don't like the lung shot. Their big bullets don't open up in an animal as small as a deer; they zip right through the critter while hitting little or no bone and produce a wound that may take hours to kill. The guys using heavier slugs in big-caliber rifles lose a lot of deer because their bullets go through the animals before they have a chance to kill by expanding. That just doesn't happen with calibers such as the .243, 6mm, and .270. Regardless of caliber, if you confine your deer shooting to bullet weights in the 100 to 150-grain class you're going to be shooting slugs that will expand in a deer's lungs. And when they expand they're going to kill in short order.

What about the "brush-buster" capabilities of the bigger slugs that so many veterans claim are so important, especially in whitetail woods? Well, in these modern times there is considerable evidence the old theory that heavy, round-nosed bullets will plow through brush and hit a deer at point of aim is pure nonsense.

The popular concept of the brush cartridge includes bullets of .30 to .45 caliber having muzzle velocities of 1,800 to 2,300 feet per second. Such bullets are supposed to plow along and push aside twigs or small branches or drill right through them with no deviation from point of aim. The concept also claims that high-velocity, pointed, and lighter slugs blow up on contact with anything much heavier than a blade of grass, or else they deflect wildly off course.

Jim Carmichel, *Outdoor Life's* respected shooting editor, says the reverse of the concept is more likely to be true.

"In a nutshell the class of cartridge usually referred to as brush busters are, in fact, about the poorest choice for the job," he told me. "The reason the high velocity, pointed, and lighter slugs have more stability in flight is their higher rotational speed. It follows that a heavy, slower-spinning bullet is more likely to tumble when it hits a twig or branch. You can validate the theory by experimenting with a toy top. When the top is spinning at high speed, strike it smartly and notice how it wobbles a bit but then trues itself back up. When the top's rate of spin slows, an identical blow will

The author recommends using fast-opening bullets in the 100- to 150-grain class. In the bullet expansion photos shown here, a Remington Core-Lokt, pointed bullet enters gelatine and begins expanding almost immediately. The mushrooming of the lead core continues until the thickest portion of the metal jacket resists further mushrooming and helps hold the bullet together. Whether hitting bone or only flesh, this kind of bullet penetrates well, while providing good shock effect on deer-size game.

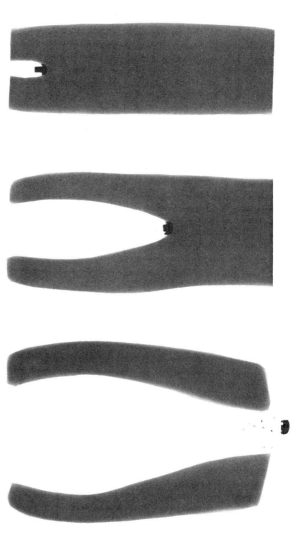

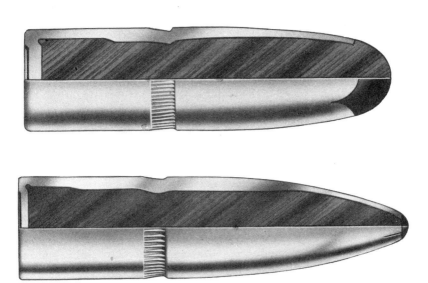

These cutaway drawings show the relationship of lead to jackets for the Remington Core-Lokt soft nose and the pointed, soft point. The greater amount of exposed lead of the soft nose is favored for short range by many hunters using rifles of .30 caliber or more because it provides maximum mushrooming and shocking power. This soft nose offers good initial wind resistance but loses velocity and energy more rapidly than the pointed bullet. The pointed bullet shoots flatter and retains energy better at long ranges.

knock it completely out of balance. The same thing can happen when a bullet of high rotational speed strikes brush. At top speed it might wobble for an instant, but then it will settle down again in a point-on direction. Slower-spinning bullets are more likely to be knocked out of kilter and begin to tumble.

"But, to be factual, we have to conclude there is no really reliable brush cartridge or bullet. When a bullet of any sort strikes a substantial obstacle—even a twig no bigger in diameter than your finger—there is every likelihood that it will be deflected to a certain degree. The real answer, with any caliber, is to try to place your shot so your bullet has a free ride to target. The hunter who takes care to line up his shots so that the bullet has a clear right of way has a good brush rifle regardless of caliber."

Another myth that is on its way out these days is the supposed superiority of semiautomatic rifles in relation to second-shot speed. A few years ago it appeared as if the semiautomatic would sweep the market, but that expected sales volume never came about. The reason is that autos will get off shots faster, but they're little faster than other models in getting off *aimed* shots. Recoil is about the same in all models of the same caliber, and you have to overcome the effect of recoil before you can aim a second shot. This process is a short one, but you must take the kick, control the rifle's movement, and get your scope back on target before you can touch off a following *aimed* shot. All of this can be done in a hurry, but the process takes more time than is required for the experienced rifleman to operate the action of a pump, lever, or bolt-action rifle.

In addition, I consider a bolt-action rifle to be of far safer design than other types. It is also more trouble-free. Sand or grit can get into a bolt-action and you still can ram the bolt home and get off a shot.

A friend of mine had the habit—like most of us—of carrying loose cartridges in his pockets. One time some dirt got into Warren's pocket. He went deer hunting that morning, loaded his semiauto, got off one shot at a buck, then had his rifle jam when the second round failed to feed into the chamber.

Since then he has always carried clean cartridges in a plastic bag in his pocket—a good trick for anyone—but I'll bet if he had been using a bolt-action he would have nailed that buck, or at least had a second shot. I'm partial to bolt-action rifles because they're safer, more dependable, and more accurate than other designs.

After reading this far in this chapter you certainly have reason to believe that I'm also partial to the .243 caliber. Well, I am, for several reasons. And those reasons might as well lead off my discussion of killing power.

Because of my profession as an outdoor writer and editor I find myself in the fortunate position of being able to make two extended deer hunts each year. During the last ten years I've harvested an average of two whitetails or mule deer each season. All of those animals were downed with 100-grain .243 slugs. One big mule deer managed to run off 60 yards after being hit just back of the lung area, a bad shot. One whitetail made it 30 yards before piling up, another whitetail buck struggled about 10 feet before caving in. All other deer (plus some antelope) I've taken during the 10-year period dropped in their tracks. So the main reason I shoot a .243 is that it's just plain amazingly deadly on deer. I don't have to have anybody tell me it's deadly; I know it's deadly from plenty of personal experience.

Why is it so deadly? Because its high-velocity, rapidly expanding bullet hits and reacts with an enormous degree of shock. Deer hunters are finally coming to realize that the heavy, round-nose, controlled-expanding bullets just aren't the best medicine for deer because these animals aren't very big. I mentioned before that a lot of big-caliber gunners lose their venison because slugs weighing much over 150 grains can go right through a deer while expanding very little unless they hit solid bone. A 100-grain .243 bullet—or others of comparable weight and design in such calibers as the 6.5mm, 6mm, .264, .270, .257 Roberts, .280, .284, 7mm Magnum, and the .30/06—begin expanding soon after contact. By the time they reach the inside of a buck they're really blowing up, and that's why they're so deadly. Quick-opening bullets hitting at high-impact velocity are by far the best for deer hunting.

Another advantage of the modern high-velocity cartridge is its flat trajectory. With such a cartridge, should a long-range shooting opportunity present itself, you have a bullet that will handle the situation. For example, if you sight in a .243 rifle to hit dead-on at 25 yards the bullet will hit only two inches high at 100 yards and only four inches low at 300 yards. This means you could aim for the lung area of a buck standing anywhere from 25 yards to 300 yards away and be reasonably sure of a fatal hit. In other words, you wouldn't have to worry about holding high for the 300-yard shot as did the old-timer with his .30/30. Today's high-velocity flat-shooting cartridges enable you to hold the same point of aim every time on any deer within reasonable range. Just get a sight picture on the lung area and touch off.

These days, deer hunters often make trips to relatively distant areas for mule deer and whitetails, and long-range shooting is much more common than it was years ago when most gunners stuck to their local areas where shooting ranges held to a norm.

The trouble with long-range work is that most hunters don't have the shooting experience to handle it. We all hear about the guys who nail mule deer across canyons with 500-yard kills, but it's best to take those stories with more than several grains of salt. Consider that 500 yards is the length of five football fields placed end to end. You could hardly see a deer that far away in most terrain conditions.

Then consider how far a bullet drops from line of sight at extreme range. Even a .243, sighted in at 200 yards—which is a fairly long range—will drop its bullet more than 40 inches out at 500 yards. In my opinion successful 500-yard shots are pure luck unless the shot is wide-open at a stationary target; even then, the rifleman has to be blessed with good fortune if he even hits the deer at that range, let alone puts his slug into a vital area.

Add to all this that the average hunter's range estimation can be pretty sloppy. It has to be. Sometime ago I mentioned practice makes perfect. How much range estimation practice have you done in your lifetime? Most of us would have to answer, "darn little." But we can help ourselves. Practice range estimation whenever you take a walk or while hunting small game. Pick a spot ahead that you guess to be 200 yards. Pace it off. You'll probably be surprised to find it's far closer to 150 yards. An estimated distance of 400 yards will be more likely to measure closer to 300. That's why you hear those stories of 500-yard kills. If the guys who made them later paced the range off, they'd most likely find they'd been toying with the truth.

Top that off with the unusual light conditions commonly confronted while you're deer hunting. Things look farther away then they really are at dawn and evening. Your buck will also look farther away in snow or fog. So practice range estimation with the pacing-off technique during the off season. This will help you improve your percentage of hits when actually shooting at deer. The guys who shoot the most deer at long range are good at judging distance.

Some experts become proficient at estimating distances by dividing the ground between the shooting position and the target into 50- or 100-yard segments. I once estimated the number of football-field lengths between my stand and a mule deer buck in Wyoming. I came up with 3½, which equated to 350 yards. When I paced off the killing shot I came up with 326 yards.

SHOOT FROM A REST

It's always best to shoot from a rest whenever the opportunity is presented. I can't emphasize this rule too strongly. Most of the shots I've missed at deer came about because I shot offhand. A big percentage of offhand shots are tried because the gunner shoots too rapidly. Most deer shot at from stands are unaware of the gunner, and are standing still or walking slowly. Stalking and stillhunting gunners are not so likely to get standing shots. But if they do their jobs right, they'll often have enough time to utilize a rest. So the guy who shoots too rapidly usually does so because he has some degree of buck fever. He tries to beat the shakes and wobbles by yanking off a quick shot. This results in flinching, which compounds the problem. The steadier your sight picture is on your buck the less likely you are to try the quick shot, and the best way to keep a steady sight picture is to shoot from a rest.

The standing position is the worst possible selection. The kneeling position is best for a quick shot if no rest is available.

The beauty of it is that some sort of rest is often at hand to use with the physical positions which, by themselves, are not desirable because the human body is wobbly to start with and becomes much more jumpy during the excitement of the shot. Nothing cures the buck-fever tendency as well as a rest.

I have yet to meet the serious deer hunter who is not occasionally subject to momentary jitters when taking a shot at a buck. The serious hunter is the one who gets a supreme thrill out of deer hunting; if there were no thrill he wouldn't go. It follows that if there is a thrill the man enjoying the excitement is subject to some degree of the shakes. Veterans are able to control the malady because they don't blow their cool as easily as in-

It's best to shoot from a rest whenever possible. This gives you a steady sight picture. On long-range shots a spotter using binoculars may be able to tell you where you hit and how you should hold for your second shot.

experienced hunters and because they have confidence in their shooting ability. But they're well aware that nothing quiets the nerves like shooting from a rest.

In some instances shooting from a standing position without a rest is a necessity. Quick shots at deer jumped in brush are the most common examples. When the gunner finds himself in weeds, grass, or thickets so high he cannot use the more reliable kneeling, sitting, or prone postions he'll be forced to shoot while standing. But he still may be able to shoot from an improvised rest such as a tree crotch. He'll be wise if he does so because nothing cures excitement like self-confidence, and nothing builds self-confidence like shooting a firearm that isn't wobbling.

Most rests are improvised, but some can be planned. I use one that I've never seen used by another hunter. When building a stand blind in white-tail country I often stretch a taut wire around the trees forming my blind boundaries. The wire is at rifle-resting height in relation to my sitting position in the blind. Regardless of the direction in which I spot a deer I can slide my rifle over the taut wire. I thereby have an immediate and soft rest.

Another good trick is to nail reasonably solid limbs or weathered boards around a blind stand at rifle-holding height.

I know a farmer in whitetail country who gets a shot at a buck almost every year from the same stand edging one of his fields. This guy is a rifle nut, so he uses his benchrest rig in his stand. He places it on an elevated small table which, in effect, enables him to shoot his buck from a benchrest.

Improvised rests can be utilized almost anywhere. In the West you sometimes can use sagebrush for a handy rest. The trick is to place a cap or jacket on a bush, settle the rifle down on it and touch off. Standers in whitetail country are often careful to select stands adjacent to stumps or windfalls that will make excellent rests. A reasonably solid rest can be gained most anywhere in deer country by grabbing the trunk of a small tree, then laying your rifle over your wrist. In some areas rock out-croppings or large stones make natural rests. But keep in mind that if you shoot off a solid surface you should pad your rifle with a cap, gloves, or other soft object. Without such padding your rifle will recoil upward and send your bullet high.

PRESEASON PRACTICE

Preseason training, whether on the target range or in the small-game field, is a fine way to insure hitting deer. Practice shooting with a .22 rifle is a great help because you can shoot many rounds at little expense. Since I'm partial to bolt-action scoped rifles for deer I have long used a bolt-action scoped .22 for my small-game hunting. I shoot at enough rabbits and squirrels with the .22 to make finding accurate sight pictures almost second nature. Shooting at running rabbits and climbing squirrels is great practice. When deer season approaches I sight in my deer rifle and shoot a few cartridges at targets to get used to the feel and recoil of the heavier firearm. Then I'm as ready as I can be for a chance at a buck.

THE RIGHT RIFLE

You may have noted that nowhere in this chapter have I gone into the subject that has drawn so much ink from gun writers: "The Right Deer Rifle—East and West." I happen to feel that the theory that eastern white-tail hunters should go with a light fast-pointing rifle, and the western hunter should go with a flat-shooting heavier rifle isn't really a true pic-ture. For one thing, there are some long-range shooting opportunities in the East, and there are a lot of mule deer shot at short ranges in the West.

In fact, North American deer are hunted in more places and over more types of terrain than any other big-game animal by far. This fact suggests that it's simply impossible to conclude that any one deer rifle is the "best" anywhere. If one rifle in one caliber was the best in a given area most deer hunters in that area would be using a specific gun and cartridge combination. You just don't see this situation in deer woods today.

What you do see is more and more hunters going to bolt-action rifles shooting high-velocity cartridges. This modern trend is noticeable everywhere in deer country, East, West or in between. I think the reason is that the "brush-buster" myth has been exposed, that such supposed truths as the advantages of the semiautomatic have not proved to be realistic, and that many of today's traveling hunters want a rifle and cartridge combination that works reasonably well in the East or West.

The important point is that the ease-of-use offered by modern rifles, and the ballistics offered by modern cartridges, have significantly narrowed the advantages and disadvantages long claimed in the East-West controversy. It's a controversy that just isn't very important anymore. And one of the main reasons, one I mentioned earlier, is that any rifle can be a good deer rifle if the man who is using it is a good deer hunter. Go with a modern rifle shooting a modern high-velocity bullet in the 100- to 150-grain bracket and you'll be well-armed wherever you hunt deer.

SHOTGUNS

Another subject I haven't mentioned in this chapter is the use of shotguns loaded with slugs or buckshot. I've never hunted deer with a shotgun, but I've talked with a lot of hunters in farm country who are limited by law to the use of these firearms. The serious ones tell me that the specially barreled slug guns equipped with low-power scopes are quite accurate out to 100 yards. They claim that regular-choked shotguns shooting slugs lose accuracy at about 50 yards, and that the use of buckshot ought to be outlawed.

The thing with buckshot is that it's extremely dangerous. A shotgun shooting buckshot sprays lethal balls in several flight patterns. Your chance of hitting someone are far higher with nine or more balls than with one slug. Further, you can aim a slug. Your chance of hitting a deer at point of aim with buckshot is practically zero. Nobody can tell where buckshot will hit a deer, so the odds of crippling zoom.

If you want to be a serious deer hunter and you hunt where rifles are legal don't even consider using a shotgun. Your investment in a good rifle and scope will average out to very few dollars per hunting season if you have a reasonable number of hunting years ahead of you. If you're limited by state or county laws to the use of a shotgun for your deer hunting, you'll be wise to invest in one of the specially barreled slug guns and a low-power scope.

17
Modern Gear

Some years ago I was on a deer hunt in which hunting from tree stands was almost mandatory because of thick ground cover. In this situation, a hunter on the ground could see only a few yards through the thickets, but had good visibility from a vantage point in a tree. My problem was my fear of climbing trees. I had to climb up into a big pine tree and sit on a branch. I didn't like any part of the deal, and when the hunt was over I told myself I was all finished with climbing trees. But thanks to modern gear I've changed my mind.

My new attitude developed after *Outdoor Life* published an article of mine about how to hunt from stands. One of the letters I received from readers came from Jim Baker, President of Baker Manufacturing Company (P.O. Box 1003, Valdosta, Georgia 31601). Said Jim: "Our Baker Tree Stand is the only patented tree stand that will actually *climb* a tree. It offers a firm, secure platform on which to sit or stand. I'd like to send you one for field testing and evaluation."

I took up Jim's offer for two reasons. First, if the contraption would climb a tree safely I could forget about my fear of climbing. Second, if it really offered a firm and secure platform I wouldn't have to worry about falling off a branch.

When I got the unit I discovered that it's light, folds up

This knock-down tree stand can be back-packed until needed for climbing a limbless tree trunk.

easily for carrying on a shoulder strap, needs no steps, does no damage to trees, and works as easily as Jim claimed it would. You merely put your feet in its platform stirrups, grasp the tree trunk with a bear hug, and walk the stand up the tree. An accessory, which works on a lever principle, eliminates the bear hug. Through a mechanical-advantage system you merely lever yourself and your stand up a tree with a series of easy arm and leg motions.

The Baker Tree Stand is a good example of how modern gear gives today's hunter advantages the old-timers never had. There are many such advantages.

Wet and cold feet are a thing of the past when you place your trust in top-quality modern boots. Browning, for example, makes a boot crafted from heavy-duty, silicone-impregnated Boulder leather. The top is hydrodynamically sealed to sure-footed crepe lug soles. These boots are guaranteed waterproof when given recommended care. In addition they are fully insulated from top to toe, incorporate German speed lacing, and offer the comfort of glove leather lining and cushioned insoles. Even the tongue is uniquely contoured for comfort and unencumbered lacing. Strong Taslan laces complement all the other features.

The hunter of years ago would have drooled over such boots. Alas for him, the materials and manufacturing processes needed to produce them were unknown in those days. Many other companies besides Browning make top-quality boots for hunters, as well as a myriad of other clothing items. You can get a Browning catalog by writing: Browning, P.O. Box 500, Morgan, Utah 84050.

The Browning "Sportsman's Check List" is the most complete I've seen. You'll find it, with minor changes, on accompanying pages. It lists equipment used by all outdoorsmen.

Are you still using that old-time tent that weighs a ton, takes four people to pitch and strike, is subject to leaking, and smells of mildew? If you are you're way behind the times. Today's tents made of such materials as nylon taffeta and cotton drill are practically condensation free. As well, they don't leak and are lightweight. I have a two-man 5x7 tent that weighs only five pounds including poles, stakes, and stuff bag. The rigging is simple and quick. The tent includes elastic shock cords at each corner which allow them to give in a strong wind. It also has coil zippers, a tough waterproof floor and a waterproof rain fly. In short, it's a far cry from the two-man tent of the old days. Today's tents incorporating modern design with modern materials come in all sizes from one-man to big wall tents suitable for a party of hunters.

One of the most dramatic examples of how hunters' gear has changed over the years is the compound bow now being used by many archers. These bows combine space-age technology with the age-old art of archery. They shoot your arrows as much as 50 percent faster than a recurve bow of

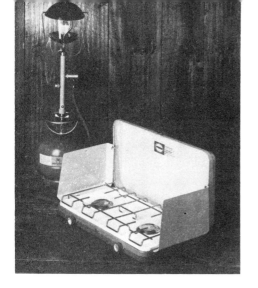

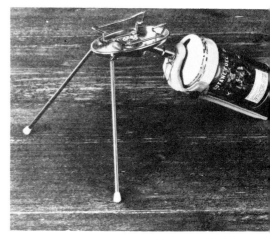

A variety of low-cost lamps, stoves, and space heaters make hunting a lot more convenient than it was in the old days. These shown are made by Primus-Sievert.

equal weight. Yet they're shorter and easier to shoot. They incorporate a system of pulleys and cables that work somewhat like a block and tackle. The mechanical-advantage system enables you to hold an arrow at full draw without tiring. Even many of today's conventional bows would make the old-timers stare with disbelief. They never heard of fold-down bows, adjustable draw weight, bow sights, stabilizer rods, sure-fold arrow rests, aluminum arrows, and other modern developments.

And how about propane-powered camping equipment such as lanterns, heaters, and stoves. The advantages of a lightweight, easy-to-operate propane stove over firewood are numerous. For example, with firewood rain can turn camping into a drab world of cold meals. Without a fire you're also subjected to shivering in the darkness. A propane stove isn't the least fazed by rain, nor is a propane lantern or heater. They'll burn on right through the heaviest downpours. With such equipment the old days of chopping wood, putting up with smoky campsites, and huddling around a fire for light or heat are gone. Deer-hunting campers of past eras might feel there is something almost immoral about the ease and convenience of camping today. They'd probably feel that things ought to be a little tougher. Maybe so, but modern equipment enables the modern hunter to spend more time actually hunting, more time being comfortable, and less time doing camp chores.

Even such minor items as sunglasses can be of extreme benefit to the modern deer hunter. Today's polarized sunglasses can reduce glare, eliminate squinting, and help to discern game that tends to disappear into backgrounds. A hunter can stretch his day by using amber or yellow shooting glasses during early morning and late evening. Such glasses intensify light and contrast. They enable you to pick out detail in poor light conditions.

Here are just a few more modern items to consider:

Unbreakable vacuum bottles. They're built like a battleship. Stainless-steel construction won't rust or stain. No glass to break. Vacuum insulation keeps contents hot or cold for many hours.

Hot-seat cushions. They use no electricity, fuel or chemicals. A scientifically developed space age filler radiates body heat from the cushion. Belt clip attached for easy carrying. They cost about $4 each. I like a hot-seat when sitting on a stand in very cold weather.

Anti-foggers. A stick-type material that steam-proofs and fog-proofs any glass or plastic. One quick smear with the stick, a follow-up buffing with a soft dry cloth, and your glasses or scope won't fog up in wet or damp weather. I once had an excellent shot at a trophy whitetail during a drizzle. When I shouldered my rifle my scope was so fogged up I couldn't find the target. That buck got away. He wouldn't have if I'd been able to use the new fog-proofing material.

Hand warmer muff. Attaches to the buttons on the front of a coat or through a belt. An inside pocket holds a conventional hand-warmer. It's

Scientifically designed archery tackle helps modern bowhunters send arrows out on faster, truer flights than ever before.

lightweight, detachable, and can be folded and carried in a pocket. It's made of quilted nylon on the outside and polyester fill inside. It's water-resistant. The unit is ideal when you're sitting on stand because your bare hands can be withdrawn in an instant from the lap-located muff.

Electric boot dryers. They dry all types of footwear from shoes to waders. Damp boots dry in one hour, wet boots dry overnight. Light, compact and rugged, a pair of dryers plugs into any 110-120 volt AC or DC outlet, draw only 8 watts, and will do no damage to any type of boot.

Freeze-dry foods. If you're backpacking or camping, the saving in weight of freeze-dry foods over fresh or canned goods is no less than amazing. No refrigeration is needed and freeze-dry foods last for a year or more. One outfit—Chuck Wagon Foods, Micro Drive, Woburn, Massachusetts 01801—offers all kinds of meal packs which are complete meals. There's no waste and everything is portion-packed and tailored to the size of your group and your plans. Each meal is plastic-packed in strong, feather-light, and waterproof containers. Preparation and cooking requires only a fraction of the time required for fresh food. Simple and easy cooking instructions are printed on every bag. One feature that's often overlooked is that there are no skins, peels, or other debris to dispose of. The bags are burnable.

Emergency signal kit. Eddie Bauer, 1737 Airport Way South, Seattle, Washington 98134, sells a kit that works in any terrain or any weather. It contains a 10-mile signal mirror, a red smoke flare, a fire starter kit with matches, tinder and instructions, and two red Skyblazer Flares. These flares are self-contained. Just unscrew the safety cap and pull the release chain. Each flare reaches an altitude of 400 feet with an intensity of 20,000 candle power that is visible up to 20 miles. The beauty of the kit is that it weighs only five ounces. You can attach it to your belt and never know it's there. If every back-country deer hunter had one you would never see all those "lost-hunter" stories that hit the front pages of newspapers every fall.

Four-wheel-drive vehicles and modern shelters make it possible to overnight economically, and far from motel crowds.

Down-filled gear. It gets better all the time and ranges from underwear and socks to shirts, vests, coats, hats and sleeping bags. The heavy clothing of years ago can't come close to down for warmth, comfort and convenience.

Four-wheel-drive vehicles and pickup campers. Back when I began hunting deer as a teenager I used to drive my mother's car to the end of a dirt road, then hike for miles back into remote country where whitetails herded each fall. Ten years ago I got into the same hotspot with practically no walking. It was a simple matter to drive in there with a four-wheel-drive (4WD) via a two-track trail. Two years ago the area—which is National Forest land—was closed to vehicle traffic because too many 4WD's loaded with hunters were putting too much pressure on the deer.

Several years ago I camped in those woods with old-fashioned camping gear. Later, when vehicle traffic was permitted, hunters would base in the area with modern pickup campers and tent trailer-campers loaded with propane equipment, portable generators, and all the conveniences of modern camping. The area held some of the best whitetail hunting I've ever experienced, but it went downhill fast when the hunting pressure increased. I was glad when vehicle traffic was prohibited. Now that it's limited to hunters on foot the deer herd has bounced back.

I believe that 4WD's and pickup campers loaded with modern camping conveniences can be too efficient in some areas. In my opinion the 4WD's and pickup campers, and perhaps even house trailers, should not be allowed in certain areas where they make the hunting too easy. Some state game departments have already outlawed vehicle traffic off established roads and trails. This is as it should be in those areas where these units are the cause of too much pressure on the game.

On the other hand, these modern vehicles—in places where they are properly and legally used—can make a camping-hunting trip a delight that was far beyond the imagination of the old-timers. Such vehicles offer so many comforts that some hunters owning such equipment take their families along on their hunts. The wife and kids often don't hunt at all; they just go for the camp life because it's almost as comfortable as staying at home.

In this chapter I've mentioned only a few of the modern conveniences available to deer hunters. You'll find scores of others in top-quality sporting-goods stores. Some of the best sources of information on what's available are the many free catalogs offered by such sales outlets as Eddie Bauer, Browning, Herter's, L. L. Bean, Gokey Company, Cabela's Incorporated and Orvis. There are many others. Check the advertisements in the outdoor magazines and you'll find the sources for dozens of free or inexpensive catalogs. Send for these catalogs and you'll get a wealth of information about modern gear.

Sportsman's Checklist
(Courtesy of Browning Arms Co.)

While planning your trip make a "/" in the boxes opposite the items you'll need. Then as you pack the item, finish the "X."

BIG GAME HUNT—BASIC ITEMS

Rifle Season

☐ Rifle (sighted in)
☐ Spare rifle
☐ Rifle cases
☐ Pistol w/holster
☐ Ammunition
☐ Belt cartridge case
☐ Rifle cleaning gear with gun oil

☐ Spotting scope
☐ Hunting regulations
☐ Check state Hunter Orange Safety Requirements
☐ General license
☐ Special tags
☐ Deer call/rattling antlers

Archery Season

☐ Bow
☐ Extra bow string (with nocking point marked)
☐ Hunting arrows
☐ Spare broadheads
☐ Broadhead cement
☐ Broadhead sharpening file
☐ Field arrows
☐ Bow sight
☐ Bow quiver
☐ Bow string silencers

☐ Brush deflectors
☐ Bow string wax
☐ Bow tip protector
☐ Armguard
☐ Shooting glove or tab
☐ Camouflage bow or tape
☐ Camouflage stick or cream
☐ Camouflage outfit
☐ Archery regulations
☐ Archery license

Include on above hunts

☐ Binoculars
☐ Compass
☐ Hunting knife
☐ Buck scent
☐ Topographical map of hunt area
☐ Block and tackle/Game hoist
☐ Bone saw
☐ Meat sacks
☐ Bulk salt (to preserve hide & cape)

☐ Plastic bag for heart and liver
☐ Rope
☐ String or wire (small piece to tie tag to carcass)
☐ _____
☐ _____
☐ _____
☐ _____
☐ _____

PERSONAL GEAR

Clothing

☐ Boots
☐ Camp shoes
☐ Hat
☐ Gloves
☐ Coat
☐ Jacket
☐ Vest
☐ Sweater
☐ Shirts
☐ Trousers
☐ Underwear
☐ Long underwear
☐ Socks

☐ Rain gear (camo, green or orange)
☐ Belt
☐ Handkerchief (Bandana)
☐ Silicone boot dressing
☐ Spare boot laces
☐ Duffle bag
☐ _____
☐ _____
☐ _____
☐ _____

Toilet Articles

- Comb
- Fingernail clippers
- Hand soap
- Razor
- Shaving cream
- Small mirror
- Toothbrush
- Toothpaste

- Towel and wash cloth
- Tweezers
- _____
- _____
- _____
- _____
- _____

Other

- Alarm clock
- Canteen
- Camera   w/spare   film/flash bulbs
- Cigarettes
- Glasses
- Pocket knife
- Pencil/Notebook
- Pillow
- Pipe & tobacco
- Pipe cleaner

- Safety pins
- Sewing kit
- Sleeping bag
- Sunglasses
- Walkie Talkie
- Wallet
- Watch
- _____
- _____
- _____
- _____

FIRST AID, DRUGS, SURVIVAL

- Stomach balms
- Antihistamine
- Aspirin
- Band-Aids
- Chap stick
- Coke syrup (for upset stomach)
- Cough syrup
- Eye drops
- First aid kit
- Insect repellent
- Laxative

- Merthiolate/Iodine
- Nose drops
- Presription drugs
- Survival kit
- Snake bite kit
- Suntan lotion
- _____
- _____
- _____
- _____

CAMPING GEAR

Shelter

- Tent (check poles, ropes, pegs)
- Tarp
- Tent stitcher
- Sleeping bag

- Mattress/Cot
- Tent heater & fuel
- Portable latrine

Cooking

- Camp stove & fuel
- Pocket stove & fuel
- Matches
- Grill/Grate/Griddle
- Skillet
- Dutch oven
- Pressure cooker
- Coffee pot
- Dish pan
- Dishes
- Knives, forks, spoons

- Spatula
- Can opener
- Butcher knife
- Dish cloth & towel
- Firewood
- Cooler
- Vacuum bottle
- Water cans
- Table
- Chairs
- Camp stool

CAMPING GEAR *(continued)*

Lighting

☐ Camp lantern & fuel
☐ Extra mantles

☐ Flashlight w/spare bulb & batteries
☐ Flares

Tools

☐ Axe
☐ Broom
☐ Buckets
☐ Hammer/Nails
☐ Pliers

☐ Rope
☐ Saw
☐ Sharpening stone
☐ Shovel
☐ Wire

Permits

☐ Fire permit
☐ Golden Eagle permit to federal lands
☐ Local permits

Other:

☐ Pack frame
☐ Backpack
☐ Day pack (for lunch, etc.)
☐ _____

☐ _____
☐ _____
☐ _____
☐ _____

CAMPER OR TRAILER

☐ Broom
☐ Propane
☐ Ice
☐ Spare tire
☐ Extension mirrors for vehicle
☐ Spare keys
☐ Spare fuses
☐ Spare mantles for propane light
☐ Jack crank (camper)
☐ Hitch lock (trailer)
☐ Leveling jacks (trailer)

☐ Fill water tank
☐ Check turnbuckles (camper)
☐ Check tire pressure & lug bolts (trailer)
☐ Check running lights
☐ Charge battery (trailer)
☐ Check propane gas fittings
☐ _____
☐ _____
☐ _____
☐ _____

BOAT

☐ Approved life jacket (one for each person)
☐ Anchor
☐ Line (tow)
☐ Lights
☐ Horn
☐ Paddle(s)
☐ Fire extinguisher
☐ Signal flag
☐ Bail bucket

☐ Boat registration
☐ Fuel
☐ Cushions
☐ Charge battery
☐ _____
☐ _____
☐ _____
☐ _____
☐ _____

VEHICLE

☐ Spare fan belt
☐ Spare radiator hose
☐ Spare heater hose
☐ Spare fuses
☐ Spare keys
☐ Spare oil
☐ Spare brake fluid

☐ Chains
☐ Jumper cables
☐ Shovel
☐ Tools
☐ Tow chain
☐ Road maps
☐ Check oil

☐ Check water
☐ Check antifreeze
☐ Check tire pressure (also on spare)
☐ Check battery water
☐ Fill spare gas cans (transport externally *only*)

☐ _____
☐ _____
☐ _____
☐ _____
☐ _____

DOG EQUIPMENT

☐ Leash
☐ Brush
☐ Whistle
☐ Dog food
☐ Kennel crate
☐ Collars and identification tags
☐ Tie out chains
☐ Feed and water pans

☐ Extra water
☐ First aid kit for dogs
☐ Health certificate (if interstate)
☐ _____
☐ _____
☐ _____
☐ _____

HORSE EQUIPMENT

☐ Halter & lead rope
☐ Feed bag
☐ Oats, grain, or conditioner
☐ Salt or trace mineral
☐ Curry comb and brush
☐ Saddle blankets
☐ Saddle pad
☐ Saddle
☐ Saddle bags
☐ Scabbard
☐ Bridle/extra bit
☐ Extra rope
☐ Utility axe & saw
☐ Chaps
☐ Spurs
☐ Pack saddle
☐ Panniers, pack bags, pack boxes
☐ Mantie (canvas pack cover)
☐ Lash rope & cinch
☐ Hobbles
☐ Bell and strap

☐ Tether rope
☐ Horse cover blanket
☐ Feed & water buckets
☐ Feed—hay° or pellets
☐ Horse shoes & nails (#5 city head)
☐ Anvil (rail) & 4 lb. hammer
☐ Shoeing equipment (rasp, hoof pick, hoof knife, shoeing hammer, hoof nippers, clinching bar)
☐ Horse cut spray/iodine
☐ Horse insect repellent
☐ Brand inspection certificate°
☐ Health certificate°
☐ Check horse trailer
☐ _____
☐ _____
☐ _____
☐ _____

°Check state regulations if interstate travel is involved.

FOOD STAPLES

Accessories

☐ Aluminum foil
☐ Charcoal
☐ Charcoal lighter
☐ Dish washing soap
☐ Garbage bags
☐ Facial tissues
☐ Matches
☐ Cups
☐ Napkins
☐ Plates
☐ Towels
☐ Plastic bags
☐ Plastic eating utensils
☐ Scouring pads
☐ Toilet paper

Baking Items

☐ Baking powder
☐ Baking soda
☐ Biscuit mix
☐ Cornmeal
☐ Flour
☐ Pancake flour
☐ Shortening

Canned Goods

☐ Baked beans
☐ Chili
☐ Chili beans
☐ Fruit (also dehyd.)

Juices:

☐ Grapefruit
☐ Orange
☐ Tomato

Meats:

☐ Deviled ham
☐ Sardines
☐ Spam
☐ Tuna
☐ Milk (also dehyd.)
☐ Soups (also dehyd.)
☐ Stew

Vegetables:

☐ Beets
☐ Carrots
☐ Corn
☐ Lima beans
☐ Peas
☐ Potatoes (also dehyd.)
☐ String beans
☐ Tomatoes

FOOD STAPLES *(continued)*

Hot drinks

- ☐ Bouillon cubes
- ☐ Coffee
- ☐ Hot chocolate
- ☐ Tea

Relishes

- ☐ Horseradish
- ☐ Ketchup
- ☐ Mustard
- ☐ Olives
- ☐ Peppers
- ☐ Pickles
- ☐ Relish

Sauces & Dressings

- ☐ Applesauce
- ☐ Bar-B-Q Sauce
- ☐ Mayonnaise
- ☐ Salad dressing
- ☐ Soy sauce
- ☐ Steak sauce
- ☐ Vegetable oil
- ☐ Vinegar
- ☐ Meat sauces

Spices

- ☐ Celery salt
- ☐ Chili powder
- ☐ Onion salt
- ☐ Oregano
- ☐ Paprika
- ☐ Pepper
- ☐ Rosemary
- ☐ Salt
- ☐ Seasoning salt

Spreads

- ☐ Honey
- ☐ Jam & jelly
- ☐ Peanut butter
- ☐ Syrup

Others

- ☐ Noodles
- ☐ Rice
- ☐ Sugar
- ☐ _____
- ☐ _____
- ☐ _____
- ☐ _____
- ☐ _____

FOOD PERISHABLES

Bakery

- ☐ Bread
- ☐ Crackers
- ☐ Hamburger buns
- ☐ Hot dog buns
- ☐ Cookies
- ☐ Pastries

Beverages

- ☐ Soft drinks
- ☐ Hard stuff
- ☐ _____
- ☐ _____

Dairy

- ☐ Butter
- ☐ Cheese
- ☐ Eggs
- ☐ Milk

Fruit

- ☐ Apples
- ☐ Apricots
- ☐ Bananas
- ☐ Oranges
- ☐ Peaches
- ☐ Raisins

Meats

- ☐ Bacon
- ☐ Chicken
- ☐ Fish
- ☐ Game
- ☐ Ham
- ☐ Hamburger
- ☐ Hot dogs
- ☐ Lunch meat
- ☐ Sausage
- ☐ Pork chops
- ☐ Steaks

Vegetables

- ☐ Celery
- ☐ Corn-on-the-cob
- ☐ Lettuce
- ☐ Onions
- ☐ Peppers
- ☐ Potatoes
- ☐ Tomatoes

Miscellaneous

- ☐ Candy
- ☐ Cereal
- ☐ Chewing gum
- ☐ Chocolate bars
- ☐ Dessert items
- ☐ Potato chips
- ☐ _____
- ☐ _____
- ☐ _____
- ☐ _____
- ☐ _____

And last but not least . . .
tell someone exactly where you're
going! It could save your life.

18

Basics of Hunting Away from Home

Because I'm a full time outdoor writer, much of my job involves hunting away from home. I've been on deer hunts over much of North America. In recent years these trips have been very successful because I've learned how to plan them. But I'll never forget some of my early hunts.

Years ago I made a trip into Minnesota that turned out to be a complete flop. A casual friend told me he used to hunt in a certain area of the state that was loaded with deer. Being a greenhorn I had visions of driving into the area, picking a hunting spot and waiting for a buck to walk by.

It turned out that it had been many years since my friend had hunted the area. Much of the woodland he had described in glowing terms had been lumbered and cleared. The game warden he told me to look up was retired. The youngster who had taken his place seemed more interested in wearing a shiny uniform than helping deer hunters. I never saw a deer in two days of hunting. By then I realized I was up against a hopeless situation. I was in strange country without local contacts and without any idea of where to get advice. I got into my car and made a very depressing journey home.

This sort of thing happens all too often to inexperienced hunters. They read glowing reports of great deer hunting in outdoors magazines, they note the area hunted, and they decide to travel out there next fall and get in on the action. This type of planning is almost bound to lead to disappointment.

Even better planning can have its downfalls. One time years ago I was on a fishing trip in northwestern Ontario. One of the businessmen-guests of the lodge shared a boat with me. I became quite friendly with the Ohio man, especially when he mentioned he owned an interest in a Wyoming ranch that was loaded with mule deer and antelope. He suggested I hunt there with him in the fall. I jumped at the opportunity. I was sure I couldn't miss on this trip.

It didn't turn out that way. As the time approached to leave for the hunt the businessman phoned me and said he had to cancel out. He assured me this was no problem because his ranch manager would take care of me. Well, when I arrived at the ranch I was advised by the manager that he had problems with his cattle and that I would have to do most of my hunting on my own.

At the time I had very little experience with hunting in the West. It took me a couple of days to find out where the deer were, and I had to settle for a much smaller buck than I'd hoped for. I was lucky in scoring on an antelope, but the hunt left a lot to be desired.

These two experiences point out several factors that can make away-from-home hunts go sour. On any hunt in an area unfamiliar to you it's necessary to have a contact who knows the area and how to hunt it, and you must be assured he will hunt with you. This is the precise reason why good guides or outfitters can charge high rates and be worth every penny you pay them. A good guide in average game country is much more likely to get you a shot at a buck than is a guide in top game country. If I'd had a guide on the Minnesota and Wyoming hunts I mentioned they might have turned into highlights of my hunting career.

I'm not saying it's a must to have a guide to insure a good hunt in un-familiar country, but it's almost mandatory to have a contact who can per-form many of the functions of a guide. Some incidents come to mind that illustrate the point.

A friend has hunted in Montana for the past five years. His first trip was a washout because he simply climbed into his car and drove out West to go deer hunting. The next year he tried a different area with the same re-sults, until he got smart. He decided to quit hunting, drive to various ran-ches, strike up conversations with ranchers, and offer to pay a guiding fee. One rancher took up the offer and showed my friend a big buck after only a couple hours of hunting. The two men struck up a fine friendship and my buddy has been going back to the same ranch every year since. Now, he never has much trouble getting his game. The system this fellow used is a great one for any hunter who has the time to scout around, knock on a few doors, and develop contacts.

Another friend of mine has an uncle who is a rancher in Wyoming. This guy didn't take up deer hunting till a few years ago, but when he did he went to his uncle's ranch. He had, in effect, a free and ready-made guide service.

Still another example concerns a fellow I know who makes summer vacation trips with his family to a new area each year. He makes it a point to investigate the area's deer-hunting possibilities. When he turns up something interesting he makes contact with local people for a fall hunting trip.

All of these men hunt away from home, but they hunt with somebody who can tell them where and how to cash in on the area's deer hunting. If you can't work something out on a free basis you'll be very wise to pay for service from a guide or outfitter. It just doesn't make any sense at all to hunt new country without being accompanied by someone who knows the ropes.

The next most important thing is to plan adequate time for your hunt. I fell into this trap several times years ago, but I especially remember a South Dakota trip. My assignment was to get a deer-hunting story, but I wanted to spend part of my time taking advantage of some of South Dakota's great pheasant hunting. I started my trip by gunning ringnecks, then I switched to sharptail grouse and prairie chickens. Soon my allotted time was running out. I had to get in my deer hunting in a hurry, and I had to settle for a small buck. I'd seen several far larger bucks while I was bird hunting, but they all seemed to evaporate when I went after them. If I'd had more time I might have scored on a trophy.

The lesson I learned on that trip is not to mix too many activities into one hunt, to concentrate on one objective, and to plan plenty of time in case things go wrong. Once, while planning a big-game hunt in Montana, I had to make up my mind whether to schedule the trip for ten days or two weeks. I decided on two weeks almost entirely on the basis of the South Dakota experience I just mentioned.

When I arrived in Montana I ran into four consecutive days of blizzards which made hunting impossible. I scored on my big mule-deer buck the last day of the hunt. If I hadn't scheduled those extra few days I would have gone home without venison.

One thing I see quite often in the field that especially irritates me is the hunter who isn't physically able to meet the rigors of the type of hunting he is attempting. It makes no sense at all for a man to plan a rigorous fall hunting trip, then sit around all summer and do nothing to get himself in shape. Deer hunting in many areas is darn hard work. Most of the bucks fall to men who are able to meet the physical demands of the hunt.

Another thing that ruins many hunts is making the trip at the wrong time. There always is a best time to hunt in any area across the nation. The best time may coincide with weather conditions, available browse, the rut or several other factors. It almost never coincides with your normal business or personal schedules. My major rule of thumb when hunting a new area is go with a man who knows how to hunt the area, and go when he tells me to go. If you go earlier or later because of personal preference you'll seriously hamper your odds on bagging a buck.

Because hunting is also my job I often have to leave for hunts alone, but it's certainly more enjoyable if I have a companion along. I make darn sure it's a companion who is going to add pleasure to the hunt, not take pleasure away. I've seen too many hunting parties in the field having a lousy time because one or more members of the group made life miserable for their companions. When you spend a lot of money for a hunting trip nothing is more disheartening than having the fun ruined by some guy who doesn't get along with the rest of the group.

It seems to me that some hunters select their partners at cocktail parties. It's almost as if a couple of casual acquaintances meet and the talk swings to hunting. One guy might say, "Why don't we plan a deer hunt in Wyoming? I'll bet Jack and Pete would go. We'll have a great time."

Well, a man may act a lot differently in the field than he does at home. You don't know how a friend feels about hunting until you've been out with him a few times when the going is rough and the game doesn't cooperate. The middle of an expensive hunting trip is not the time to find that you and your buddies don't see eye to eye. Game hogs, bemoaners of not getting meat, and complainers about weather or accommodations can ruin the best of trips. The time to find out if you want to make an extensive trip with a man is after you know him well enough to be sure he enjoys the outdoors the same way you do.

Elsewhere in this book you'll find an entire chapter on the subject of shooting deer, but now seems to be a good time to emphasize the importance of being able to put bullets where you want them to go. Many hunters save money for years for "one big hunt," then blow the opportunity of a lifetime by missing an easy shot. Suffice it to say here that you should be very familiar with your firearm and with what it will do. A man doesn't become efficient at shooting deer by taking his gun out of the closet once a year. You should sight in your rifle and shoot plenty of practice rounds before heading for deer country. That's another lesson I learned the hard way.

One of the finest trophy whitetail bucks I ever saw ran across an open field in front of me during a Wisconsin hunt many years ago. I emptied my rifle at him and missed every shot simply because I'd had little experience with shooting at running deer. I didn't lead him enough, but I didn't discover that fact till the following spring when I began practice-shooting at moving targets. The day I missed that enormous whitetail was the day I decided a deer hunter was plain foolish if he didn't learn how to handle his rifle expertly. Good chances of nailing a buck come all too seldom.

So far in this chapter I've covered the general thoughts that should be considered in planning a hunt away from home. Now let's get into some specifics. You should come up with answers to the following questions before deciding on an area you want to hunt:

1) Do you want to hunt big country—but want creature comforts at the end of the day with nights in town and good surroundings?

2) Do you want to camp where you can get swallowed up in solitude or enjoy spectacular scenery?

3) Would you prefer to hunt good deer country with a top outfitter who can provide you with shooting opportunity and take care of all camp chores, dressing game, and so forth?

4) Do you want to make a short hunt with just meat in mind, or do you want to make a longer hunt for a trophy in big, rugged country where bucks live long enough to grow trophy antlers?

5) Do you want to hunt mule deer or whitetails?

6) How much money can you afford to spend?

7) How much physical exertion are you capable of? Few middle-aged and elderly men are capable of keeping up with normal activities of guides who are used to working in high mountain ranges. The average hunter deceives himself more about his physical condition than anything else, especially if he has led a well-fed and sedentary life. You may want to eliminate a hunt at high elevations where a lot of climbing is required, or where you'll have to pack out your game.

8) Where do you get information on license costs, season dates, permit applications, names and addresses of guides and outfitters, and best times and places to go?

I've found the answers to all the above questions during my many deer hunts in unfamiliar country. You are very likely to feel differently than I about some aspects of hunting, but here is how the answers look to me:

Question Number 1. Being a Michigan flatlander, the thrill of hunting big country—mountain ranges or foothills—offers a special appeal to me. Being in my late 40s, I'm not really as excited about roughing it as I used to be. If I can find creature comforts at the end of the day after hunting in good deer country I'll take them. There are a couple of ideal ways of doing this. They are advantages the old-timers didn't have.

The boom in motels across the country during the last decade or two has reached into the boonies. Some of the little towns boasting populations of only a couple of thousand or so have surprisingly nice motels, especially if they're in vacation country. I've based in motels during several deer hunts in the prairie and intermountain states, and they worked out fine. A town that has at least one decent motel generally has at least one good eating place. The thing to remember about motels in good hunting country is that they fill up fast. Some hunters returning to the same area year after year make their reservations a year in advance.

Another excellent way of enjoying creature comforts at the end of a hard day of hunting is to base in one of the newer fold-out trailer campers. I well remember a deer hunt four of us made in Wyoming a few years ago. One of my partners and I decided to drive to our host's ranch, pull a rental fold-out trailer, park it near the ranch, and enjoy life. Our two other partners decided on different transportation, and they accepted our host's invitation to base in one of his outbuildings that had been used as a bunkhouse years earlier.

Warren and I were extremely cozy in our rented trailer. We had good heat, lights and plenty of room. Our two companions shivered because of inadequate heat, and they put up with mice and cobwebs in the run-down bunkhouse. For my money fold-out trailers are great. They're compact, easy to tow, and you can get them into almost any back-country that's open to cars or trucks.

Plusher accommodations are more readily available to deer hunters than they are to most other types of hunters and fishermen simply because deer can live close to man if good habitat is available. One of the finest small-town inns I've stayed in is in Chamberlain, South Dakota. There were four of us on that trip, and we all downed fine bucks within a few miles of town. We lived about as well as you can anywhere and still enjoy good hunting. Such a hunt would be ideal for elderly, out-of-condition, or physically handicapped hunters.

Question Number 2. A few years ago my conception of the ideal deer hunt was to camp far from the crowd. Getting away from other hunters usually means pack trips with horses or backpacking trips. Recently I was on a December pack-trip hunt in the Colorado Rockies. I figured our group had to be the only hunters on the mountain because we were 11 miles up from the nearest road. I was really surprised when one of our guides told me he had met two young deer hunters who had backpacked up that mountain. When he had come upon the two men they were boning out a big four-point buck.

The best way to get some solitude and enjoy spectacular scenery is to book a pack-trip hunt with a good outfitter. Backpacking trips can get you into lonely country, too, because most hunters won't walk more than a short distance from their cars. If you take a day to backpack into a remote area you'll leave the great majority of hunters far behind. A couple of my deer-hunting friends go this route. They select their hunting areas by studying topographic maps. They pick regions far from roads. They hike in and wouldn't think of hunting in any other way.

Right here is a good place to mention that it isn't always necessary to hire a good guide or outfitter to get you into remote back country. One of the best ways is to use a guide or outfitter when you hunt new country for the first time. That first hunt will acquaint you with the lay of the land, where the deer are, and how to hunt them. After that you can return year after year and camp on your own. This approach works well in areas where there are large chunks of public hunting lands. Most guides have no more control over access to those lands than you do.

Another good bet is to contact state game departments and ask specific questions concerning where you'll find the type of hunting you want. If you're just interested in meat you should ask which sections of the state produce the most deer and which sections have the highest harvests. If you're interested in a trophy you should ask which sections produce the biggest bucks. I've asked the game departments of every state in the nation these questions. It was surprising to discover that in most cases the biggest deer are not found in the same areas that produce the most deer.

Though I've mentioned it in other places in this book, I want to emphasize that game departments in most of the better deer states no longer try to attract nonresident deer hunters with the enthusiasm that they used to years ago. Many state game officials are now worrying about too many deer hunters rather than too few. Many of these officials no longer have any problems selling their high-priced nonresident deer licenses, so it makes sense that they have cut down on the reams of deer-hunting information they used to supply to prospective nonresident hunters. But it's a different story with tourist associations, state travel agencies, and outfitter or guide associations. Such organizations want your dollars, and they spend a lot of promotional money to get them. If you ask, most state game departments will give you the names and addresses of the organizations that will be of most help to you.

Because of the factors I've mentioned and because most modern hunters have more leisure time and more money than ever before, and because of the advantages of modern camping equipment, the possibilities of camping and hunting where you can be alone are far better now than in the so-called "good old days."

Question Number 3. If you prefer to hunt deer country with a top outfitter who can provide you with shooting opportunity and take care of all camp chores, dressing game and so forth, your opportunities have never been better. Most of these opportunities are in the West where increased numbers of hunters have led to increased numbers of outfitters and guides.

The easiest way to make contact with top outfitters is to get the names and addresses of the organizations from their advertisements in outdoor magazines. Of course, not all outfitters advertise, so another good bet is to ask state game departments for addresses of guide and outfitter associations. Then contact such outfits, mention what type of hunting you want to do, and you'll get more information than you need.

Still another approach is to write the National Rifle Association, 1600 Rhode Island Avenue, N.W., Washington, D.C. 20036, to order a copy of *Hunting*. The book costs less than five dollars, and it lists details on many guides and outfitters including names, addresses, services, accommodations and facilities. The book also includes hunting season dates for all states and provinces, license costs, incidental information, and many articles helpful to all hunters. The book is updated annually.

Question Number 4. Short hunts with the primary purpose of just getting venison is what many hunters have in mind. If this is your idea of how to go your first decision should be to travel to one of the states showing a high hunter-success ratio, as mentioned in Chapter 2. Write to the game department in the state of your choice and ask for information on which area of the state shows the highest deer harvest. Most of these states are in the intermountain area, which means they contain guide and outfitter services. Check guide and outfitter names and addresses through one of the systems I've mentioned. Then write for information on rates, services, and best times to schedule hunts. When you get the dope you can make your decision on where to go.

If you want to score on a trophy mule deer, the odds are you'll have to make arrangements with a guide or outfitter who operates in trophy country. As I've mentioned, the best heads taken from each state seldom come from the same areas that show the highest hunter-success ratios.

If you're really serious about the subject I'd suggest purchasing a copy of the book *North American Big Game.* It's a joint venture of the National Rifle Association and the Boone and Crockett Club. The book lists hundreds of the best trophy deer taken in North America, the precise areas where the animals were killed, and the year they were killed. Study the book carefully and you can make a list of the major areas producing trophy bucks. Then, if you're interested in mule deer, you can contact guides or outfitters in the areas you select. I'd suggest picking an outfit that recommends a pack trip back into remote areas. Few big muley bucks are killed in areas easily reached by the average hunter. Most of the big brutes don't grow those enormous racks by being dumb enough to try surviving in heavily hunted areas.

From my experience, your best chance of downing a trophy whitetail is in southeastern Saskatchewan. I've never seen as many big bucks in other areas. There are some guides there, but in general you won't find guides and outfitters in most of North America's whitetail country.

Question Number 5. There are several things to consider when you're trying to decide whether you want to hunt mule deer or whitetails. If you want an outstanding trophy it's best to go after mule deer for the reasons I just mentioned. Hook up with a good guide or outfitter and your chances soar because those fellows know where the deer are and they know how to hunt them.

Also, mule deer usually have larger racks than whitetails and they are easier to hunt. The major drawbacks to a mule-deer hunt for most of us are the expenses involved in traveling to western areas and paying for guided hunts. Other factors to consider include the type of hunting you enjoy and the kind of country in which you want to hunt.

If you enjoy stillhunting or stalking it's best to forget whitetails. These two methods are far more effective with mule deer. If you like to hunt on your own from a stand, then going after whitetails should be your choice. Mule deer should get your vote if you enjoy the terrain in the West and if you would prefer to hunt from a camp.

Question Number 6. How much money can you afford to spend? I live near a small town in northern Michigan and can walk out my back door to go after whitetails. Last fall I nailed a buck only a half-mile from where I'm writing these lines. Later on during the fall I hunted mule deer with an outfitter in the Colorado Rockies. That trip cost me close to $700. The meat of my Michigan whitetail cost me practically nothing. The mule-deer meat was expensive somewhere around $7 per pound. That example serves to illustrate how the differences in costs of deer hunting can go.

There are other variables. The deer hunter who already owns a camping outfit can camp much more cheaply than the man who has to rent one. The man who rents a fold-out trailer and camps can make a hunt in a given area for less money than the man who bases in a motel and eats in restaurants. Four men sharing the costs of a trip can get by for less money than two men who make the same trip. A week's hunt with an outfitter costs less than a ten-day hunt. The list of variables could be almost endless. Cost of transportation alone can be a big item. If you and one or more partners share the costs of driving to a distant hunting area the cost per man would be much less than if you used air transportation.

If you live in the East it will cost you a lot more money to hunt mule deer than whitetails. Vice versa for most of the hunters who live in the West. What we have discussed in this chapter should give you the basic information you need to decide what kind of a hunt you want to make. The answers to letters you write to game departments, outfitters or guides, tourist associations, and state travel agencies will give you solid clues to how much various trips will cost. Then it's up to you to plan one that will fit your wallet.

Question Number 7. I have already talked about how much your physical condition can affect the outcome of your hunt, but there are a couple of other important points: the most important is that you can do a lot to improve your physical condition before you go on a rugged hunt. As an outdoor writer I talk to lots of deer hunters who make trips away from home. A few years ago I began to get the distinct impression that many of the most successful gunners are those that prepare themselves physically for the type of hunting they're going to do long before they make the trip. They set up training programs that may include dieting, jogging, playing tennis, or any number of regular exercises. These men figure that if they invest a lot of money in a hunting trip they want to be able to get the utmost enjoyment out of it. That theory certainly makes sense to me, and I follow it.

The other important point is that some types of deer hunting are much easier physically than others. Stillhunting, for instance, demands less physical exertion than participating in drives. Hunting from a stand requires less exertion than climbing mountains. If you choose to hunt in mountainous terrain it's a lot easier to reach the back country by horseback than by backpacking. You should consider all such details if you're concerned about your physical condition.

Question Number 8. I've also pointed out the basics of how to get information on license costs, season dates, permit applications, and so forth. I've talked about how to go through official channels, but I want to emphasize that there's another route that's more available today than ever before. It will save you some time in planning away-from-home hunts.

In the old days most deer hunters operated relatively close to home. In these modern times more and more gunners are making trips to distant states and provinces in attempts to bag their deer. A guy who has made a trip to the area you want to hunt is a valuable source of information. If you want to hunt deer in Wyoming the chances are there is somebody in your neighborhood who has been there, knows the ropes, and has the answers to many of the questions you're likely to ask.

If you can get in touch with the right man you'll save yourself a lot of trouble in planning a hunt. A good bet is to ask questions in sporting-goods stores. Many gunners who hunt away from home buy gear from their local dealers, and they like to mention that they're going to such-and-such a state to get their buck. Most hunters like to talk about their experiences, especially with strangers. Sporting-goods dealers are often able to suggest the names of great contacts.

And don't pass up chance meetings at such places as service clubs, golf clubs, and sportsman's clubs. If you let it be known that you're looking for information on out-of-state deer hunts you'll be surprised at the contacts you'll make.

19

Fine Points of Hunting Away from Home

Let's say you're going to hunt mule deer in Montana. You have never hunted there before. You've decided that your best bet is to book with an outfitter, that you prefer to fly West on a commercial airliner, that you have applied for a nonresident deer license, and that you have the names and addresses of several outfitters operating in the area you have chosen to hunt. Everything seems to be well organized, doesn't it?

Not by a long shot. You still have to choose a specific outfitter, and it's just as easy to select a bad one as a good one. There are more bad ones today than there used to be because there is more demand for outfitters. There are fly-by-night operators in the guiding business just as there are in any other business.

Even planning your plane trip involves plenty of details. What airlines offer the best connections to where you want to go? And, of course, you won't know where you want to go until you have made specific arrangements with your outfitter as to where he can pick you up. And when can he pick you up? That detail enters into scheduling your flights. There are considerations involved in how to pack your gear for plane flights. And you may not have thought about how you're going to get your venison and antlers back home with you. There are tricks of the trade in making hunting trips whether you go via commercial aircraft or other modes of transportation.

And how about the hunt itself? If you've never hunted the area you're considering, how do you know what type of clothing to pack, and how much? What types of personal gear should you take? Does your guide supply sleeping bags? How about air mattresses and rifle scabbards and other gear? And when the hunt is over who is going to butcher, package, and freeze your meat? What's the best way to pack it for transportation home? These are the types of questions I'll answer in this chapter.

First I want to emphasize how important it is to choose a top outfitter. Recently a friend of mine and five companions went on a mule-deer hunt in the Colorado Rockies. They made a very poor selection when choosing an outfitter, though they didn't know it when they booked him. During a week's hunt they managed to score on one small buck for the entire group.

That same fall I also went on a mule-deer hunt in the Colorado Rockies. There were three other hunters in my group. We scored on four big bucks in only one-and-a-half days of hunting. The difference was that my hunt was well planned and executed because I worked with a top outfitter. Though I paid slightly more for my hunt than my friend paid for his, I enjoyed one of the finest hunting trips of my career while his was a miserable flop. That's the best example I know of why it's so important to know how to choose an outfitter or guide.

My first rule is to contact several outfitters or guides in the area I want to hunt. When I get replies I examine them carefully. Those that promise the moon are automatically rejected. It seems that too many nonresidents have the wrong idea that game in the western states is so plentiful they'll find big bucks stepping out of cover all over the place. Unscrupulous guides and outfitters prey on this false belief. They assume that if they promise exceptional and easy hunting they're sure to book plenty of clients. They worry about producing, later.

It's simply impossible to consistently produce what they promise because deer hunting isn't that easy anywhere. Sure, some hunters are lucky, but by and large it takes a lot of work and knowledge on an outfitter's part to get his clients reasonable shooting opportunities. And there are many contributing factors an outfitter can't control. Bad weather, game populations that may be up or down, and heavy or light hunting pressure all have good or bad effects on a client's opportunity to bag a buck. The good outfitters are aware of these things, and they're aware they'll get some clients who can't hunt hard enough and can't shoot straight. These men don't promise you great trophies and easy hunting. Instead they'll tell you how long they have been in business, what facilities and services they can offer, and that they'll do everything possible to make your hunt safe, comfortable and rewarding. When you get replies along those lines you're usually dealing with honest men.

The next step is to get references. The reputable men will be more than happy to supply the names and addresses of hunters they have guided during recent years. Your letters or phone calls to a few of these hunters will get opinions as to whether the men they dealt with produced a satisfactory or unsatisfactory hunt.

Another system can work, too. I often get letters from gunners who read my deer-hunting stories in *Outdoor Life*. In the stories I always mention the names and addresses of my guides and outfitters. Quite often readers will ask me if I'd recommend the men I hunted with. You can use the same system. When you read the story of a deer hunt that intrigues you, why not follow up on it? Write the author in care of the magazine's editorial offices and ask whatever questions you want answered. Many authors reply to these letters.

Once you make firm contact with the man you want it's time to ask some specific questions. As I mentioned earlier you should know what types of gear to bring along. Little things like knowing whether insulated boots would be more suitable for the hunt than regular hiking boots could make a world of difference in comfort. The one thing that ruins many hunts is boots that don't match the type of hunting that's required.

You should know what type of shooting opportunities you're likely to get so you can sight-in your rifle to meet them. You should know what the weather conditions will probably be so you can pack clothing that will be most comfortable and efficient.

You should also know what type of personal gear you'll have real use for. A lot of hunters expect an outfitter to pack half their worldly goods into the back country for them. There's no sense in bogging down a hunt with equipment that won't be used. How can a hunter make good use of a month's supply of clothing, six pairs of boots, and a lot of unnecessary stuff like tape players and other convenience items? A few changes of clothes, some for warm or dry weather, some for cold or wet, are all a man requires. Check with your guide or outfitter on what he recommends.

One situation that's a modern trend, but which varies from state to state, is the use of Blaze Orange outer garments. Some states require them, others don't. Check with your guide on such items so you won't waste time shopping before the actual hunt begins.

Long before the hunt, arrange the meeting place with your man and when you'll meet him. It's best to try picking a time that's most convenient for both of you. A guide who has been working all day doesn't take kindly to meeting a plane in the middle of the night. Attention to such details always makes hunts run smoother.

When it comes time to pack for your hunt and leave home there are more things to think about. If you're flying it's good to keep in mind that airlines occasionally lose baggage, and they're always very particular about the carry-on hand luggage you bring aboard. Now that all passengers and hand luggage on commercial flights must be inspected prior to boarding there are some rules to follow.

Inspectors are suspicious types. Your favorite skinning knife would look perfectly normal on your belt in deer country, but it would be sure to raise suspicions in carry-on luggage. So would ammunition or other apparently lethal items. Stow such items in your main baggage containers. The big bags going into cargo areas of planes aren't opened, except for spot checks.

I never pack my rifles as baggage items for two reasons. First, baggage sometimes gets lost. If you end up at your destination without your rifle you're in tough shape. Second, cargo-baggage items really get tossed around. Such handling is an excellent way to jar scopes out of line. The best procedure is to bring your rifles aboard and surrender them to a stewardess who will place them in an up-front compartment. You'll get them back at your destination. This is standard procedure on commercial flights routing through hunting country. It provides better handling of your firearms and it insures against losing them.

The best way to insure against your baggage getting lost is to get to the airport at least one hour before flight time. Last-minute loading of baggage is when most items get mixed up.

Though I've advised against packing too much gear it's also a mistake to pack too little or to pack unwisely. I was on a hunt years ago with a man who had lost one of his bags through an airline baggage-control foul-up. He wasn't overly concerned because he had experienced the same problem before.

"The first time it happened I put in a lousy hunt," he told me. "The one bag I did have contained light hunting clothes and light boots, the stuff I expected to wear around camp. The lost bag contained the heavy clothes and foul-weather gear. I hoped for nice weather so I wouldn't freeze, but we got blizzards. At the time I was young and healthy so I toughed it out, but I was wet and cold most of the time.

"Since then I've divided my gear between my two bags. Instead of putting my heavy coats, shirts, and rain gear in the same bag I'll put some items in one bag and some in the second bag. If one bag gets lost at least I have a fighting chance to be halfway comfortable. I divide all my hunting clothing that way. Another thing I do is not to dress up for airline flights to hunting country. Dress clothes are worthless for the hunt, so why wear them? I look respectable enough in a clean hunting shirt, sweater, light hunting pants, and lightweight boots. That's the type of clothing I'll use for some of my hunting anyway. The point is if I'm already wearing those items there's no chance they'll be lost if something happens to my baggage.

"One other point," he continued. "One time one of my bags got lost and I never saw it again till I returned home. Somehow the airline baggage tag came off the bag, so the airline returned it to the address shown on the bag's identification tag. Since then I use new identification tags when I'm flying out to a hunting area. The tag shows my name, but the address is that of my outfitter. In case of a mix-up the bag may show up at my out-fitter's home within a day or two. All is not lost when that happens. For my return trip home I just switch to tags showing my home address."

That fellow shares my conviction that it's better to pack two smaller bags (I use duffel bags) than one large one. Two lighter bags are easier to handle, you can split your clothing items as mentioned, and if one bag gets lost you're still in business.

You may disagree on the best way to pack firearms. The two arrangements available are the usual snug-fitting gun cases and the modern suit-case types lined with foam or soft plastics. The new types are ideal from a protection standpoint, but I've found them a bit clumsy in the field. What I've done is to incorporate the protection features of the suitcase type into my regular gun cases. I've taped two-foot-long strips of cushion foam ma-terial inside my gun cases so that when the cases are zipped shut, the strips of protection encase my scopes and mountings like buns around hotdogs. The system offers fine protection against scopes being jarred out of line in transit, and I still have a regular gun case in the field. Everybody to their own opinion, but I feel a regular gun case is a lot handier in bouncing jeeps and in similar situations than the suitcase types.

Because I write for my living it's second nature for me to carry a note-book while I'm hunting. This enables me to keep an accurate record of what happens during my trips, what details I overlooked in planning, and the names and addresses of people I meet. When you're out in the back-country on a hunting trip a lot happens in a hurry, and unless you have notes of the developments as they occur you'll forget a lot of them by the time you return home.

Such notes are always of value for planning other trips, and I've found they often lead to new trips. Several times I've struck up acquaintances with hunters I've met in the field. Later correspondence, based on notes I'd made, led to friendships which in turn led to planning hunts together. Some of these hunts have been the best I've had. In any event, notes of the details of your hunts can lead to the same personal satisfaction as photos. Long after a hunt is over, rereading notes and viewing photos brings back all the enjoyment in vivid detail.

One handy piece of equipment I haven't mentioned is a small, hand-carried tote bag. I've used one for years to pack such items as binoculars, extra skinning knife, hand warmer, extra gloves, extra ammunition, sun glasses, candy bars, lunch thermos, matches, aspirin, smoking material, and so forth. I don't load my pockets down with all these things each day be-cause I might not need them. But the tote bag goes with me when I go into hunting country whether I go by car, jeep, boat, or horseback. The object of the system is to keep all these miscellaneous items in one place and to keep them handy so they can be reached without much trouble. It's a simple trick that makes my hunting more efficient and more enjoyable.

Many out-of-state hunters suddenly find themselves in financial trouble far from home. The biggest mistake is in assuming that the cost of a guided hunt covers everything. It doesn't cover many expenses you would have if you made the hunt on your own. For example, guides don't include in their fees the expenses of butchering, wrapping, and freezing your meat. Those expenses come out of your pocket. So does the cost of shipping your meat home. Shipping a trophy head to a taxidermist is another item. You also may have to purchase new items during the hunt. Ripped clothing, broken sunglasses, boot laces, and other incidentals easily might have to be replaced.

A big unplanned expense item can be a change in schedule from the planned end of a hunt. This can happen when you fail to get your buck and want to hunt a few more days. Weather might cancel plane flights, which means you'll be faced with an extra day or two in town. If you don't have the cash in your pocket to meet unexpected expenses you'll be in sorry shape. Hunters who travel to hunting areas in personal cars don't have to worry about cancelled plane flights or air freight costs of frozen meat, but they can run into problems that are just as bad.

One time I had just finished a deer hunt in northwest Nebraska. I planned on beginning my drive home the next morning, but a forecast of a severe snowstorm moving in from the west prompted me to get into my car and start driving toward home right away. The blizzard caught up with me outside of North Platte, Nebraska. By the time I approached the town the freeway was drifting with snow so rapidly I knew I'd be a fool to continue. The blizzard proved so bad that it forced me to hole up in a mo-tel for two days. If I'd been without cash or credit cards, I'd have been in trouble.

Another time a pal and I had driven into Manitoba on a moose hunt—it could just as easily have been a deer hunt. We hauled a snowmobile trailer behind our car, intending to use it to pack our meat home. As luck would have it the trailer broke down on our return trip. Not only did we have to come up with cash for an additional day's expenses, we also had to pay for considerable repairs to the trailer.

My rule of thumb on budgeting the expenses for a hunting trip is to total all planned expenses, then pocket an additional 15 percent to cover unex-pected expenses. The additional money should be in cash because people don't like to cash personal checks for strangers any more. In many places they refuse. Credit cards also get a negative response in many of the small backwoods communitites. If it turns out you don't need the additional money it makes a tidy little sum to bank when you get home.

The largest normal expense item that many hunters fail to plan ade-quately for is the cost of taking care of their meat. Years ago it was com-mon practice to hang deer from tree limbs in a cool area until the hunt was finished. Then the carcasses were tied to car tops or lashed to trailers for the drive home. This procedure involved no cost at all until the hunter arrived home. Then he had his local butcher cut up the meat. This expense was little noticed, for it was paid from the regular family budget.

Today it's obvious that you can't take a whole deer carcass home with you if you're traveling by commercial aircraft. Another important factor is the relatively new government control of meat-cutting plants. Regulations covering the cutting of noninspected meat are far stricter today than they were years ago. Today's butcher who wants to cut up game meat has to have certain facilities and has to follow specific regulations in order to be licensed to handle game.

Many of the smaller operators—those who used to handle game a few years ago—no longer will accept the meat. These men figured that it would cost more money to follow government regulations than they would take in by processing wild animals. In many areas of the East and Midwest it's now impossible to find a butcher who will process, cut up, and freeze game. So, in many cases, nonresident hunters have found it mandatory to have their meat taken care of in the area they hunt. It's no problem to find game processors in prime hunting regions.

It seems to me this is a far better deal than hauling a carcass home. For one thing, the sooner you process game the less chance you run of meat spoilage. Also, you eliminate a lot of problems when you get home. Last year, for example, I picked up my three cardboard boxes of frozen venison in the baggage area of our airport shortly after my plane landed. I loaded them into my station wagon and drove home. It took me only minutes to unpack my meat and stash it in my freezer. I've been doing the same thing for several years. It's far better than hoping unprocessed meat won't spoil on the way home, worrying about getting it into a cold-storage locker, worrying about finding a butcher to cut it up, and worrying about when he'll find time to do it.

Processing meat in the hunting country is my idea of the proper way to handle it regardless of whether my trip is made by plane or car. If I'm driving and it will take me two or three days to get home, I'll have the frozen meat packed with dry ice to keep it from thawing. And don't worry if it does thaw a bit. The old belief that frozen meat which has partially thawed out should not be refrozen has little basis in fact. It can be refrozen once with no damage at all. It should not be refrozen twice. This principle does not apply to fish and other more perishable foods. Once defrosted they should be eaten; refreezing can spoil them.

In the better deer areas of the West many game processors do a great volume of business. I've seen groups of hunters arrive at processing plants in pickup trucks loaded with game carcasses. I've seen cold-storage rooms crowded with deer hanging from meat hooks. I mention this to point out that it's not wise to expect a processor to be able to handle your animal on short notice.

If you're working with a guide or outfitter, chances are he'll have a system worked out with a processor for handling his clients' meat. But don't depend on it. Ask your man at the beginning of the hunt if he can handle your meat processing connections for you. If he can't, or if you're on your own, you should do some planning to avoid delay in heading for home. A mix-up here, in terms of a day or two delay, is another example of how unexpected expenses can dent your wallet.

I've found it best to make contact with a game processor before beginning my hunt in a new area. Find out if he will handle your meat, his hours of operation, and his phone number. When I down a deer I prefer to get it skinned out and hung in cold storage as soon as possible. So when I come in after a successful day I phone the processor and ask if I can bring the carcass right in. If this isn't convenient for him I'll make arrangements to have my animal at his place of business at the agreed-upon time. Businessmen appreciate this kind of consideration, and they'll go out of their way to take care of your needs.

If I'm hunting with companions we follow the same procedure. One man in the group may get his deer the first day of the hunt, another man the last day. If the first animal has been processed early, a lot of last-minute details are avoided at the end of the hunt.

If I fly to my hunting area I ask my meat processor to pack my meat so that each box weighs a bit less than 50 pounds. Such boxes are often accepted by airlines as excess baggage at no extra cost. I discovered that by accident one time in Colorado. The processor who had put up my meat was temporarily out of his larger-size boxes, so all of my venison went into smaller boxes. I checked them in at the airport, asked for charges, and was advised there was no cost for parcels weighing under 50 pounds. The technique won't always work, but in that case I flew a big mule-deer buck 1,500 miles without paying a dime for air freight.

Your boxes of frozen meat should be marked plainly. One time my frozen air frieght meat was mostly thawed when I picked it up at the baggage counter of my home airport. It had been placed by a heater. If I'd labeled the boxes "frozen meat—do not store near heat," that problem wouldn't have developed. Another time one of my boxes of meat was half-thawed because I hadn't taken the time to mark the top side of the box, "this end up." The significance is that when dry ice is put in a box it's always put in the top because cold air flows downward, not up. In effect, the dry ice in the upside-down box wasn't accomplishing its purpose. It's no problem at all to mark boxes with a black marker.

20

Typical
Away-from-home Hunt

Advising you about the considerations involved in planning a deer hunt in unfamiliar country is fine as far as it goes, but such material can't give you a feeling of the experiences you'll run into. I'll tell the story of one of my typical hunts, it's an adventure that illustrates many of the points I've made in the two preceding chapters of this section. Here is how the excitement went:

"There's a buck!"

Those electrifying words were shouted at a time when they didn't make sense. Our eight-man group was in a spike camp at the end of a narrow clearing along Bordeaux Creek in northwestern Nebraska. It was noon. Two big campfires were crackling under the makings of our lunch. We were moving about in warm sunshine and talking about the morning's hunt. That buck should have been aware of our activity long before he reached the clearing.

I was standing near one of the fires with a cup of coffee in my hand when somebody bellowed the startling news. I whirled so rapidly that some of the steaming liquid sloshed out of the cup and burned my wrist. I dropped the cup as if it were on fire. The three-point (Western count) mule deer had come upon us at a dead run. He was almost across the clearing before I spotted him.

Dan Contonos was closest to the deer, and he had his

rifle slung over his shoulder. I've never seen a man react faster. He leveled his sporterized .30/06 Springfield in a blur of motion. His snap-shot missed the streaking buck as the animal melted into cottonwood thickets.

Fred Nelson, my hunting partner, looked at me and grinned. "I didn't expect to have a buck run through camp," he said. "But just about anything can happen when you're hunting away from home."

He was right. Let's start from the beginning.

Fred is a long-time acquaintance who lives in Lincoln, Nebraska. He's the public relations director for that state's Department of Roads. I'd met him on another hunt and we had become good friends. Several of his letters during recent years mentioned Pine Ridge deer hunting. The subject sounded so intriguing that I asked him for more details.

"Hunting the Pine Ridge is hard work," he replied in a letter. "The area is as rough as any country you've ever hunted. It's all jumbled up with hogbacks, outcroppings, buttes, pinnacles, and canyons. Most of it is timbered with Ponderosa pine, buckbrush, and stunted cedar. Little clearings dot the woodlands, and many of them are slashed with dry washes and creek beds.

"The huge area offers stillhunting at its best. There's little driving done since the bucks have too many escape options in that broken country. There's no hunting at all by vehicle because you can't get vehicles across the buttes and canyons. You have to walk in, and it's tough going up there a mile high.

"But the Ridge is fascinating because it's beautiful country. It's ideal for a man who likes to hunt hard, and it harbors both whitetails and mule deer. If you like the combination come out and join me this fall."

That information told me about the kind of terrain and type of hunting I was getting into. Through corresponding with the Nebraska Game and Parks Commission I got additional information I needed. I learned that the nonresident deer-permit fee was $30, that applications would be accepted after July 1, and that the season would run from November 13 through November 21. That year, both residents and nonresidents could apply for a second permit after August 1. I decided to apply for two permits. They arrived in my mail during September. Fred had arranged for us to hunt with a part-time guide who he knew was an excellent man. That solved my problem of selecting a guide.

I drove to Nebraska from my home in Michigan, then checked into a motel in Chadron where I was scheduled to meet Fred the evening before the deer season opened. Fred had told me to be sure to plan on hunting the first few days of the season. He had explained that's the time the most hunters are in the woods, and that the deer don't travel much unless there are plenty of hunters to move them. When he arrived at the motel he was accompanied by Don Berlie, our guide. Don's part in the hunt was to be considerably different than that of the usual guide.

"I'll be out with you fellows mostly to have fun," he explained. "Deer season is my vacation from my job at Chadron State College. I like the atmosphere of old-time deer hunts with a little camp life and some hard work. That's why I set up a spike camp. It's mostly a gathering place for my hunters now. Years ago we used to sleep and eat there. I still prepare lunches over open fires, but my hunters all base in motels as you men are doing. That's more convenient these days.

"I won't do much hunting with you," Don continued. "I believe a man should work at getting his own deer. I'll tell you where to go, but it will be up to you to walk in there and do your own hunting. My small fee reflects the fact that I do little actual guiding. I charge a flat rate of $10 per person per day, and that includes lunch."

Don went on to tell us that he would spend much of his time on horseback. He enjoys riding his Morgan horses almost as much as he does hunting. He pointed out that our hunting area—on two huge ranches and thousands of acres of public hunting territory on state forest land—would be on some of the roughest terrain in the Pine Ridge.

"Some of our bucks are killed so far into the back country that it's difficult to drag them out," Berlie explained. "That's one of the reasons I keep a couple of horses in camp. When the need arises I can ride one of my Morgans to a kill site and pack out a deer with little trouble. It's one of the services I offer, but I also ride so I can keep in contact with my scattered hunters. It's big country, I don't want anybody to get lost back in there."

"How many hunters do you have in your group?" I asked.

"Five in addition to you two. We'll all start from camp in the morning, but I'll send my group east while you fellows will hike west."

Long before dawn Fred and I drove down a ranch trail leading to Berlie's camp eight miles southeast of Chadron. We arrived early, so my partner told me what to expect.

"Right now the deer are probably down in ranch fields feeding," he began. "At dawn they'll move back into the high country to bed down. If conditions are normal you should see about twenty-five deer today."

A half-hour later Don gave me instructions that fired my enthusiasm even more. Dawn was a haze of orange working into the sky of stars when he pointed toward a ridge top that was a black silhouette in the sky.

"The bigger bucks should work up high," he told me. "Climb up to the top of that ridge and pick a vantage point. There are deep canyons on the far side that deer use for runways. Watch 'em closely till noon, then walk back to camp."

Fred hiked off ahead of me while the other men walked toward a high ridge in the east. The temperature was about 35 degrees. There were scattered patches of snow remaining from a previous blizzard. I decided I wouldn't have much of a climb, so I donned my heavy snowmobile suit and insulated boots. That gear is too warm for hiking but ideal for sitting.

I soon came to a creek bottom that I hadn't noticed. I headed down a hill, through cottonwoods and elms, up another hill, and across a glade. I was already puffing, and the ridge looked as far away as when I had started.

Several hundred yards farther I knew I was overdressed, but full daylight was coming on fast now so I hurried on. The glades became steeper and dotted with pines and buckbrush. Finally they angled up like steep ski slopes, but my real climb began when the pine clumps became thicker and intermingled with outcroppings of butte rock.

Several times I scouted around steep rock cliffs for draws I could climb through. Often I stopped to rest my pounding heart and aching lungs. By the time I reached the end of my climb the sun was well into a blue sky. I mentally kicked myself for failing to have asked Fred or Don about the proper outer clothing to wear.

I found I'd peaked out on a north-south ridge edging the valley harboring our camp. I noted pasture lands and fields of winter wheat and sorghum stubble far below me. A timbered creekbottom wandered near our vehicles which appeared as toys in the distance.

Closer, around and below me, pines and red cedars shimmered various shades of green as sunlight and shadows mixed in draws and canyons. I walked to an outcropping of rock, sat down and glassed the entire area with my 8x40 Gottinga binoculars. I didn't spot animal life of any kind. I stayed put all morning without seeing a single deer. Then I made the long hike back to camp.

Fred arrived as I was discarding my snowmobiling gear in favor of lightweight hunting clothes and hiking boots. He'd seen a mule-deer doe and a small whitetail buck that he'd passed up. He was amazed at the scarcity of deer. Our disappointment evaporated when the rest of the group arrived. They rolled into the campsite in Don's pickup camper. I could hardly believe my eyes when I looked in the back of the truck and inspected three fine mule-deer bucks.

"We saw dozens of deer," Don reported happily. "One of the boys missed a good buck, and they passed up a spikehorn. Deer were running like rabbits on that east ridge."

Don seemed puzzled when I mentioned that I hadn't seen a single deer. His typically western eyes squinted from under the brow of his cowboy hat as he weighed my statement.

"Well," he drawled, "I know every inch of that country and I can guarantee you there are plenty of bucks up there. I was sure deer would be moving, but apparently they bedded down early. We'll get the rest of the gang up on those ridges this afternoon, you're going to see deer running. I figured there would be other hunters up there, but it's no problem. This early in the hunt we've got plenty of manpower to get those deer moving."

The rest of the gang turned out to be Don's son-in-law, Dan Contonos;

Ray Berlie, Don's California-based brother; Gus and Roger Peiper, a father-and-son team from near Lincoln; and Don Anderson, a horse-raising friend of Don's. We were preparing lunch when the buck I mentioned at the beginning of this story almost ran through camp.

The afternoon's activities were planned around flanking maneuvers combined with stillhunting. Don told Don Anderson, Fred, and me how to get around to the far side of the west ridge. When we arrived there we were to hunt toward the east. Dan, Gus and Roger were to hike north along the creek bottom. Their plan was to travel a couple of miles, then stillhunt up and across the ridge in a westerly direction. In effect, both groups would be traveling toward each other. The plan was designed to move deer in several directions. Since we would all be well scattered we could stillhunt, and there was the possibility of seeing deer jumped by other members of the group. The plan was a good example of how a guide knows the best ways to hunt his area.

"Later in the afternoon Ray and I will ride horses up into that back country to check on you fellows," said Don as we left camp. "If anybody gets lost, or gets a buck, stay put. We'll find you."

After hiking a couple of miles I topped out on a ridge and sat down on a boulder to glass the area. Movement suddenly caught my eye. Then I spotted two deer walking down a timbered slope a quarter-mile ahead of me. They were mule deer and they were traveling straight toward me but they were moving through thick pines and I couldn't tell if either animal wore antlers.

I stayed on the boulder for half an hour without seeing those deer again. Just as I was about to move on I caught another flash of movement 100 yards below me, again in thick pines. I made out the broken outlines of two deer heading toward a small clearing. I figured the mule deer had circled, but when the two new deer stepped into the open they were whitetails, a fat two-point buck and a doe. I had that buck dead to rights, but I was hoping for better trophies so I let him go.

During the next couple of hours I saw several more deer in the distance as I continued stillhunting. Most of them were sneaking through timber, an obvious indication that our flanker movements were working.

While climbing over still another high ridge I spotted Fred sitting on a rock outcropping below me. After I dropped down to compare notes Don Anderson walked in behind us. He had hunted this country before with Berlie, so he made a suggestion.

"A lot of deer are probably in that big timbered canyon below us," he began. "You're in a good spot right here, Fred. I'll post John farther down this rocky ridge, then I'll drop off into the timber and see what I can move out. I'm just hunting for exercise anyway. I killed one of those bucks this morning."

I didn't go as far down the ridge as Don told me to, mostly because I'm not too keen on heights. The sharp finger of butte rock kept getting narrower and its cliffs seem to drop straight down. I picked a place where I could see into clearings bordering both sides of the 10-foot-wide ridge, then I sat down.

The clearing on my left was a narrow opening in pines that stretched away for 50 yards. It harbored some buckbrush, yucca plants, and high brown grass, but it was basically an open alley in the timber. I happened to be staring straight down that alley when a big whitetail buck materialized along its edge. I don't know where he came from. He was just suddenly there.

He was moving when I first glimpsed him but he came to a sudden halt. As he stopped he seemed to be looking directly at me. My heart almost choked in my throat as I realized that he could jump into cover before I could begin to raise my rifle and get a sight picture.

As luck would have it he hadn't spotted me. I knew that when he turned broadside to me and looked down into the canyon. As he moved his head his thick-beamed antlers flashed in sunshine. His shoulder area was behind buckbrush but his back offered a clear, 40-yard shot. I settled the crosshairs of my Redfield 3x9-power scope on his spine and fired. The buck went down dead in his tracks.

I stayed on my high vantage point for an hour. Then I spotted the Berlie brothers on horseback near the bottom of the canyon. They saw my signal as I waved my bright orange cap. As they worked up to my position they spooked at least a dozen mule deer through the little clearing. Two were small bucks, but I had no intention of filling my second tag so soon. This was the first day of a scheduled five-day hunt, and I wanted to see more Pine Ridge action.

The cliffs below my perch dropped straight down for about 20 feet, so I backtracked to Fred's location. From there we hiked down into the canyon to the kill site. I found that my buck had five points on one antler, four on the other. Don arrived, took a rope off his horse, and dragged my fine trophy up a ridge. Fred and I hunted the rest of the afternoon, and walked into camp just as darkness was falling. We figured we'd hiked about eight tough miles that day. It had been quite a session of deer hunting.

The next morning I stillhunted by myself in high ridges west of camp. I'd move slowly, then stop and glass canyons and draws. I found that if I took my time in studying alternate routes I could hike over the rough terrain quite easily. I prided myself on that thought until after a hot lunch of hunter's stew and soup.

I'd sneaked down a bare ledge of butte rock that knifed out between the almost sheer walls of two deep canyons. I glassed from near the end of the ledge for twenty minutes without seeing movement. Then I pitched a rock down into a thick clump of pine and buckbrush. A doe mule deer bolted out of there, and ran up and over the canyon rim. Moments later a three-point buck sneaked out of the far edge of the clump and headed downhill. He didn't have much of a rack, but he was a big deer. I decided to take him.

The mule deer was 150 yards away when I found him in my scope, but I didn't shoot because he was traveling in thick cover. Finally he walked into a small stand of pines. He didn't reappear. I figured he wasn't too spooked and that he hadn't seen me. He probably had bedded down, so I tried stalking him.

I backtracked to a cut in the ledge where I eased downhill by grasping handholds in rock crevices. A few minutes later I came to a grassy slope so steep that I had no choice except to slide downhill 30 feet on my rump. Several times I came to dry washes so sheer-walled that I had to backtrack to get around them. By the time an hour had passed I'd taken so many different and difficult routes that I'd lost all track of the pine clump where the buck was. My main thought now was that I was very thankful for the physical conditioning effort I'd put in prior to making this hunt.

The bottom of the canyon was so rough it looked as if it had been blown apart with dynamite. Snow drifts were still deep in shaded cuts and they were laced with deer tracks. But the tracks became of less and less importance as I concentrated on getting out of that hole. By the time I reached the canyon's rim I was bushed. I remembered Don saying, "I want my hunters to work, to get exhausted, to know they've been hunting the way hunting was meant to be." It was dusk when I got back to camp. Fred greeted me with a fine story.

"I walked about five miles back into the hills and took a stand on the edge of a canyon," he said. "I just got settled when a doe mule deer walked up a trail 50 yards away. Minutes later a forkhorn buck took the same route. About every fifteen minutes a mule deer walked by. I heard some of them coming before I saw them. I just knew a big buck had to show sooner or later.

"Finally I spotted an enormous mule-deer buck walking down the opposite side of the canyon. He was a big brute with a white muzzle, but he was close to 1,000 yards away. I watched him for a while, then he just disappeared. Tomorrow I'm going back in there and try to find him again."

The next morning Don and I took my big whitetail to a locker plant in Crawford. He believes in getting his clients' meat processed as soon as possible to avoid delay at the end of the hunt, and also to eliminate the possibility of spoilage. Don makes preliminary arrangements with the processor so the man expects to have several deer to handle during a specific period. During the drive he filled me in on some of the details of Pine Ridge deer hunting.

"The state Game and Parks Commission issues around 4,500 deer permits covering the Pine Ridge Management Unit," he began. "The hunter-success ratio averages a bit better than 50 percent.

"The stranger who comes out here would have no trouble finding a place to hunt if he stayed on the 27,000 acres of public hunting land, but the ranchers are touchy about their private holdings. They're tough on trespassers because they're very concerned about their livestock. If a stranger wants to hunt on private land he should make contact with a rancher before applying for a deer permit."

"What's the best way of doing that?" I asked.

"Write the chamber of commerce in Chadron or Crawford," Don replied. "Ask for names and addresses of ranchers who take in hunters. Some landowners offer room and board and part-time guiding services for very reasonable fees. Many ranchers now recognize that their deer can be a cash crop, and they're anxious to make arrangements with legitimate hunters. That's another reason why they have no use for trespassers."

"Are there any other guides in the area who operate as you do?"

"A few," Don said. "I wish there were more because I have all the hunters I can handle. The five men you met are leaving tomorrow and a few more are coming in. Most of those fellows hunt with me each year, so I'm not looking for more clients. A stranger should definitely have a local contact before coming out here."

During most of the fourth day Fred continued stillhunting the area where he'd spotted the giant mule deer buck. He didn't see the animal again. Finally he gave up his hopes for a trophy, and scored on a small mule-deer buck with his Winchester Model 70 .308. That same day three of the men in Berlie's new group downed bucks. All three deer were whitetails, one a big four-pointer. The total score for the camp was now nine bucks. As has happened so often during my many years of deer hunting, I was impressed with the fact that the way to get bucks in unfamiliar country is to hunt with someone who knows the local picture.

Snow fell during the night, a thick dusting of light powder that covered everything. The snow was so soft on top of the unfrozen ground that it made for ideal stillhunting. Don suggested I work the thickets that stretched for miles along the creek.

"There are always deer in these flats," he said. "You can't get close to 'em when the ground is bare because they hear you moving in leaves. And it's normally tough to see a deer in there because the cover is so thick. New snow solves both problems. A deer will really show up against this white background."

I hadn't gone a mile when I spotted a flock of about thirty wild turkeys feeding in a sorghum field. It was the third flock I'd seen during the hunt. I practiced stalking them. When I got within 25 yards of the closest bird I knew that my approach must be virtually soundless. Suddenly they spotted me and ran off like streaking shadows.

An hour later I walked almost on top of a bedded whitetail buck. I didn't know he was there until brush busted to my left. I whirled and spotted the animal trotting off through timber 70 yards away. I noted a three-or-four-point rack when the buck crossed a tiny clearing. My Winchester Model 70 .243 flew to my shoulder and I found the deer in my scope. I held my fire till the buck reached another tiny clearing. Now or never!

At the crack of my rifle the deer leaped into high gear and streaked away. I assumed that my bullet hadn't found its way through branches, but I trailed the buck for more than a mile hoping to find signs of blood. I didn't, and there was no second chance. I'd blown a good opportunity.

But my stillhunting luck held out. I spotted two mule deer on a sidehill, and I stalked close enough to determine that they were does. They never knew I was in the area. I was about four miles from camp when I decided to head back. Right after that I walked almost on top of another whitetail buck.

He was drinking from the creek as I rounded a bend in the stream 30 yards away. We spotted each other at the same time, and we were both startled. He was a small buck—one antler had two points, the other was a long spike—but my hunt was about over and I was elated with this opportunity.

The whitetail made a fatal mistake when he decided to run up a steep hillside instead of bolting for the cover of thickets. It was a difficult shot, but I'd had enough practice with shooting my rifle to know where to hold on an animal running uphill. My 100-grain bullet caught him when he was halfway to the ridge. (Note: By 1974 deer-hunting pressure in Nebraska had become so heavy that it was difficult for a nonresident to secure a deer-hunting permit. Nebraska no longer promotes nonresident deer hunting, but many states do. For "where-to-go" information see Chapter 2.)

21
Notes on Trophy Hunting

It stands to reason that if a physically healthy man has unlimited time and money he can enjoy the best hunting on earth. Does it follow that if he buys his way into the best game country he is also likely to take a trophy head? Not necessarily, and particularly not if he wants a trophy whitetail deer.

The odds on taking a trophy good enough to make the record book go with the man who hunts big-game other than deer. Consider wild sheep as an example. All but the desert bighorn inhabit the wildest and most remote mountain areas of North America. A sheep hunter has fair odds on downing a record-book ram because he pays top dollar to hunt country that is never seen by the average hunter with average means. He hunts animals that live long enough to grow trophy heads. The same reasoning applies if you go after other wild animals such as grizzly bear, Alaskan-Yukon moose, lion, greater kudu, or what have you.

It's the opposite story with deer, especially whitetails. Most deer live close to man, consequently they are hunted hard by almost anyone who owns or can borrow a rifle. Few bucks live longer than 1½ years. Consider that it often takes a whitetail or mule-deer buck four to six years to grow the best set of antlers he'll ever produce. Such a buck has to make it through at least several hunting seasons before he has the slightest chance of becoming a candidate for the record book.

From what I've said so far you might conclude that it's impossible today to bag a real trophy buck. It's extremely difficult, but not impossible. In another chapter of this book I pointed out that the world-record mule deer was killed in 1972 by Doug Burris, Jr., of San Antonio, Texas. He nailed his monster buck in Colorado. Nearly all of the top twenty typical mule deer listed in the Boone and Crockett Club record book were taken in the 1960s and 1970s. Many of the best whitetails were also taken in relatively recent years. But let me illustrate how difficult it is for you to make the record book with a deer.

During the last Boone and Crockett Club big-game awards period—which covered three years—only two whitetail deer qualified for the record book, in which 290 heads are ranked. Because there are roughly 1.5 million whitetails bagged annually in North America—or roughly 4.5 million during that three-year period—the odds against any one hunter bagging one of those two bucks was 2.25 million to 1. Not only that, but the second-best buck entered in the Club's last awards program scored 172⅛ points, a bare 2⅛ points above the minimum 170-point score required for a typical whitetail's entry into the record book.

A trail-watcher's dream come true! Four bucks trot by. A hasty, heart-pounding evaluation says that the partially hidden buck at the back sports the best rack. He's a rare ten-pointer with good spread and long tines. The problem now is how to stay cool.

Ten years prior that magical minimum figure was only 160 points, but still within range enough to give me the flying twitches for months one season. That fall I killed a typical whitetail buck in Saskatchewan that astounded me. When I approached the downed animal after I shot him I couldn't take my eyes off his enormous antlers. The beams were so thick and the tines so long they seemed unreal. At the time I wasn't involved with trophy hunting as I am now, so I was more impressed than I would be today. In my mind there wasn't any question that my buck would make the record book; the question was how close to the top he would rank.

That evening I received an unpleasant shock. I had guessed that the rack would score over 180 points, but when I scored it with a tape measure I came up with 166 points. I knew that no big-game antlers or horns can be officially scored until 60 days after the kill date, to allow for natural drying and shrinkage. So my hopes of scoring high in the record book were dashed. Now I knew I'd be lucky if I made the book at all.

I didn't. The final official score was 156 points, just four points short of the minimum requirement at that time.

I mention this story for several reasons. Even though I was a veteran deer hunter when I shot that buck, I honestly believed he was one of the best typical whitetails that ever walked in North America. He certainly wore the best rack of antlers I've seen on a live whitetail before or since. But he wasn't nearly as good as he looked as far as the record book was concerned. Because of my position as Midwest Field Editor of *Outdoor Life* I run into somewhat similar situations every year.

One time in Nebraska I was accused of not knowing what I was talking about. One of the members of my guide's camp downed a ten-point whitetail. He asked me how high it would rank in the records. The buck had an immense, impressive rack, but I knew after studying it that it wouldn't score more than 140 points. The hunter didn't believe me. "That's the biggest buck by far that's been killed around here for years," he said. "They just don't get bigger than this one. You're wrong. Score him out and we'll see."

I obliged the fellow. He double-checked each measurement as I made it. We came up with 131 points. He was crestfallen.

Here's another story along the same lines.

After I nailed that Saskatchewan giant I had the head mounted. It hangs in my office where it is seen by many visiting outdoorsmen. Once a visitor from another state studied it closely, then said, "Damn nice buck. But he'll take second place to the one killed by my cousin a couple of years ago."

"Did your cousin have his rack scored by the Boone and Crockett Club?" I asked. "If his buck is a lot better than this one he's a cinch for the record book. And that's a tremendous honor because getting a whitetail buck into the book is hunting's toughest job. You'd do him a great favor by having him get in touch with the Club."

It didn't work out that way. My visitor thought it would be a better idea for me to see the mounted head, so he brought it with him on his next trip through my area. When we compared the two heads side by side I felt sorry for the fellow. He stammered when he said, "I can't believe it. Your buck's rack is wider and its tines are longer. It didn't look that big on the wall by itself. Before we matched those racks I thought my cousin's was the best I'd ever seen."

And therein lies a misconception about trophy hunting. A better-than-average whitetail rack coming out of my home area—the northwestern part of Lower Michigan—would be only fair in the big-buck country of northern Michigan. It wouldn't even draw notice in southeastern Saskatchewan where bucks with huge racks are fairly common. The same story holds true with mule deer.

In the foothills of Wyoming I once downed a mule-deer buck which had the best rack I'd seen in four days of hunting. At the time I thought the head was plenty large enough for mounting. It hangs on a wall in my office, too. Three years ago I left the rack of a far larger mule deer buck in the mountains of Montana where I shot him. By then I'd learned how large a really trophy mule deer's rack is. Recently, I brought home the five-point (Western count) antlers of a fine mule deer I killed in the Colorado Rockies. Though it's far more impressive than the antlers of the mounted head on my wall, I didn't even bother to cape the head. I won't pay the expense of another mule-deer head mount until I down a buck that's considerably larger. That accomplishment is possible because I now know the areas where the truly big mule-deer bucks roam.

So trophy hunting can mean two things. If you hunt your local area exclusively, and it's a region that doesn't produce big racks, your goal should be to take a buck that's one of the best ever taken in your surrounding locale. Such an achievement would be a milestone in any deer hunter's career. But if you want to reach for the stars and hit the big-time nationally, then you'll have to hunt the regions where big bucks live. If this is your goal you'll probably have to spend some time and money and hunt hard.

The best key to finding big-buck areas is serious study of the record book, *North American Big Game,* part of the North American Big Game Awards Program, now jointly sponsored by the Boone and Crockett Club and the N.R.A. The book is published about every six years. (Recent publication dates: 1964, 1971, and 1977.) Cost of the 1971 edition was $15. Mail order instructions are at the end of this chapter. The book lists the specific areas where all ranked trophies were taken. This is very important because the same areas that have produced big deer with big racks will continue to produce big deer. And the answer isn't all in mineral content of soil, the factor that produces the browse that produces large racks.

Any big-buck area has the right combination of cover, water, escape routes, and the most nutritious browse. If the area is large enough several big bucks will share it. When they die or are killed off other large bucks will move in because the region offers ideal living conditions. This is the precise reason why you sometimes hear of hunters who take trophy bucks quite frequently. These lucky fellows happened to find big-buck country and they hunt it year after year.

But back to the record book. Serious trophy hunters who have studied the book know that many of the best mule deer racks were taken in New Mexico. Further study shows that a fair share of those bucks came from the Jicarilla Apache Reservation. I once helped a fellow write a story of his hunt on the reservation for *Outdoor Life*. We titled the story "Three Bucks for the Book." That title indicated that all three men on the hunt took bucks that made the record book. They planned their hunt after serious study of the record book.

Colorado produces the most record-book mule deer. You can find the best areas by making a list of the Colorado kill sites tabulated in the book. Mark them with X's on a map of the state. When you're finished with that job you'll find that some of the groups of X's tend to concentrate in specific areas. The next step is to write to the Colorado Guides and Outfitters Association, P.O. Box 983, Glenwood Springs, Colorado 81601. Ask for a list of outfitters operating in the region in which you're interested. (Write the state game agency in any western state for the address of outfitter associations or guides.) Once you make connections with an outfitter or guide in the area, you'll know you're organizing a hunt in big-buck country.

It's a different story if you're interested in trophy whitetails. Most record-book whitetails are taken in the eastern half of the nation, in country that's harder to hunt and is far more heavily hunted than is most of the West. Whitetails are much more clever than mule deer, especially the mature bucks. Also, there aren't as many big-buck areas in whitetail country as there are in mule-deer country. You can pinpoint a few areas such as parts of Arkansas, Ohio, the western end of Michigan's Upper Peninsula, the southeastern part of Saskatchewan, the northeastern part of Missouri, and southern Texas, but in general an enormous whitetail buck might show up almost anywhere. He'll be an animal that just happened to be a giant, just as our giant basketball and football players seem to come from most anywhere.

Some of these bucks are hunted unsuccessfully for years by hunters who are aware of their presence. A local friend is now in his fifth year of trying for a specific buck he jumped while grouse hunting. He hasn't seen the animal since, though he often has found his tracks. Such stories are common.

Another factor pointing to the cleverness of whitetails is that some of the antlers recorded in the record book are referred to as "pickups." Some of these antlers have been found in the woods, still intact with the skull, long after the buck died. One of the best was found by a farmer on his own property. This guy is an avid deer hunter who thought he knew just about every deer that lived on his place. When you realize that this man had never seen the buck alive, and that the average whitetail's home range is about one square mile, you can appreciate how difficult it is to score on a trophy whitetail.

There are several general tips that should up your odds on whitetails. First, hunt from a stand. See Chapter 9 for all the details. I'll just emphasize here that the average stillhunter, stalker or driver is trying to match his eyes, ears, and knowledge of his area against an animal whose same facilities and knowledge are far superior. Almost all trophy whitetails are downed by hunters working from stands because the trail-watching hunter is the only one who has the odds in his favor.

RIFLE PROFICIENCY

Being an expert with your firearm is all-important. You may get only one chance at a real trophy buck during your lifetime. To blow it because you can't shoot well enough is almost inexcusable. Today the interest in shooting clubs and rifle ranges is higher than ever before. Even if you're a city dweller it's likely there's a place near you where you can practice shooting.

I don't know why, but many deer hunters wait until opening day before picking up their rifles. Except for deer season their rifles are stored away. How proficient would you be with your car, camera, or any other piece of equipment if you used it only once or twice a year? Any firearm is only as good as the man using it.

I'll tell a little story proving the point, even though it doesn't involve deer hunting. I once knew an Indian guide in northwestern Ontario named Charlie. He told me about the time he had two moose-hunting clients in his canoe. They were canoeing silently along the shoreline of a fly-in lake. Charlie eased his canoe around a sharp point of land and put his hunters almost on top of two bull moose feeding on shallow-water lily pads.

The two Americans shouldered their expensive scope-sighted rifles and began blazing away. The two moose, unhindered by any lead ballast, ran for shore. Water sprayed in glistening sheets as the bulls' hoofs and legs ripped through the water. They dashed out on the beach and melted into thick shoreline brush.

While the shooting was still going on both clients suddenly realized they couldn't hit their targets. One yelled, "Damnit, Charlie, shoot!"

Charlie wasn't normally interested in shooting moose for customers, but this case was different. It was now or never for these guys because it was late on the last day of their hunt. Charile wanted them to go home happy, but even so he waited till they emptied their rifles and the bulls had disappeared. Then he went into action.

The Indian knew the lay of the land. He figured the animals would run parallel to the shoreline, and if they did they would run around the tip of a narrow peninsula. So he dug in his paddle and rammed the canoe ashore. Then he jumped out and ran up the hill toward the other side of the peninsula. He was almost too late. Just as he cleared the top of the hill he spotted the two bulls running through brush below him. He threw up his old Winchester .30/.30 and dropped both moose. Each took a single slug in the neck.

How can a man with a battered unscoped rifle outshoot two men armed with superior rifles? And how could he do it from an offhand position while panting for breath? Simply because that old Indian was so familiar with his rifle that he could use it as efficiently as he used his canoe paddles and skinning knives. The average deer hunter will never become that fine a shot, but he certainly can improve with practice.

GETTING A GOOD BUCK

It seems to me that there are two other major reasons why more trophy bucks *are not* shot each year. When the average hunter gets a chance at an average buck his thoughts are predictable. "I've waited all year for this hunt," he says to himself. "This buck is a good one. I may not spot a better trophy. I may not even get another shot. I'd better take him."

So he shoots. If he is successful his hunt is ended. The larger buck that he might have spotted if he'd kept hunting is therefore safe for the rest of the year as far as this hunter is concerned. The second reason why more big bucks aren't killed is that they're far more clever than average bucks. The average hunter may have the skill to outwit a small buck, but most don't have the skill or patience to compete with the big bruisers.

RECOGNIZING RECORD HEADS

Skill and patience aren't the only things required to nail a trophy. First you have to know what a trophy is. I've already mentioned that most hunters have little understanding of how outstanding a rack of antlers must be to make the record book. Most of us can forget about ever seeing a buck that will qualify for the book, but we're all very interested in taking bucks that will make above-average head mounts for our dens or offices. Any outstanding deer head, professionally mounted, serves to bring back the memories and thrills of a great hunt each time it's viewed. Such memories are what makes hunting so intriguing.

It's very easy to overestimate the size of a rack on a deer before you shoot. I've been hunting deer for many years—I killed my first buck in 1943 when I was sixteen years old—but my heart still tries to jump into my throat when I spot a buck in the woods. My mind seems to shout, "There's a buck." I'm well-convinced this same sort of thing happens to all dedica-

This is a superb whitetail. But he'd probably not meet the minimum qualifying score for the records. Here's why. Record heads almost always carry five or more points to a side, unless symmetry, massiveness, and wide spread of over 21 inches drive up the score. A big whitetail buck's body width is about 15 inches and eartip-to-eartip spreads are 11 to 14 inches. Using these comparisons, it would appear that the spread of the rack in the photo would be 17 to 19 inches. Corresponding tines are uniformly long with the exception of the odd point. And the main beams are fairly massive. Though a fine head, this one is not a "record-book head."

ted deer hunters. If it didn't, there wouldn't be much thrill in going deer hunting.

Anyway, when we first sight a buck—if he's wearing a rack of noticeable size—we all jump to the conclusion that the antlers are larger than they really are. I'll be the first to admit that I've shot bucks I expected to be decent trophies, only to run to the kill site and find an animal wearing antlers far smaller than I expected. That's why—when a man spots a buck with an exceptional rack—he's apt to overestimate its dimensions. When such animals are missed they become the basis of the stories that begin with: "Today I missed the biggest buck in the state. I swear that old bruiser would rank near the top of the record book." Well, in reality, the deer probably wouldn't even have qualified for a low ranking.

This is a superb nontypical mule deer. For field estimation of trophy qualities it's safe to figure on an eartip-to-eartip spread of 17 inches. This would put this buck's spread at about 24 inches, or about average for record-book mule deer in both the typical and the nontypical categories. In the nontypical category, lengths of points in addition to the brow tines and two "Ys" on each side are added to the score. In the typical category, lengths of extra points are subtracted. Another rule of thumb: If the spread looks about half again as wide as the body and the general sweep of each antler equals the spread, you may be looking at a record.

Again, most hunters just don't realize how massive a buck's rack has to be to be good enough for record-book status. My latest realization of this fact came during my 1975 whitetail hunt in south Texas. During this hunt I stopped at Lionel Garza's Texaco station in the town of Freer.

Lionel runs the annual "Muy-Grande" contest which recognizes outstanding whitetail bucks killed in Texas. Garza is dedicated to the sport of trophy hunting. His displays of mounted heads and racks, which were taken by many hunters, cover the walls of his station and a special trophy building behind the station. In addition, he has photos of all the outstanding bucks entered in his contests. Visit Garza's station and you'll be overwhelmed with the evidence of enormous whitetail bucks. Yet, of all those mounted heads, only one was good enough to make the record book.

Antlers and diet. Before I get into telling you what to look for when trying to decide if a trophy buck is good enough to shoot, I want to mention a
factor that has an effect on antler development. I've pointed out that deer
develop largely on the basis of what they eat. But how much they eat is
also important.

How much they eat depends on weather. If a given year in a given area
comes up with an early spring, plenty of rain during the summer and a late
fall, the area will produce deer with larger than average racks simply because the animals had plenty of nutritious browse during a long period.

In northern states, where deer are subject to extreme physical hardships
during severe winters, weather adds another dimension. If the winter is
tough and long-lasting, antler development will get a slow start in spring,
not only because a buck's physical condition is poor, but also because the
new foods he needs are slower than usual in growing. Top that with an
early fall and the year simply doesn't produce enough days to promote
good growth of browse. Just as farmers experience poor years for crop
growth, so a buck experiences poor years for antler growth. This is the reason there are years of good heads and years of poor heads.

*Here are four young mule deer bucks. Since just-decent mule deer racks
tend to stand higher than those of spectacular whitetails, eastern hunters
after record mule deer for the first time tend to be very impressed with the
first few mule deer bucks they see. Experience and study of exceptional
racks help bring evaluations nearer reality.*

Judging heads. There *are* methods of judging the quality of antlers before you shoot. A beginning hunter should keep in mind the difference in size of mule deer racks compared with whitetail racks. As I have pointed out earlier, a whitetail buck boasting antlers measuring 20 inches across the outside spread is really an excellent trophy. But a mule deer's rack measuring 20 inches would hardly rate notice in big-buck country.

If a buck's body is aligned straight toward you or straight away from you, the accepted procedure for estimating antler quality is to compare the width of the rack with the width of parts of the animal's body. The body width of a big whitetail will measure about 15 inches across. This means that even if you manage only a fleeting glimpse of a whitetail wearing antlers wider than his body you're looking at a very good trophy.

But this rule of thumb doesn't hold true with mule deer because a mule deer's rack has to be much wider than a whitetail's to rate as a trophy. The assumption is that a muley buck is a trophy if either antler overhangs the body by at least half the body width.

Another body feature used in trophy estimation is a buck's ears. With ears cocked the eartip-to-eartip measurement on whitetails is 11 to 14 inches. The same measurement on mule deer is 16 to 18 inches. So if you see a buck of either species with a rack spreading far out beyond his ears you better nail him, especially if he's a whitetail.

The familiar white flag (tail) of a whitetail is also a comparison feature. Since this flag is often raised when a buck is running it's a dominant feature. If its length is comparable with the height of the buck's antlers the rack is likely to be a great one.

This trick won't work with a mule-deer buck because he has a stingy little tail that he doesn't raise, and also because the trophy rack of a mule deer measures far higher than a whitetail's. The measurement to consider on a broadside muley is the animal's body height from withers to brisket. If the height of the rack approaches the withers-to-brisket dimension he's a beauty.

TROPHY FIELD CARE AND MOUNTING

Once your trophy buck is down there are several things that must be done properly before the mounted head will end up as one you'll be proud of. The first consideration is the correct removal of the cape. Don't cut your buck's throat or make any incision in the neck skin. To do so would seriously hamper your taxidermist in preparing a lifelike mount. It's necessary to leave intact much more neck skin than you'd think would be necessary for a full head-and-neck mount. Most poorly mounted heads result because the taxidermist doesn't have enough cape to work with.

Start the job by making a cut through the skin beginning on top of the buck's head just behind the ears. Cut rearward along the top of the neck to

This is Doug Burris Jr. and some of his mule deer mounts. The head in the center, taken in 1972, ranks as the world record in the North American Big Game Awards Program. With only one abnormal point on its right antler, the head shows excellent symmetry, long points, good mass, and an extraordinary inside spread of $30^6/_8$ inches. The score: 226.

a point behind the front shoulders. Then make two vertical cuts—one down each side of the body—to a point where they meet. That point should be at least behind the brisket. Some taxidermists prefer to have these cuts meet just ahead of the forelegs. In any event, when you finish these cuts you'll realize that plenty of skin is required for a good mount.

The trick now is to get the head and cape removed from the rest of the carcass. Start peeling the skin at the point where your horizontal and vertical cuts meet behind the front shoulders. With the aid of a skinning knife, peel the flaps of skin away from the body toward the head. Continue until the freed skin is removed to the base of the skull. Then cut the head free of the carcass by cutting through the neck.

You should get your buck's head and cape to a taxidermist within a few days after the kill to eliminate spoilage. I once found this impossible to do, so I froze the head. I folded the cape, put the works in a cardboard box, sealed the box, and took it to my local meat-packing plant. The box remained in a freezer room for two months.

One definite advantage the modern deer hunter has over hunters of yesteryear is that good taxidermists are far more plentiful. They're far more professional, too. Most old deer heads you see in bars are poor mounts. The

Here are the general knife-blade lines for removal of the cape as described in the accompanying text. The key here is to give the taxidermist plenty of neck and shoulder skin to work with.

majority were done years ago by amateurs who took up taxidermy as a hobby or part-time job. Such shoddy work has been replaced by the extremely lifelike mounts produced by today's professionals who realize that they'll stay in business only if they do excellent work. And it's easier to do professional work now because of modern materials and methods.

Even so, you should check out your taxidermist. Look at his displays. Note how realistic they are. If you can't check him out personally, ask for his brochure and a list of references. Contact a couple of those references by phone. They'll tell you in a hurry if they're satisfied with the man's work. The key question to ask is how long it will take to get your head mounted. If the answer is a few weeks I'd advise looking for another tax-idermist. The good ones tan their hides before mounting them, and tanning takes time. You won't get a good mount unless the hide is tanned. Tanning is expensive, too. If a guy offers to mount your head for less than $100 you can expect a poor job.

One other thing to consider is where you're going to hang your mount. It's likely there will be one best spot on your office or den wall, and that the mount will look most dramatic if the head is turned either right or left with a curve in the neck. The old-fashioned way of mounting deer so the heads were high and looking straight forward is out. You have to decide which way the head should be turned, and you have to be sure to give these instructions to your taxidermist.

Still another detail to discuss with your taxidermist is how lifelike you want your buck to appear. Many taxidermists have beauty in mind more than reality. If you nail a real old buster of a buck he isn't going to be very pretty. Likely he'll have a torn ear, a grizzled snout, and a thick neck. Many taxidermists have a tendency to pretty up rugged features and make the finished job look more like the bucks you see in paintings. It's up to you to decide what you want. Personally, I prefer deer heads that are more on the rugged side. But be sure to discuss this point. If you don't, the odds are your taxidermist will lean toward a pretty deer.

The vast majority of deer hunters are not trophy hunters. Most have little or no knowledge of the Boone and Crockett Club records or the official scoring system. Consequently, many big bucks are shot and never scored because the hunters aren't aware of the excellence of their trophies. The most dramatic example of this is the current world-record typical whitetail. The antlers were discovered hanging on the wall of a bar near Sandstone, Minnesota. When the buck was killed, and by whom, is unknown. But some interested citizen noticed the enormous rack and had it officially scored. It totaled 206⅝ points.

So if you do come up with an enormous rack you owe it to yourself to see if you're due some recognition. Some states have big-buck clubs that recognize outstanding bucks taken within the state. Minimum score totals for state clubs are always lower than those specified by the Boone and Crockett Club. For information on state clubs write to the information-and-education division of your state's conservation department or department of natural resources.

In 1974 the Boone and Crockett Club and the National Rifle Association joined forces to conduct the big-game record keeping previously handled only by the Boone and Crockett Club. For information on obtaining score charts and on how to get your trophy buck scored write to the National Rifle Association, 1600 Rhode Island Avenue, N.W., Washington, D.C. 20036. By return mail you'll get the name and address of the official scorer living nearest you. Then it's up to you to contact him.

22

Your Attitude Makes the Difference

You would think a guy who has been hunting deer for over three decades would know better than to pull the dumb stunt I managed a couple of years ago.

It was late in our Michigan deer season. Everything had gone wrong. As the days wore on it began to look certain that I'd miss getting my buck for the first time in eleven years. That's the way it worked out, all because of the dumb stunt.

Ben Gregory, a local florist, his son-in-law Gerry, and my son Jack were also in the bad-luck category. None of us had had a shot all season. We decided to change our fortunes by hunting a new area.

"I know a place," Ben said. "It's one of the farm areas where I hunt rabbits. My beagle jumped two big bucks there one day last month. There's a creek bottom laced with alders and cedars. It's an ideal place for clever bucks to be hiding this late in the season. Tomorrow I'll put you guys on stands, then I'll try moving some deer."

Shortly after dawn Gerry, Jack and I were on stands overlooking tangles edging the creek. It took Ben a couple of hours to work his drive. None of us saw a deer.

Ben and Jack took other stands while Gerry and I drove a wider part of the heavy cover. Again, no deer.

We decided to separate and scout in various directions, then meet back at the jeep about noon. I went on down the creek, hunted some timbered hills, and finally angled back toward our vehicle, parked in an apple orchard. Just before entering the orchard I noted a thick stand of pines covering several acres in a stubble field off to my left. I was so discouraged I paid those pines no heed. I was convinced the area's deer had long since moved out.

Ben was leaning against the hood of his four-wheel-drive vehicle drinking coffee when I walked up. We were discussing our inability to find a single deer when the boys arrived. They hadn't seen a fresh track, but they didn't want to quit hunting.

"The only area we haven't covered is that stand of pines out in the field," Ben said. "There could be some deer bedded in there."

"I'll walk out to the edge of the orchard, take a look at those pines, and decide how we should drive it," I offered.

I had cased my rifle and put it in the vehicle moments before. The thought occurred to me that it would be smart to take it with me. But I was only going to walk about 50 yards. Besides, no self-respecting deer would be standing out in that stubble field.

I had barely made it to the edge of the orchard when nine whitetails burst out of the pines. They were running toward a wooded ravine to my left. Then they noticed me and stopped in their tracks.

The last two deer in the line were bucks. One wore a fine rack, the other was a forkhorn. They were only 150 yards away and there wasn't a twig between us. Without my rifle I felt as though I was practically undressed. I'd blown my entire deer season with one moment of negative attitude.

After mentioning this story several times to veteran deer hunters I was surprised to learn that similar incidents are not uncommon. All have involved a momentary negative attitude. Several guys told me they missed getting deer when they left rifles on their stands while moving off a short distance to answer a call of nature. Leaving a rifle in a vehicle while walking off to glass or inspect the surrounding countryside has cost many a man a fine shooting opportunity. So has putting a rifle aside while taking a smoke break or making a warming fire.

One time in Montana I was part of a five-man group of mule-deer hunters. We had parked our two vehicles in a clearing and were beginning to set up spotting scopes when a buck bounded through the opening. He was only 50 yards away but he might as well have been 50 miles because we'd left our rifles in the vehicles.

I'd bet that most deer hunters can recall incidents of seeing deer in places and at times they least expected to see them. The obvious cure for this sort of thing is to develop the positive attitude of expecting to see a buck at any time. Maintain this attitude and you'll never leave your rifle behind.

From what I've experienced in the deer country of many states I'd say that physical fitness definitely helps to develop the positive attitude necessary for successful hunting.

I learned my lesson the hard way during my first hunt in the mountains of the West. I thought I was in good shape, but I lost a trophy mule deer because I wasn't.

I spotted the buck feeding slowly across a logged-off clearing a half mile above me in Wyoming's Rockies. My binoculars showed a high and heavy rack on the deer. There was a thick stand of pines leading from my position all the way up to and around the clearing. Stalking cover was no problem. Six inches of snow on the ground would deaden the sounds of my approach. That buck was mine if I could make it up to the clearing before he fed across it and disappeared into cover. At the speed he was moving I figured I had no more than ten minutes to make the uphill hike.

By the time I made 250 yards my breath was coming in gasps. When I closed half the distance to the clearing my momentary rest stops were coming all too frequent, but I had to pause and pump air into my lungs because I wasn't in shape for fast climbing through snow at an altitude of 9,000 feet.

Still, I almost got that deer. When I reached the end of the cover I sneaked up behind a pine blow-down and peered over the tops of its dead branches. My buck was at the edge of the clearing, and he was scratching an ear with a hind hoof. By the time I got my scope on him he was just beginning to step into the timber. I was puffing so hard my rifle's barrel was waving all over the mountainside. My only chance was to shoot in a hurry. My bullet didn't touch the deer.

I'm certain that a little pre-hunt physical conditioning would have enabled me to reach that clearing in plenty of time for a steady shot. If you're in shape you can hunt harder and longer, have more fun doing it, and be more efficient.

Another thing I've noticed frequently is that certain groups of hunters seem to down more deer each fall than other groups which appear quite similar with respect to age and physical characteristics. I'm convinced the reason is compatibility. Hunting groups that share mutual desires and common goals develop good hunting plans which in turn promote better results. It's best to have companions who want to hunt in much the same manner as yourself, then your group will have an overall positive attitude because then there won't be any complaints.

I once hunted for several years with a group that went into a section of rugged back country with 4WD vehicles. It was federal land, open to public hunting and ideally suited for hunting whitetails with the driving technique. We were very successful at collecting venison because we got a kick out of getting into that country with 4WD's (it's practically inaccessible to walking hunters), we enjoyed the marvelous scenery, and we worked well as a team of drivers.

The group fell apart several seasons ago when the feds closed the area to vehicle travel. The common bonds that held us together and made us function as a smooth-running team were gone.

I have since done much of my Michigan hunting with an entirely different group of men who favor working from stands. As I got interested in hunting from a stand I came to the conclusion that it's a more productive technique than driving. As my interest developed so did my compatibility with my new group because we shared common desires. Developing a positive attitude was the natural result.

Somewhat along the same line is my conviction that many hunters don't have enough determination to be successful. I once kept a record spanning several years of my Michigan deer hunting. Noted were such things as number of days I hunted, deer seen (broken down into bucks, does, and fawns), number of shots taken, and number of deer bagged.

When I figured out the averages I discovered that I hunted 2.7 days to see one buck. It follows that the Michigan fellow who puts in one full day of unsuccessful hunting, then gets discouraged, is almost sure to develop a negative attitude at precisely the time he shouldn't. If he'd only realize that the odds say he'll see only one buck in nearly three days of hunting he might very well maintain a positive attitude.

Similar statistics will vary from state to state. In the mountain states, for example, it's been my experience to see up to two or three bucks per day in the better deer country. If a man knows what he's up against in terms of how many deer he's likely to see during a day's hunt he's less apt to develop a negative attitude. Too many hunters expect to see far more deer than the odds predict. It just doesn't work that way.

Doug Burris, Jr., of San Antonio, Texas, downed the world-record mule deer in Colorado's San Juan National Forest in 1972. I talked with Doug at length about his hunt, and I'll never forget his comments about how determination ties in with positive attitude. His common-sense statement came after I asked him about the weather during his hunt.

"It rained every day for three straight days," Burris said. "I had good rain gear, but when you hunt from dawn to dark in wet woods you're going to get at least partially wet no matter what you wear."

"Must have been miserable hunting," I opined.

"Yeah, but I'll tell you something," Burris emphasized. "You won't get 'em unless you stay out there with 'em."

Doug's mention of good rain gear leads to the all-important point of having adequate equipment. The guy that doesn't check his hunting clothes and gear until the day before the season opens is well on his way to developing a negative attitude while in the woods. The deer hunter whose boots leak or whose clothes won't keep him warm will give up much more easily than the man who stays dry and comfortable.

Sleeping bags, clothes, and other gear which haven't been properly selected can lead to all kinds of negative attitudes. It's best to avoid getting "bargains." Go with equipment of dependable quality and you'll be a lot happier on your hunt. Your chances of bagging a buck just about disappear when you can't keep your mind on hunting because of discomfort.

Another big thing that can ruin a man's morale when hunting deer is to miss a shot at a buck. Ask any deer guide or outfitter about the shooting ability of his clients and you'll likely hear something like this: "Most deer hunters seldom have more than the basic knowledge of how to hit with a rifle. They can't have because they won't spend the money or time to learn the correct techniques."

This is true, but it's also true that a lot of experts miss deer, too. Three years ago in Montana I was hunting whitetails with Dave Wedum, a man who spent many years as a guide and outfitter. At one point in our hunt we spotted a small buck of just the size Dave wanted for winter meat. Wedum dropped to one knee, leveled his rifle at the target standing 200 yards away, and touched one off. The buck leaped into high gear and ran around a ridge.

"I'll be darned, I missed him," Wedum said with a wry grin.

There are several conclusions about this incident that stand out. First, Dave didn't get all shook up because he missed. He had missed before and he'll miss again because it's easy to miss a deer whether you're an expert shot or not. Knowing this, Dave didn't let it effect his attitude the least bit. If you think it's almost a crime to miss a deer, forget it. Brood over it and you'll develop a negative attitude which will breed buck fever the next time you get a shot.

However, practice makes perfect applies as much to shooting skill as it does to anything else. If you do some practice shooting with your rifle before deer season opens you're bound to gain familiarity with your firearm. This breeds confidence, which in turn develops a positive attitude. The best shots don't expect to miss because they know their guns and they know what they're capable of, but they also know that no man can nail every buck he shoots at.

The same type of thinking should be applied to every other skill used in deer hunting. Only if you're enthusiastically motivated to sharpen your skills can you develop them to the point where you'll become more successful than most other hunters. And when you become more successful, you'll develop a positive attitude that will be hard to shake. This is why expert hunters continue to be experts. They know they've harvested a lot of deer and they know they'll harvest a lot more because they believe in themselves and their equipment.

Patience is another key to success which many hunters underrate. I'm still a member of the hurry-up group, but I'm not nearly as impatient as I used to be. Every time I feel a tendency to get a day's hunt moving faster, I reflect on an incident that occurred years ago.

Ben Gregory and I had driven to South Dakota to hunt pheasants, sharptail grouse, and deer. We were hunting with Ron Hoffman and Barry Betts. Both men were game biologists with the South Dakota Department of Game, Fish, and Parks.

Our schedule called for hunting birds for a few days before the deer season opened. It turned out that the upland gunning was so great we found it difficult to get charged up for deer hunting.

Still, Ron nailed a ten-point whitetail early on opening morning. Ben got an eight-point whitetail later in the day. Barry didn't have a permit to hunt deer that year, so I was the only guy left in the group with an unfilled deer tag. I wanted to get a deer in a hurry, so Ron decided he'd try helping me get my buck.

The next morning he took me into an area harboring lots of mule deer. In addition to many does we jumped one small forkhorn while stillhunting along the edges of brushy draws. When I shouldered my rifle to try for the buck Ron said, "We'll find something better than that."

Several times Ron told me I was walking too fast. One time after he got me slowed down we spotted a second small buck bedded in brush edging a dry pothole. I decided to take him.

"Go ahead," Ron said. "But it seems to me you give up awfully easy. You traveled a long way and spent a lot of money to hunt deer out here. If you'll develop a little patience we'll find a better trophy. The successful deer hunter is the guy who is willing to put up with a little waiting."

I felt pretty sheepish. I told Ron I was just trying to hurry things a bit.

"Never hurry when you're hunting deer," he answered. "When you're stillhunting you have to spend quite a bit of time getting in tune with what's going on in the area around you. By this I mean you can blunder around while hunting birds and get shooting, but you're not going to see deer unless you fit into the rhythms of surrounding outdoor activity. You can't expect to get a buck unless he's unaware of your presence until you have a shooting opportunity. To do this you have to be so quiet you can startle game. And the only way you can do that is by not making unnatural noises. That's why I have the patience to stillhunt slowly. If we keep it up we'll get your buck."

We did. Late in the afternoon we spotted a fine three-pointer bedded in a very narrow gully of rocks. We had approached the gully so quietly and slowly the deer was unaware of us. All I had to do was stalk him from behind the cover of some low brush. I must not have disturbed the rhythms of the area's activity one iota because I sneaked to within 100 yards of that buck and he still wasn't aware of me. He died in his bed without knowing what hit him.

This incident probably had as much to do with Ron's knowledge of local deer habits as it did with his theories on patience. His attitude was extremely positive because he knew the tendencies of deer in his area and he knew the type of range they were using. You can get the same type of knowledge by reading everything you can find on deer hunting, going into your deer woods as often as possible, and talking with local experts. When you gain a lot of knowledge it's almost impossible to have a negative attitude. After all, the guys who have the most knowledge about any given field usually come out on top because they have what it takes to be winners.

Through the years I've come to one conclusion about attitude that overrides all others: there's a world of difference between a meat hunter and a deer hunter. The true deer hunter goes afield because he has the *desire* to enjoy everything he sees from brilliant sunrises in wild country to blizzards swirling at dusk. He enjoys everything he hears from the sounds of wildlife to the conversations of compatible companions. He enjoys everything he touches—from a treasured rifle to the hot handle of a pot of campfire coffee. In short, his senses are attuned to the joys of deer hunting simply because he has a tremendous desire to participate.

Uppermost in the mind of the meat hunter is venison. He wants it any way he can get it and as soon as possible. For this type of man the killing of deer becomes more a business than a sport. Anyone who doesn't like what he's doing doesn't do well at it.

Warren Holmes, one of the most successful deer hunters I know, hates venison. When he was a small boy his grandfather forced him to eat a deer steak. It made him sick. From that day on he hasn't tasted the meat.

But he loves deer hunting because he desires the thrills he finds in the sport. He gets a buck every year because of his extremely positive attitude, even though the meat is enjoyed by other members of his family. Warren gets deer because he enjoys hunting so much he never wants to quit. When you develop that type of desire your odds on succeeding go way up.

23

How to Get Hotspot Information

Modern deer-management programs have been so successful that there is now good deer hunting in all of our forty-eight contiguous states. This surely doesn't mean you'll get action in any patch of woodland you may select to hunt. You have to search out the best areas. If you haven't made determined efforts to find the choice hunting locations there can be little doubt that some topnotch hunting exists in places relatively close to your home.

The explosion of whitetail herds into farming country has offered excellent hunting in areas where there were no deer as recently as ten years ago. Plenty of fine bucks are now harvested within a few miles of some of our larger towns and cities. Deer aren't everywhere, but they can be almost anywhere. Your job is to find them.

Regardless of where you live, or the type of terrain you hunt, you can locate top deer areas if you use certain techniques. Even if you make a trip into a distant state you have never hunted you can find deer hotspots. One of the best systems to use in strange country might be called "buying information."

You don't really buy information, you get it as a byproduct when you buy something else. The idea is to purchase a good share of your hunting needs when you get into the area you're going to hunt. The average nonresident hunter purchases most of his needs at home, thereby eliminating any chance of utilizing the technique of buying information. It works like this:

Say you go into a sporting-goods store in unfamiliar country and you buy only a hunting license. The merchant could care less about how your hunt turns out because he makes next to nothing from sales of hunting licenses. Suppose, on the other hand, that in addition to your license you also purchase some ammunition, new socks and gloves, a shirt or sweater, fuel for your camp lantern, or any one of dozens of other items.

When you do this the average merchant takes a lot more interest in you because he's putting your money into his cash register. If he happens to be a hunter he'll have current information on hotspots, condition of back-country roads, camping areas, and all sorts of helpful details. He'll know the names of guides and landowners. And if he gets enough of your money he may become quite free with good advice.

The most dramatic experience I've had with this sort of thing occurred several years ago when I was on a hunt in Wyoming. I was the guest of a rancher who showed me a great time with antelope and mule deer. I got my buck antelope the first day of the hunt, and I scored on a three-point mule deer the second day. The next morning we took my field-dressed and skinned animals to a local processing plant.

When we drove up to the plant we parked behind a pickup truck that was half loaded with antelope and mule-deer bucks. It was an astonishing sight. I don't think I've ever seen so much legal game piled in one spot. It seemed obvious that a group of local hunters—wise in the ways of hunting the area—had driven in to get their animals butchered by the plant operator who most likely was a good friend.

Then I noticed that the truck bore Wisconsin license plates. I was intrigued immediately with the situation. How, I wondered, did out-of-state hunters score so well in strange country? The answer most likely was that they had been hunting this area for many seasons and that they had an "in" with a local rancher whose property harbored a surplus of game. Still, I wanted to find out if my assumption was correct. So I struck up a converstion with the Wisconsin men.

"You fellows sure did well," I said to one member of the five-man group. "Have you been hunting out here many years?"

"No," he said with a grin. "We were just very lucky. This is our first trip to Wyoming. All we had when we left home was our nonresident licenses, a few basic items of clothing, and camping gear, and our rifles. We didn't know what we'd run into because we didn't have any experience with this country. So we decided to get local advice when we bought supplies and the equipment we'd need.

"We were lucky enough to pick a sporting-goods store owned by a guy who had hunting access to several ranches. By the time we finished buying ammunition, some hunting clothes, a few camping supplies, and odds and ends, the man was quite concerned about the success of our trip. He not only got us permission to camp on a ranch, but he told us where to camp and how to hunt the area. We had great success because we were lucky enough to go into that store. We've already made arrangements to hunt out here next year."

These fellows were lucky in a way, but the real reason they were so successful is that they "bought" prime information according to the principle I mentioned earlier. It's a principle that will work wherever you go.

Another trick along the same line can be used near your home. It involves little more than buying something from landowners. Farmers often sell produce from their gardens during the summer. Some sell fire wood year-round. Some are part-time machinists, mechanics, painters, or handymen. The point is that if you buy something from these men you make new contacts in the process. If you're good at developing these contacts you'll eventually get on fine terms with landowners who might have great deer-hunting potential on their property.

Don't overlook the possibility of finding farmers or ranchers who are having problems with crows, coyotes, barnyard pigeons, or other pests. Many of these men will welcome you if you suggest helping control their pest problems with off-season shooting. And, of course, while you're doing the off-season hunting you should also be looking for deer sign. I've found some excellent deer-hunting areas while I was crow shooting during spring and summer.

The rule is to keep your eyes and ears open no matter where you go in rural areas at any time during the year. I've stumbled onto deer hotspots while trout fishing along brushy creeks, picking mushrooms in the spring, and walking into flooded timber enroute to jumpshoot ducks. I mark such spots on a map and check them out for deer prospects just before the season opens.

I have a local deer-hunting friend who finds potential hunting country from an airplane. He has a buddy who is a pilot, so he gets his plane rides for free. The important thing is that he uses a system for his scouting from the air. He times his flights for late winter or early spring while there is still snow on the ground. It's remarkable how easily deer can be seen from a relatively low-flying plane when the ground is white and trees have no leaves. The system is significant in whitetail country because these animals usually live their entire lifetimes in about one square mile. If you spot whitetails in early spring they'll often be somewhere in the same area when fall comes.

When my friend spots a concentration of deer—they'll most often still be herded while snow remains on the ground—he marks the location on a map so he can find the precise area from the ground. Anybody can use this technique by paying for plane rides. Most small-plane pilots will fly you over a lot of country for about $10.

In this day of rapid change in the economy, a good many of us find ourselves changing jobs and moving our residences into unfamiliar country. When we do this we have no idea of where the best deer hunting may be. If I moved to another state in which I didn't know any outdoorsmen I would write a letter to my new state's conservation department and ask for the name and address of the department's deer specialist. After I got this dope I would write the specialist and ask for general information on the state's deer-hunting picture. I would point out that I was a new resident and that I had to start from scratch in learning about hunting opportunities.

All state conservation departments now have deer specialists who have a wealth of information. These men work with statistics concerning deer herds and deer-hunting success year-round. They have results of hunter surveys, deer population centers, and similar information for all areas of their states. A lot of this information is often available in leaflets, booklets, or other printed forms. It's very possible that one letter of inquiry will get you more general deer-hunting information than you could dig up on your own over several years.

Some of the dope you get can be truly amazing. Many states now have special maps showing deer concentration areas. Some states have devoted entire issues of conservation-department magazines to deer hunting and deer management. In addition to maps and general information, many of these magazines list deer harvests by county. Such lists need little more than a glance to clue you in on where deer hunting is likely to be great.

Further, many conservation department deer specialists can suggest other sources of information on where to go. Texas may top the list for information in this category. As I write these lines I have on my desk the following three publications:

1975 Hunters' Guide To Texas. This 185-page book has 16 chapters devoted to Texas deer hunting. It has hundreds of names and addresses of ranchers and farmers who offer hunting for a fee by day, week, or year. It covers all of the state's hunting regulations and is full of other details the deer hunter needs to know. You can order a copy of the book from The Pemberton Press, 1 Pemberton Parkway, Austin, Texas 78767. The book costs $4.95.

1975–76 Texas Hunter's Directory. This 130-page book sells for $2.75 and lists over 1,000,000 acres of free hunting in addition to more than 400 lease listings. It also contains outstanding articles on deer hunting and lists the state's 1974 deer harvest statistics by county. You can order the book from Outdoor Worlds, 2909 North Buckner, Suite 104, Dallas, Texas 75228.

Texas Hunters Hotline. This is a magazine published quarterly by the Texas Trophy Hunters Association, P.O. Box 29327, San Antonio, Texas 78229. Most of the material in the magazine is devoted to Texas deer hunting.

Other states and regions of the country often have private sources of information that are separate from or in addition to conservation department sources. Many states now have big-buck clubs that publish newsletters. Regional outdoor magazines are often a big help. Don't overlook guide or outfitter associations. In any event, when you make contact with your state's deer specialist be sure to ask him if he knows of other sources of deer-hunting information that may be useful to you.

Such sources of information can be windfalls to the modern deer hunter. Consider that the old-timers had nowhere to turn when they wanted dope on how to find the best hunting areas. They had to depend on locating good areas on their own.

Here are some other ways of getting leads on where the deer are:

Always remember that 20 percent of all hunters in any given area bag 80 percent of all game harvested. This small part of the hunting population represents the local experts. No matter where you may go in deer country there are always experts who know the local situation intimately. If you can establish good friendships with some of these men your problem of finding deer will just about evaporate. How do you get these guys to reveal their hotspot secrets?

A top bet is to join a local sportsman's club. Get involved in the work projects and show real enthusiasm. Once you're accepted as a dedicated worker you're likely to make friends with dedicated deer hunters. When you reach this point you won't have much trouble getting into discussions loaded with deer-hunting where-to and how-to information.

You can also work on getting names of local deer-hunting experts from the better sporting-goods dealers. Such dealers come into frequent contact with their area's top outdoorsmen. You may or may not strike it rich when you introduce yourself to these veteran hunters. If you're a knowledgeable hunter in your own right your past experiences may be food for discussions which will lead to fine friendships. Keep in mind that some deer-hunting groups may be looking for new members.

Never forget that your local conservation officer knows where the deer are because he's in the field year-round. And public relations is part of his job. You will draw a blank trying to get information from a local expert who wants to keep his secrets to himself, but your officer generally will answer your questions to the best of his ability.

Not only will he tell you about deer-concentration areas but he'll offer information concerning public hunting grounds, special hunting problems, tips on hunting technique, and so forth. You can get the same sort of advice from forest rangers. In some states you'll find county extension agents or their counterparts are good bets. You'd be wise to make contact with any county, state or federal employee whose work keeps him outdoors in deer country year-round. These guys know where the deer are, and as public servants they're expected to help you as much as they can.

Another way to get good information is employing what I call the "looking-for-evidence technique." Here are a couple of examples of how the technique works.

A deer-hunting friend of mine once wanted to build a cabin in some of Michigan's best whitetail country. He selected several possible areas, then he spent a good deal of time during one hunting season traveling to the small-town deer-processing plants in the areas. He talked with the operators and asked questions as to the numbers of whitetails processed, what percentage of the animals were big bucks, and whether the numbers of deer processed were increasing or decreasing in recent years. He built his cabin in the area that appeared to have the most deer and a good proportion of trophy bucks. Since then he has scored extremely well.

Another hunter I know asks his state's deer specialist for statistics on how many deer were checked through each of the state's deer-check stations during the previous season. Such information helps him determine which areas of the state hold the largest herds. This fellow uses his summer vacations for camping with his family in these areas. One of his major objectives during camping trips is to scout for deer runways, feeding areas, and bedding areas. By the time deer season opens he knows exactly where he'll hunt.

Another way of looking for evidence is to look for potential deer hotspots by studying maps. Maps can be fine starting points for pinpointing land features that are likely to harbor deer. I'll discuss the use of maps for deer in Chapter 24.

There is still another way to get good deer-hunting information, but it will work for you only if you live within easy driving distance of rural neighborhoods. In these areas it has become popular to stage rural church dinners as money-raising projects. Tickets are always available to the public.

Go to one of these affairs and you'll meet lots of farmers and landowners. And you'll meet them while you're cleaned up and neatly dressed. Take your wife and kids along to establish the fact that you're a respectable family man. Strike up conversations about just about anything except serious hunting. Save that pitch until you get quite well acquainted. Concentrate on making new friends while enjoying a delightful evening. Eventually, such contacts can easily lead to great tips on where to find deer. It's even possible that you'll hit it off with a landowner who will invite you to hunt with him on his private property. A landowner who hunts his own spread knows exactly where the deer are and he knows how to hunt them. You can't get a better deal than that.

24

Maps Can Work Wonders

A few years ago, in wild tangled country in northern Michigan, a deer hunter walked away from his camp on an overcast morning. He jumped and followed a deer in an area heavily tracked up earlier by other members of his party.

Several hours later, worn out from hiking through swamps and across ridges in deep snow, he lost the deer track and started back to camp.

He was no beginner. He had hunted deer for the better part of twenty years and knew his way around the woods. But he was in country he had never seen until that November, and he had made the grave mistake of not looking at a map at the start of his hunt. He was carrying a compass, but had only the vaguest notion of where he was and which way to go.

He ran out of matches the first night, slept under logs after that without a fire, circling, wandering, lost in swamps and beaver ponds. He staggered out of the woods onto a road at the end of seventy-two terrible hours. He came out only six miles from camp, but had traveled more than thirty miles to get there. He came very close to freezing to death, all for want of taking a good look at a map in the beginning.

That ordeal serves perfectly to illustrate the most common and urgent reason deer hunters need maps if they are planning a trip in unfamiliar territory. Similar stories are read in newspapers each fall. But not getting lost is far from the only reason for utilizing good maps. Consider the following letters I've received because of my position as a staff editor of *Outdoor Life:*

"I've heard about the great deer hunting near the Marais des Cygnes waterfowl area and I'd like to hunt there next fall," writes a Kansas reader. "Some of the area is closed to hunting. I've never been there. Where can I get a map of the area?"

Here's a similar letter from a Minnesota reader.

"I've read that Minnesota's northeastern counties harbor a lot of deer. I want to hunt there next fall. I've heard that the region is rugged wilderness and I'll surely need a good map of the area. Where can I get one?"

Here's another inquiry from a reader that is almost word for word like dozens of letters in my files:

"I've dreamed for years of going deer hunting in Colorado. My two partners and I have decided this is the year. We want to hunt the western part of the state. Where are the best locations and where can I get maps of the areas?"

That deer hunter's problem is typical of an ever-growing segment of outdoorsmen, especially deer hunters, who want detailed information on where the action is outside their home states. Letters flow in asking for information on map sources in many states and provinces.

I can get accurate answers to most where-to-go questions because I work closely with state fish-and-game officials throughout North America. But answers to questions regarding availability of specific maps often stumped me.

Recently I decided that I knew far too little about the subject. I wondered just how many types of maps are available to outdoorsmen. How good are they? Who distributes them? How much do they cost? What's the latest word in maps that will benefit deer hunters?

To find out, I conducted an in-depth investigation. I sent lengthy questionnaires to state, federal, and private agencies in the United States and Canada. I asked for specific information on various types of maps that are of value to hunters, and where outdoorsmen could get those maps.

My mailbox was soon loaded with maps of all descriptions. A resulting study of the piles of material revealed that there are far more maps available (many for free distribution) than I had imagined. You should know about these maps. The facts I dug up are so interesting that I'm devoting an entire chapter to the subject of maps.

THE OVERALL PICTURE

I was surprised to learn that many state fish-and-game departments have taken a new attitude on maps, an attitude that you'll be happy to hear about.

"Everyone seems to be map-conscious these days," one official in a western state told me. "Our department is well aware that we haven't been able to supply the outdoorsman with the specific type of maps he needs. Frankly, we've just never had the money to publish all the maps, directories, and charts that the public wants.

"The answer is for state game-and-fish departments to cooperate with federal and private agencies in map production and distribution. We can supply hunting and fishing information—the other agencies can supply engineers, artists, and map-making facilities. The results would be maps that sportsmen would have real use for. That's the direction we're heading in."

So are other states. Here's what the Chief of Information and Education for South Dakota's Department of Game, Fish and Parks told me:

"Our department is currently working with the U.S. Forest Service and the Bureau of Land Management on a series of nine recreation maps. The maps are scaled at a half-inch to the mile. They'll cover approximately 3.5 million acres of state and federal public land. With the exception of obvious places like the Black Hills, most South Dakotans are unaware of these holdings. The maps are a boon to deer hunters looking for new places to hunt. They are available from our department office in the State Office Building in Pierre, 57501."

An official from another state said to me:

"Right now there isn't any substitute for the U.S. Geological Survey quadrangles when it comes to helping the deer hunter. These maps show topography (relief features and surface configuration) like no other map shows. But our game-land maps (hotspot areas) show the best hunting and game-concentration lands, again something no other map shows. We're superimposing game-land maps onto topo maps. These maps are ideal because they show the best hunting areas and exact terrain conditions."

Private enterprise also is recognizing the ever-growing demand by outdoorsmen for accurate maps. Here's what C. Ross Anderson, President of AAA Engineering and Drafting Company in Salt Lake City, Utah told me:

"After years of preparing relatively useless recreation maps for various government agencies, our company launched a private mapping program. We cooperate with every private, state and federal agency that can supply information that answers real needs for the sportsmen. We are working very closely with park services, forest services, U.S. Geological Survey, Bureau of Land Management, state highway departments, tourist and publicity councils, chambers of commerce, snowmobile associations, etc.

"We have produced several maps of areas in western states. These maps are indexed to show best action areas, campsites, public lands, accommodations, boat ramps, and just about everything a sportsman wants to know. We hope to produce similar maps covering other areas of the nation. A lot of the information on these maps is excellent for deer hunters."

Another map producer, Clarkson Map Company, produces special recreation maps designed for outdoorsmen in the Midwest. The company has produced several different books of hydrographic (depth contour) lake maps covering the most popular fishing lakes in Michigan, Wisconsin and Minnesota. Another of their productions is a book of maps covering every county in Michigan. These maps show dozens of legends including campgrounds, roads, trails and conservation department units. Similar books of maps cover Wisconsin and Minnesota. You can get details by writing the company at 725 Desnoyer Street, Kaukauna, Wisconsin 54130.

Government agencies are also publishing special-use maps. A good example is the U.S. Bureau of Sport Fisheries and Wildlife map of Waterfowl Production Areas in the Midwest. That agency is responsible for the purchase and easement of 300 areas totaling 103,516 acres of wetlands in North Dakota. The areas are managed to provide the most favorable conditions for duck reproduction and to provide hunting opportunities for waterfowl, upland birds and deer. The areas are open to free hunting and are not to be confused with refuges. You can get these maps by writing the Division of Wildlife Refuges, Federal Building, Fort Snelling, Twin Cities, Minnesota 55111.

WHY ARE GOOD MAPS SO IMPORTANT?

Obvious examples are state highway maps. You wouldn't think of driving your automobile through unfamiliar states without road maps. Yet many deer hunters head into areas where they've never been and they don't even think about getting maps that would help their hunting activities. That's a major mistake. I learned the lesson well many years ago while hunting deer in Saskatchewan.

My partner Bob and I found that our hit-and-miss hunting of woodlots and swales wasn't very productive. One day we drove into a tiny town to find lunch and we walked into the hamlet's only restaurant. We sat down next to a booth holding four exuberant stateside hunters. Their luck with whitetails had been great. Bob and I couldn't help wincing as we overheard their talk of seeing lots of deer.

Finally we could stand no more. We introduced ourselves and hinted that we sure would like to know where we could find some bucks.

"No problem," grinned one of the hunters. "We found a hotspot this morning that's loaded with deer. We didn't spook those animals much because we only needed one buck to fill our take-out limits."

"Great," exclaimed Bob, "where do we go?"

"About 10 miles northwest. You might have a problem getting there because it's off the highway, way back in over a series of back roads. I'll draw you a map."

A few minutes later it was obvious that the hunter couldn't draw a reliable map because he couldn't recall the locations of many crossroads and landmarks. We asked the proprietor of the restaurant for an area road map. He didn't have one. I went across the street to a gasoline station and found no maps of any kind. We were licked.

Our new friends did their best to explain how to get to the area. But Bob and I never found it though we spent hours in the search. For the lack of a simple map we probably missed out on a great adventure.

Another time I was in Manitoba on a camping deer hunt when my Cree Indian guide decided we should follow some fresh deer tracks. We paid a lot more attention to those tracks than to the direction we were going. An hour later we jumped the animals but they crashed away unseen in the thickets. The guide decided to take a short-cut back to where we had parked our canoe along the bank of a small creek.

Two hours later we hadn't found the canoe and I figured we were lost. Three hours after that the guide finally admitted he didn't have the slightest idea of where we were. The only thing I knew for sure was that we were at least 10 miles from the closest road and 20 miles from the nearest town. We knew we would be in serious trouble if we didn't find that canoe.

Late in the afternoon we stumbled out of the bush onto the bank of a large river. The guide breathed a grunt of relief and said, "That's our river, but current going wrong way."

Soon he decided that the current was going the same way it always had, but that we had been traveling west instead of east. We walked downstream along the bank for a mile before the guide suddenly recognized a landmark. We were out of trouble then and we walked almost straight to the canoe. I've often wondered what would have happened if I'd been by myself in that totally unfamiliar wilderness.

I later obtained a topographic map of the area, and I was able to trace the progress of our misguided journey. If I'd had that map when we became lost I could have saved a day's anxiety with a simple compass reading. I've never gone into any wilderness since without a map or maps covering the area I was going to hunt.

That logic was emphasized in many replies to the questionnaires I sent out asking about the value of maps. Denton H. Hartley, Chief of Information and Education for the New Hampshire Fish and Game Department, was particularly impressed with the lost-hunter problem. Here's what he said:

"Just ask a natural-resource warden or conservation officer in any state or province whether he wished sportsmen knew more about maps and listen to the answer. Lots of deer hunters get lost in the woods, but their number is small compared with those who are lost before they ever enter the woods. Plenty of gunners drive down old roads running in various directions, see a likely looking spot, get out, and start hunting. They don't know what road they're on, where it goes, or which way is north. It's amazing to me that many outdoorsmen don't even carry highway maps."

Maps are especially efficient in planning deer drives. I once joined a group of Wisconsin hunters who consider their topographic maps indispensable, not only for a successful hunt but also as safety tools.

Before a drive begins a map of the area is spread out. Each hunter is shown (by landmark features on the map) where the drive will originate, where it will end, and where each posted hunter will be standing. Because of the map each member of the group knows exactly where to go and what area he should cover. The military-type planning pays off with lots of venison.

Good maps are also perfect tools for deer hunters trying to discover back-country regions that are naturals for feeding, bedding, and runway areas. Whatever your reason for getting off the beaten track you'll find that maps are your best planning aids.

Another great advantage of carrying maps is that local people can point out hotspot locations. Many times I've had filling-station attendants, farmers, and resort operators pinpoint choice hunting areas when I pulled a map out of my pocket.

Maps also have a value as souvenirs of hunting trips. They're great for helping to explain to friends where you were, what terrain conditions you found, and where you killed your buck. A map brings back memories in a hurry and helps you relive all of the excitement.

Finding an all-purpose map covering a specific area is practically impossible. But several maps of the same area obtained from various sources can supply you with a wealth of valuable details. George A. Kaminski, Information and Education Chief for Wyoming's Game and Fish Commission, summed it up well when he told me this:

"Our commission is obligated to put out maps that clarify deer-hunting regulations and the areas of the state to which they pertain. They are economically designed for mass distribution and they show little more than where a sportsman may hunt.

"But once a man selects his area he can turn to other agencies for detailed terrain information. The Bureau of Land Management, the U.S. Geological Survey, and the U.S. Forest Service are the best bets for maps showing topographic features and public ownership boundaries.

"Highway department maps emphasize all types of roads, driving distances, and locations of towns. County maps go into detail on local trails, streams, and woodlands. If a sportsman has all those maps he has the finest information available."

FEDERAL MAPS

The topographic sheets are sold for a small sum by the U.S. Geological Survey. These maps are approximately 16½x20 inches and are drawn to scales from one-half inch to two inches per mile, depending on the character of the country charted. Bodies of water are printed in blue, man-made features in black, and features of relief (hills, mountains, and valleys) are indicated by brown contour lines. Woodlands show up in green. These maps are the best available for sportsmen wanting to know the lay of the land.

Topographic maps are produced for all areas of the U.S. that have been surveyed. Begin by requesting free index maps on the states of interest. These indexes will show areas covered by quadrangular maps and prices of each. To order maps east of the Mississippi River, including Minnesota, write Branch of Distribution, U.S. Geological Survey, 1200 South Eads St., Arlington, VA 22202. For maps west of the Mississippi, including Alaska and Louisiana, write Branch of Distribution, U.S. Geological Survey, Federal Center, Denver, CO 80225.

The U.S. Forest Service publishes maps of lake and forest regions in the various national forests. Write the U.S. Forest Service, Washington, D.C. 20250 for a key map that shows areas covered. That index lists regional offices where you can obtain the detailed maps that interest you.

The Bureau of Land Management (B.L.M.) is a top bet for maps showing lands open to public hunting. Most of the maps are printed in colors denoting public lands, Forest Service lands, state lands, game-and-fish department lands, national wildlife refuges, and private lands. These maps are a boon for sportsmen looking for action areas in the midwestern and western states holding large acreages of public-access lands.

Many of the B.L.M. maps cover entire states, but some are limited to sections of states and these maps carry an amazing wealth of detail. They show all roads (by special symbols), from paved highways down to trails suited only for seasonal travel by four-wheel-drive vehicles. They show power lines, creeks, marshes, township boundaries, railroad tracks, and just about anything else that can be identified. One of these maps, combined with a Geological Survey map of the same area, would give a deer hunter a better picture of the land than an aerial photograph. Write the U.S. Department of Interior, Bureau of Land Management, Washington, D.C. 20240 for details and an index of available maps.

CANADIAN TOPO MAPS

To order Canadian topo maps in various scales from one inch to ¾ mile and from one inch to about 4 miles, request instructions from the Canada Map Office, 615 Booth St., Ottawa, Ontario, Canada KIA OE9.

SPECIFIC HOTSPOT MAPS

Although topographic and other terrain-feature maps give you a clear picture of the physical characteristics of a given area, they can't give you any information on hunting hotspots. That information has to come from local sources or game-and-fish officials who are close to the scene in their individual states or provinces. Some conservation departments have done a remarkable job of reducing their best hunting information down to maps and charts.

An official in Nebraska's Game and Parks Commission told me:

"Hunting maps are exceedingly difficult to keep up to date because of the fluctuation of prime hunting areas from year to year. But we do publish pamphlets showing general hotspot areas. The pamphlets include maps of the state showing which sections harbor the highest numbers of deer. With this map a hunter could pinpoint one of the best counties for his hunting area."

Some of the best aids to Minnesota hunters are fire-plan maps. What's a fire-plan map? It's a map drawn from aerial photos and designed primarily to aid in fire prevention and control. It shows all roads, lakes, streams, trails, railroad grades, ponds, and other details including power-transmission lines. Most of the maps cover a 36 square-mile area. The scale is two inches to one mile.

Minnesota's Departments of Natural Resources and Administration are cooperating to make these maps available to sportsmen. They cover most wooded areas of the state and sell for 50 cents each. You can get an index of the maps by writing: Documents Section, 140 Centennial Building, St. Paul, MN 55101.

Several excellent maps are available covering Minnesota's famous Boundary Waters Canoe Area. A map folder listing canoe routes and other useful information on the entire Superior National Forest is available free from: Supervisor, Superior National Forest, Box 338, Duluth, MN 55801.

"In Kansas we have a good number of maps on public hunting areas," said Thayne Smith, a veteran deer hunter from Wichita. "We get maps from various agencies—U.S. Army Corps of Engineers; Bureau of Reclamation; Kansas Park Authority; the Forestry, Fish and Game Commission; and others.

"Our commission game-management area maps, designed principally for hunters, cover most of the state's thirty-plus areas. They're very detailed, showing open-hunting lands, roads, streams, camping areas, and so forth. The back side of these maps carries text explaining best hunting techniques, pertinent regulations, and other details that will help the sportsman enjoy himself."

From the foregoing statements it's obvious that it's a good idea to direct all your questions about maps to the Information and Education Division in the Conservation Department of the state you're interested in. If they don't have a particular map in supply they'll know where to get it. Here's another example of what I mean:

"We keep a batch of material that falls under the heading of maps," says Joel Vance of the Missouri Department of Conservation. "Some of it is published by other organizations such as the U.S. Forest Service, the U.S. Army Corps of Engineers, and the Upper Mississippi River Conservation Commission.

"I'd say that Missouri is very well mapped from a deer hunter's standpoint. Outdoorsmen can obtain any of the maps I'm talking about by writing to: Information Department, Missouri Department of Conservation, P.O. Box 180, Jefferson City 65101."

Here's still another viewpoint from a western state:

"Our Game and Fish Department publishes very few maps because so many good ones are available from other sources." That's the word I got from that agency's public-relations chief.

"Whenever someone asks for the best deer hunter's map available I tell them to contact the State Highway Department," he told me. "I'm not talking about road maps. I'm referring to individual county maps that the highway people publish. These maps show remarkable detail, down to seldom-used trails and abandoned farm buildings. They're far more complete than regular highway maps. They sell for 50 cents to $1, depending on size.

"A good bet for particular areas is the state forest maps put out by several colleges and forestry schools in the West. They contain symbols denoting public lands open to hunting, parks closed to hunting and refuges. Lakes, roads, creeks and boundary lines are all detailed.

"Another fine map (published by the U.S. Department of Agriculture in Missoula, Montana) shows public hunting areas in most western states.

"In addition to those publications I'd suggest the Geological Survey and B.L.M. maps. They're hard to beat. Any state conservation agency can tell you where to get maps."

LOCAL MAPS

No matter where you go it's a good bet that chambers of commerce, guide associations, and sporting-goods stores will have maps offering great detail on local areas. They're often extremely accurate because they cover small localities. Often they pinpoint hunting hotspots, little-known trails, and other very valuable details that are seldom included on state and federal maps. When you get into new country always ask if such local maps are available.

HOW TO CARRY MAPS

For the sportsman who makes full use of maps and carries them on hunting trips, protecting them from wear and weather and keeping them in usable condition can be a problem. A map not taken care of has a short life. Properly protected, it will last a long time.

I used to think maps should be rolled and carried in tubular cases. But after fighting those rolled maps with cold hands in semidarkness for years, and having them flap like runaway window shades just as I was about to see what I wanted, I changed my mind.

My maps are folded now to make neat, flat packages. For instance, I fold topo maps to 7x11, with the name of the quadrangle exposed on both sides. Folded this way, any map is easily carried in the field in a waterproof envelope, and easily unfolded for use.

Some hunters eliminate the waterproof envelope by reinforcing their maps with a cloth backing, such as a piece of muslin sheet. Here's how to do it:

The basic trick is to glue your map to the cloth with wallpaper paste. To insure overall contact between map and cloth the cloth should be stretched and tacked to a flat surface such as a plywood board. The cloth should be larger than the map to allow for trimming after the paste dries.

Small maps can be pasted in one piece. Large maps should be cut into sections to eliminate bulky folds. Fold the map so that it fits your pocket, unfold, and cut into sections along the fold lines. Paste the sections (in their proper relationship with each other) to the cloth. Leave a space about 1/16 inch between the sections so the finished product will fold easily and compactly.

To insure complete contact between the map and cloth it's necessary to wet the map—or sections of it—for a moment in warm water. Then apply the wallpaper paste to the back of the map with a paint brush. Pressure by hand will insure contact between the cloth and map. Wipe off excess paste with a damp rag. Let dry for at least one day, then trim the edges with a pair of scissors. The reinforced map is now ready for years of use.

An outdated map may show a road that no longer exists, or it may not include new roads, trails or other features. It's not a good idea to use maps that somebody gives you. They could have been stored in closets for years. Note the publishing date on any map of questionable accuracy. If it's old, order a new one from its publisher. Address information is contained on most maps.

25

Poachers are Making a Fool of You

Did you get your buck last fall? If you didn't it may be that a poacher killed your deer before the hunting season opened. It could be that he shot three or four in the area you hunt. Do you doubt this possibility? I'll bet I can change your mind.

During a recent winter twenty-five field-dressed deer—bucks, does, and fawns—were found lying on snow-covered ground near Chelsea, Vermont. The whitetails were shot at night in the countryside surrounding a base camp used by four Rhode Island poachers. When the carcasses were found by wardens they were covered by softwood boughs. The culprits were caught just before they could transport the illegal venison out of the state.

In Indiana two does were shot in Brown County State Park before the deer season opened. Both does had been captured earlier by biologists and fitted with radio collars as part of a deer-study project. This project, intended to benefit all Indiana deer hunters, went up in the smoke of poachers' rifles.

Here's an incident that's even more disgusting. Here's what happened, according to Albert H. Henson, Director of Law Enforcement, Kentucky Department of Fish and Wildlife Resources:

"In early November of 1974 we experienced an outbreak of illegal deer killing in several counties. Many of the deer were shot and left where they fell with no attempt made to retrieve the carcasses for consumption. In some cases the killing was apparently done from a warped sense of enjoyment at seeing the animals suffer and die."

Last fall Warren Holmes and I were hunting ruffed grouse near his cabin in the wildlands of Lake County, Michigan. We came out of a swale onto a dirt two-track and headed for our car 200 yards down the road. In that short distance we found three freshly fired .30/06 cases glittering in the sunlight. They obviously had been used by deer poachers shooting from the road long before deer season opened.

"A few of the natives around here shoot deer whenever they feel like it," Warren told me. "Many of the bucks are shot off before the legal sportsman gets a chance at them. These guys figure it's worth it to poach venison even if they do get caught once in a while. All they have to look forward to is a minor fine, no court costs, no jail term and no loss of hunting privileges. The local judges don't take violations of game laws very seriously."

The worst violating situation I've personally encountered came to light during a Wyoming hunt I made a few years ago. There was an old homesteader's shack way out in a remote part of Ken McKibben's ranch. One day while we were hunting that part of the ranch Ken noticed a pickup parked by the old shack. He didn't recognize the truck and he hadn't given any strangers permission to hunt, so we drove up to investigate.

The inside of the log shack held a startling sight. There were thirteen carcasses of freshly dressed antelope and mule deer hanging from the rafters.

"Damned professionals," McKibben grunted. "They move into an area, shoot every animal they see, process 'em neatly, and sell the meat. Let's get back to the house and report this."

The poachers were professional in more ways than one. They must have had a lookout watching the shack. When we returned with a warden the meat and the pickup were gone.

I was told about a somewhat similar operation that's carried out in the foothills of Colorado. In this case a gang of violators work massive deer drives. They don't worry about such details as asking permission to hunt.

The key is to move into an area, drive a certain section of land and shoot every deer seen. The areas selected are those which can be traveled with 4WD trucks. Some of the men are expert riflemen who do the killing. A few are spotters who direct the truck drivers to fallen deer. These poachers move into an area, make their kills, load the carcasses, and move out within an hour or two. They run their operation with such swift military precision that it's almost impossible for law-enforcement officers to catch them in action. They process the meat, then wrap and freeze it in marked packages. These guys sell venison during hunting season to unsuccessful and unscrupulous nimrods.

Early in January 1975, conservation officials in the Emmett, Idaho, area learned that four illegally killed elk had been offered for sale. Investigations turned up the pickup which had been used to transport the animals, but the meat was gone. A fifth elk was found by conservation officers where it had been dumped over a road embankment. They also found the heads and hides of seven elk and six deer.

In November 1974, undercover investigator Joe Rubesch of the Special Investigation Section in Wisconsin's DNR, bought a spike buck for $100 at a small-town tavern. Before charges were placed the poacher offered to sell additional deer at $50 each (for orders of six or more) and said he'd already poached thirty deer that year.

As Midwest field editor of *Outdoor Life*, I see a lot of such sickening reports. During recent years I've had the impression the incidents are increasing rapidly. I wondered if poaching was hitting new heights. My desire to get the facts hit a peak last fall when I stopped at a local friend's home.

Bob Wolff was wild. He's an avid bowhunter, and his beef about deer violators hit me hard.

"Something has to be done about those bums," he began. "Last evening I got on my stand near an apple orchard. Just about dusk I noticed a pickup traveling very slowly down a two-track across a field from me. Suddenly the vehicle stopped, a man jumped out, laid his rifle across the hood, and blazed away at a deer. That guy stole my deer, and he killed it a month before firearms season opens. The same sort of thing is going on all the time. I want it stopped, and so does every other legal hunter."

I began my project of finding out how serious poaching is by working up a questionnaire loaded with questions regarding every aspect of the deer-poaching problem. I mailed the questionnaires to game officials in all of the lower forty-eight states. The response was great. Not only did I get detailed answers to my questions, but I got dozens of letters elaborating on the answers. I received such a pile of information that I compiled it and used the statistics to work up the charts which accompany this chapter.

The consensus of several game officials is that we have some hunters who will break laws, just as we have some criminals in every large representative group, and that the general increase in overall poaching of deer, other big game, small game, and waterfowl reflects little more than the increased numbers of hunters, which automatically increases the number of poaching incidents. Some officials went so far as to tell me the increase in general poaching may be negligible because modern enforcement techniques nail a higher percentage of violators than the techniques used years ago. In other words, more violations are detected.

But it's a whole different ball game when it comes to the single subject of poaching deer. Poachers seem to have gone wild at the mere thought of venison. Law-enforcement officials in some states reported violation statistics that were astonishing.

Published by the Missouri Department of Conservation, this "WANTED" poster depicts jacklighting, or the illegal taking of deer by means of spotlights. Since many poachers are as willing to harvest someone else's livestock as they are deer, the poster aims at both poachers and rustlers.

One north-central state reported its deer-poaching increase during the past 10 years at 400 percent. Another state reported an estimated 41,000 deer poached each year. A neighboring state claims its illegal deer harvest amounts to over 90 percent of its legal kill. One state in the northeast put the same statistic at 95 percent. In the intermountain and western areas my statistics show that yearly illegal deer kills total over 10,000 animals in some states. Now, are you still wondering what happened to that buck you didn't get?

It's more than interesting to note that the north-central state with the 400-percent increase has judges that assess an average fine of only $69 for illegally killing a deer. I compiled statistics from all the other states where the illegal deer kill is high and found that the average fine is slightly under $100. No wonder the poachers are stealing your deer.

If you're mad enough about this you can do something about it. In most states the maximum fine a judge could assess for the illegal killing of deer is far higher than the one he actually assesses. Legal sportsmen are a part of the citizenry who elect judges, and they can have an effect on how an individual judge looks at violations. Sportsmen can organize and visit their local courts to inform their judges of their concern for the lack of control over deer poaching.

If you don't think this will help, consider some examples. In Missouri the average fine for shooting an illegal deer is about $300. Though this state's whitetail herd has increased during the past 10 years (giving more opportunity for poaching), the estimated increase of deer poaching is only 15 percent. In one of the western states where deer poaching has increased 215 percent the convicted violator can look forward to a fine of only $48.70.

Another thing you can do is recognize that the effectiveness of a conservation law-enforcement officer is largely a matter of the public cooperation he receives. For example, Minnesota consists of about 84,000 square miles or nearly 54 million acres. There are 129 conservation officers spread over this area, which means each officer is responsible for some 650 square miles. Statistics say he isn't going to learn of more than about one out of 50 violations. But statistics also say that for each case of poaching at least six people not directly involved may be aware of the violation.

"The reluctance of these people to report violations becomes a direct aid to the poacher," Harold H. Spitzer, North Dakota's Chief Warden told me. "Along with this is the great apathy of much of the public in not recognizing that the poacher steals from them and not from the game warden. The ultimate in game-law enforcement will be a reality when honest sportsmen and concerned citizens become involved and transmit information to conservation officers. When the poacher realizes he no longer has the shield of public silence his operations will diminish."

John Hall, of the Vermont Fish and Game Department, makes the point a little differently:

"The answer is not more wardens, it's public responsibility. The honest hunter has to accept the fact that self-government within the ranks of all people who kill deer is the answer. The stamping out of poaching will come only if everyone decides to turn in the spoilers. All it takes is a phone call to the local warden. Law-enforcement ethics demand that he keep the source of his information strictly to himself or others working on the case."

This reluctance of the public to turn in the poacher is vastly more significant now than it was years ago. The theory that the poacher needs the meat to feed his family is far outdated. Government subsistence support is available for the needy, and "needing the meat" isn't an adequate excuse.

Another significant factor involves modern technology. Some violators wouldn't care if the fine for illegally shooting a deer were $10,000 because they know their local conservation officer won't catch them in the act. They keep track of his whereabouts with citizen-band radios.

The only way to lick this problem is having the public become involved. A good example of how it can work is illustrated by the South Carolina Wildlife and Marine Resources Department's toll-free "Hot Line." Game violations can be reported to the law-enforcement section at any time, day or night. From a Columbia radio dispatcher, conservation officers are directed to a poaching scene in minutes anywhere in the state.

Still another factor is the public's continuing belief that deer poaching is insignificant. Well, Professor Sidney W. Wilcox of Arizona State University compiled data showing that the legal 1973 harvest of vension nation-wide had a dollar value of $139,214,338. Because of continuing inflation we could raise this value significantly higher today. I averaged my deer-poaching statistics from across the nation and came up with an illegal deer-kill figure equaling 67 percent of the legal harvest. This means deer poachers are stealing the equivalent of $100 million from the public each year. How does this hit you?

Part of the apprehension problem is that there is no "composite" poacher. Conservation officers can't flesh out the violator and look for a guy in a certain age bracket who has a certain IQ and who lives in a certain type of neighborhood. Deer poachers live in all types of neighborhoods, come in all ages, and have varying educational backgrounds.

But it is known that the violator goes into action for one of the following reasons: ego, profit, or taking what he feels is his.

The poacher who operates because of ego is the guy who suddenly decides to go out and get a big thrill out of life. This is the type of fellow who gets a charge out of outwitting the game warden. He may or may not want the deer he poaches. He's the same type of nut who shoots up road signs, vandalizes and commits other crimes just because he's determined to do things the law says he can't do.

The violator who poaches for profit could be termed a gone-wrong businessman. His operation has nothing to do with ego; he's in it for money.

He's often a skilled deer hunter and he's willing to take calculated risks just like any other businessman. He expects to get caught once in a great while, and he considers fines as nothing more than a business expense.

The third type of poacher often includes the fellow who figures his deer-hunting license entitles him to a deer—not just an opportunity to hunt. He'll get his buck in any manner possible and whether or not the deer season is open. Also in this category is the guy who figures that all wildlife should be utilized without regard for game laws. He explains his hunting with a statement something like: "Those deer out there are as much mine as yours. I'm taking mine while the getting is good."

The man in this category could care less about hunting for ego or profit. He wants venison to eat and he gets it whenever he wants it. Game officials say it's astonishing that so many poachers fit into this category, and that their occupations run from cab drivers to bank presidents.

The fact that game-law violators are not sportsmen was brought up in many letters accompanying my completed questionnaires. Some poachers shoot at almost anything. Some of these bums have shot livestock. On October 26, 1974, near Glendale, Idaho, five horses were shot. In the spring of 1975 several cows and a bull were shot on a ranch near Ellsworth, Kansas. Such gunmen are the spoilers who give all hunters a black eye with the nonhunting public. So poachers are not only stealing your game, they're also threatening all the rest of your hunting.

This fact was brought further to light by some of the answers to my questionnaire. For example, one question read: "A theory that has been advanced as to the cause of ever increasing amounts of posted land is that landowners are becoming fed up with the increased numbers of slob hunters who poach. Do you agree with this theory?" The answers totaled 86 percent "yes."

Another question read: "Do you think that poaching will continue to increase in the years ahead and continue to decrease the amount of deer available to the legal hunter unless we find new and better ways to stop it?" The answers were 88 percent "Yes."

The consensus of several officials who elaborated on their answers was that the average legal hunter doesn't seem to realize that game laws are designed to perpetuate a harvestable surplus of game, and that if these rules are not followed it will be necessary to invoke more stringent laws. This policy will mean nothing to the violator, but it will definitely hurt the honest sportsman.

There is some evidence that concerned outdoorsmen are beginning to agree that personal involvement is the answer. During November of 1974, near Creswell, Oregon, three poachers were caught with the meat of at least eight deer. After they pled guilty in district court, the judge gave them only a token penalty, which so angered local outdoorsmen that they circulated a petition of complaint about the leniency of the court.

In the state of Washington, preceding a recent elk season, the State Department of Game distributed handbills asking for the cooperation of hunters in stopping poaching. Illegal kills were reduced by 50 percent. This state has also trained over 3,000 individuals in a civilian organization known as the Civilian Wildlife Patrol. Members were instructed in the methods of taking information relative to game-law violations while they are in the field. Such information is then turned over to wildlife agents.

The Izaak Walton League in Oregon has initiated a similar approach: it's circulating wallet cards on which citizens are urged to jot down information about game poachers, vandals, and other law violators. Completed cards are mailed to the Oregon State Police.

Similar wallet cards issued by the National Rifle Association have led to several convictions in deer and elk cases. You can get these cards from the National Rifle Association, 1600 Rhode Island Avenue, N.W., Washington, D.C. 20036. The cards contain space to record specific details of any violation witnessed and can be mailed to any law-enforcement agency.

Hunter safety programs are doing their bit, too. The purpose of these programs when they got off the ground a few years ago was to reduce hunting accidents through teaching of firearms safety. Now a second major purpose is to teach the beginning hunter the respect and responsibility that go with hunting.

And here's something else to think about. Legally bagging a buck is a tough challenge with nothing guaranteed. If a guy does score, he brings home prime meat which will be the makings of some of the most memorable meals of the year. The violator who does it the easy way may treat his deer like hamburger—sell it or let it rot and then brag about it. This guy is suckering you out of some of life's most pleasant dinners, in addition to depriving you of the joys of successful hunts.

Top this off with the fact that the violator is making the honest sportsman seem like a culprit in the eyes of the nonhunting public. This segment of the public far outnumbers outdoorsmen, and if the question of whether or not to hunt ever comes to the ballot box we could be voted right out of our sport. Pretty strong stuff, but it points out that we have a definite responsibility to see that our sport does not continue to be tarnished. Now are you mad enough to fight the poachers?

If you are, you can help the cause in more ways than I've mentioned. Perhaps you have some ideas that would check the poaching problem. If you do, your local conservation officer would like to hear about them.

In discussing the problem with honest hunters I heard some interesting comments that may give you food for thought. One fellow had an idea that could work well in small- to medium-sized towns and cities where many people know each other and read a local newspaper.

"A lot of violators don't mind the fines much because they can afford them," he told me. "What would cause these fellows to stop poaching would be the threat of front-page publicity. Some of our so-called re-spected citizens wouldn't take the chance of getting caught violating laws if they knew their convictions would be top local gossip. Such convictions now are buried in the back pages if they're published at all. If newspaper editors would cooperate, we could make public fools out of poachers."

My local friend Bob Wolff pointed out how state police departments have drastically reduced highway accidents on certain holidays by tripling their road patrols. During these special times they cancel all vacations, stop desk jobs and other functions, put all available personnel into patrol cars, and crack down on speeding. State conservation departments have conducted similar operations by grouping officers and other personnel from several counties and concentrating their efforts in specific high-poaching areas at specific times.

"These crackdowns on poaching work," Bob said. "The problem is that they're too few and far between. Think what would happen if our con-servation officer could suddenly enlist the help of several police and sher-iff's deputies for occasional patrols through deer woods. The poacher who keeps track of our officer's whereabouts by citizen band radio would be shocked if he was tapped on the shoulder by a sheriff's deputy. A lot of violators would quit if they knew law-enforcement efforts could be vastly increased at any given time. Why can't such cooperation be organized?"

Probably because each law-enforcement agency is already swamped with more of their own work than they can handle. Maybe you have new suggestions that nobody has thought of. If you have, tell your conservation officer or write your state conservation department.

Appendix

This appendix contains copies of the official score charts now used for deer antlers in the North American Big Game Awards Program. For decades the sole sponsor of the program, the Boone and Crockett Club in 1973 entered into joint sponsorship with the National Rifle Association of America. Awards programs for new trophy entries of all big game are held every three years, and a record book is published about every six years (1964, 1971, 1977). To obtain score charts, record books, lists of measurers, or other information, write North American Big Game Awards Program, c/o Hunting Activities Department, 1600 Rhode Island Avenue NW, Washington, DC 20036. (Charts here are reprinted with permission.)

OFFICIAL SCORING SYSTEM FOR NORTH AMERICAN BIG GAME TROPHIES

RECORDS OF NORTH AMERICAN BIG GAME COMMITTEE

Minimum Score: Deer
Whitetail: Typical 170
Coues: Typical 110

BOONE AND CROCKETT CLUB

RETURN TO:
N.A.B.G. Awards Program
1600 Rhode Island Ave., N.W.
Washington, D.C. 20036

WHITETAIL and COUES DEER

KIND OF DEER _____

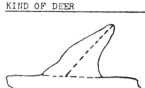

DETAIL OF POINT MEASUREMENT

SEE OTHER SIDE FOR INSTRUCTIONS	Supplementary Data R.	Supplementary Data L.	Column 1 Spread Credit	Column 2 Right Antler	Column 3 Left Antler	Column 4 Difference
A. Number of Points on Each Antler			/////			/////
B. Tip to Tip Spread			/////	/////	/////	/////
C. Greatest Spread			/////	/////	/////	/////
D. Inside Spread of MAIN BEAMS Spread credit may equal but not exceed length of longer antler				/////	/////	/////
IF Inside Spread of Main Beams exceeds longer antler length, enter difference			/////	/////	/////	
E. Total of Lengths of all Abnormal Points			/////	/////	/////	/////
F. Length of Main Beam			/////			
G-1.Length of First Point, if present			/////			
G-2.Length of Second Point			/////			
G-3.Length of Third Point			/////			
G-4.Length of Fourth Point, if present			/////			
G-5.Length of Fifth Point, if present			/////			
G-6.Length of Sixth Point, if present			/////			
G-7.Length of Seventh Point, if present			/////			
Circumference at Smallest Place H-1.Between Burr and First Point			/////			
Circumference at Smallest Place H-2.Between First and Second Points			/////			
Circumference at Smallest Place H-3.Between Second and Third Points			/////			
Circumference at Smallest Place between Third and Fourth Points or half way between Third Point and H-4.Beam Tip if Fourth Point is missing			/////			
TOTALS						

ADD	Column 1		Exact locality where killed
	Column 2		Date killed By whom killed
	Column 3		Present owner
	Total		Address
SUBTRACT Column 4			Guide's Name and Address
FINAL SCORE			Remarks: (Mention any abnormalities)

I certify that I have measured the above trophy on_____ 19 _____
at (address)_____City _____ State _____
and that these measurements and data are, to the best of my knowledge and belief, made in accordance with the
instructions given.

Witness: _____ Signature: _____

                                                                    Official Measurer

INSTRUCTIONS

All measurements must be made with a flexible steel tape to the nearest one-eighth of an inch. Wherever it is
necessary to change direction of measurement, mark a control point and swing tape at this point. To simplify
addition, please enter fractional figures in eighths. Official measurements cannot be taken for at least sixty days
after the animal was killed. Please submit photographs of trophy front and sides.

Supplementary Data measurements indicate conformation of the trophy, and none of the figures in Lines A, B and
C are to be included in the score. Evaluation of conformation is a matter of personal preference. Excellent, but
nontypical Whitetail Deer heads with many points shall be placed and judged in a separate class.

A. Number of Points on each Antler. To be counted a point, a projection must be at least one inch long AND its
length must exceed the length of its base. All points are measured from tip of point to nearest edge of beam as
illustrated. Beam tip is counted as a point but not measured as a point.

B. Tip to Tip Spread measured between tips of Main Beams.

C. Greatest Spread measured between perpendiculars at right angles to the center line of the skull at widest part
whether across main beams or points.

D. Inside Spread of Main Beams measured at right angles to the center line of the skull at widest point between
main beams. Enter this measurement again in ''Spread Credit'' column if it is less than or equal to the length of
longer antler.

E. Total of lengths of all Abnormal Points. Abnormal points are generally considered to be those nontypical in
shape or location.

F. Length of Main Beam measured from lowest outside edge of burr over outer curve to the most distant point of
what is, or appears to be, the main beam. The point of beginning is that point on the burr where the center line
along the outer curve of the beam intersects the burr.

G-1-2-3-4-5-6-7. Length of Normal Points. Normal points project from main beam. They are measured from nearest edge of main beam over outer curve to tip. To determine nearest edge (top edge) of beam, lay the tape along
the outer curve of the beam so that the top edge of the tape coincides with the top edge of the beam on both
sides of the point. Draw line along top edge of tape. This line will be base line from which point is measured.

H-1-2-3-4. Circumferences - If first point is missing, Take H-1 and H-2 at smallest place between burr and
second point.
                              * * * * * * * * * *

TROPHIES OBTAINED ONLY BY FAIR CHASE MAY BE ENTERED
IN ANY BOONE AND CROCKETT CLUB BIG GAME COMPETITION

To make use of the following methods shall be deemed UNFAIR CHASE and unsportsmanlike, and any trophy
obtained by use of such means is disqualified from entry in any Boone and Crockett Club big game competition:
    I. Spotting or herding game from the air, followed by landing in its vicinity for pursuit;
    II. Herding or pursuing game with motor-powered vehicles;
    III. Use of electronic communications for attracting, locating or observing game, or guiding the
         hunter to such game.
                              * * * * * * * * * *
I certify that the trophy scored on this chart was not taken in UNFAIR CHASE as defined above by the Boone
and Crockett Club.

I certify that it was not spotted or herded by guide or hunter from the air followed by landing in its vicinity for
pursuit, nor herded or pursued on the ground by motor-powered vehicles.

I further certify that no electronic communications were used to attract, locate, observe, or guide the hunter to
such game; and that it was taken in full compliance with the local game laws or regulations of the state,
province or territory.

Date _____ _____ Hunter _____

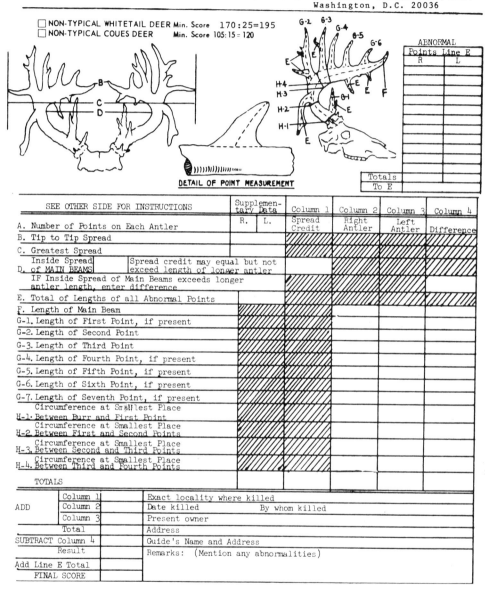

OFFICIAL SCORING SYSTEM FOR NORTH AMERICAN BIG GAME TROPHIES

RECORDS OF NORTH AMERICAN BIG GAME COMMITTEE

BOONE AND CROCKETT CLUB

RETURN TO:
N.A.B.G. Awards Program
1600 Rhode Island Ave., N.W.
Washington, D.C. 20036

☐ NON-TYPICAL WHITETAIL DEER Min. Score 170:25=195
☐ NON-TYPICAL COUES DEER   Min. Score 105:15 = 120

ABNORMAL
Points Line E

	R	L

Totals
To E

DETAIL OF POINT MEASUREMENT

SEE OTHER SIDE FOR INSTRUCTIONS	Supplementary Data		Column 1	Column 2	Column 3	Column 4
	R.	L.	Spread Credit	Right Antler	Left Antler	Difference
A. Number of Points on Each Antler						
B. Tip to Tip Spread						
C. Greatest Spread						
D. Inside Spread of MAIN BEAMS	Spread credit may equal but not exceed length of longer antler					
IF Inside Spread of Main Beams exceeds longer antler length, enter difference						
E. Total of Lengths of all Abnormal Points						
F. Length of Main Beam						
G-1. Length of First Point, if present						
G-2. Length of Second Point						
G-3. Length of Third Point						
G-4. Length of Fourth Point, if present						
G-5. Length of Fifth Point, if present						
G-6. Length of Sixth Point, if present						
G-7. Length of Seventh Point, if present						
H-1. Circumference at Smallest Place Between Burr and First Point						
H-2. Circumference at Smallest Place Between First and Second Points						
H-3. Circumference at Smallest Place Between Second and Third Points						
H-4. Circumference at Smallest Place Between Third and Fourth Points						
TOTALS						

ADD	Column 1		Exact locality where killed	
	Column 2		Date killed	By whom killed
	Column 3		Present owner	
	Total		Address	
SUBTRACT Column 4			Guide's Name and Address	
	Result		Remarks: (Mention any abnormalities)	
Add Line E Total				
FINAL SCORE				

I certify that I have measured the above trophy on _____ 19_____
at (address)_____ City _____ State_____
and that these measurements and data are, to the best of my knowledge and belief, made in accordance with the instructions given.

Witness: _____ Signature: _____
Official Measurer

INSTRUCTIONS

All measurements must be made with a flexible steel tape to the nearest one-eight of an inch. Wherever it is necessary to change direction of measurement, mark a control point and swing tape at this point. To simplify addition, please enter fractional figures in eighths. Official measurements cannot be taken for at least sixty days after the animal was killed. Please submit photographs of trophy front and sides. Supplementary Data measurements indicate conformation of the trophy, and none of the figures in Lines A, B and C are to be included in the score. Evaluation of conformation is a matter of personal preference.

A. Number of Points on each Antler. To be counted a point, a projection must be at least one inch long AND its length must exceed the length of its base. All points are measured from tip of point to nearest edge of beam as illustrated. Beam tip is counted as a point but not measured as a point.

B. Tip to Tip Spread measured between tips of main beams.

C. Greatest Spread measured between perpendiculars at right angles to the center line of the skull at widest part whether across main beams or points.

D. Inside Spread of Main Beams measured at right angles to the center line of the skull at widest point between main beams. Enter this measurement again in "Spread Credit" column if it is less than or equal to the length of longer antler.

E. Total of Lengths of all Abnormal Points. Abnormal points are considered to be those nontypical in shape or location. It is very important, in scoring nontypical heads, to determine which points are to be classed as normal and which are not. To do this, study carefully the character of the normal points on the diagram, which are marked G-1, G-2, G-3, etc. On the trophy to be scored, the points which correspond to these are measured as normal. All others over one inch in length (See A, above) are considered abnormal. Various types of abnormal points are shown (marked with an E) on the diagram. Measure the exact length of each abnormal point, over the outer curve, from the tip to the nearest edge of the beam or point from which it projects. Then add these lengths and enter the total in the space provided.

F. Length of Main Beam measured from lowest outside edge of burr over outer curve to the most distant point of what is, or appears to be, the main beam. The point of beginning is that point on the burr where the center line along the outer curve of the beam intersects the burr.

G-1-2-3-4-5-6-7. Length of Normal Points. Normal points project from main beam. They are measured from nearest edge of main beam over outer curve to tip. To determine nearest edge (top edge) of beam, lay the tape along the outer curve of the beam so that the top edge of the tape coincides with the top edge of the beam on both sides of the point. Draw line along top edge of tape. This line will be base line from which point is measured.

H-1-2-3-4. Circumferences - If first point is missing, take H-1 and H-2 at smallest place between burr and second point. If fourth point is missing, take H-4 half way between third point and beam tip.

* * * * * * * * * * * * *

TROPHIES OBTAINED ONLY BY FAIR CHASE MAY BE ENTERED IN ANY BOONE AND CROCKETT CLUB BIG GAME COMPETITION

To make use of the following methods shall be deemed UNFAIR CHASE and unsportsmanlike, and any trophy obtained by use of such means is disqualified from entry in any Boone and Crockett Club big game competition:

     I. Spotting or herding game from the air, followed by landing in its vicinity for pursuit;
    II. Herding or pursuing game with motor-powered vehicles;
    III. Use of electronic communications for attracting, locating or observing game, or guiding the hunter to such game.   * * * * * * * * * *

I certify that the trophy scored on this chart was not taken in UNFAIR CHASE as defined above by the Boone and Crockett Club.

I certify that it was not spotted or herded by guide or hunter from the air followed by landing in its vicinity for pursuit, nor herded or pursued on the ground by motor-powered vehicles.

I further certify that no electronic communications were used to attract, locate, observe, or guide the hunter to such game; and that it was taken in full compliance with the local game laws or regulations of the state, province or territory.

Date_____ Signature of Hunter _____

OFFICIAL SCORING SYSTEM FOR NORTH AMERICAN BIG GAME TROPHIES

RECORDS OF NORTH AMERICAN BIG GAME COMMITTEE

BOONE AND CROCKETT CLUB

RETURN TO:
N. A. B. G. Awards Program
1600 Rhode Island Ave. N. W.
Washington, D. C. 20036

Minimum Score: Deer

| Col. Blacktail: | Typical — 130 |
| Mule: | Typical — 195 |

MULE and BLACKTAIL DEER

KIND OF DEER:

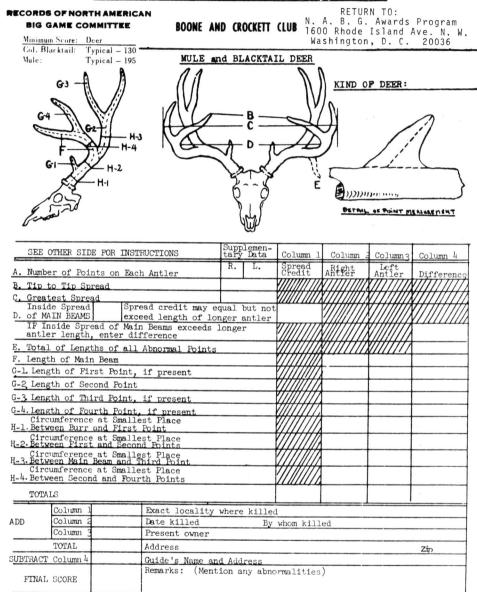

DETAIL OF POINT MEASUREMENT

SEE OTHER SIDE FOR INSTRUCTIONS		Supplementary Data		Column 1	Column 2	Column 3	Column 4
		R.	L.	Spread Credit	Right Antler	Left Antler	Difference
A. Number of Points on Each Antler							
B. Tip to Tip Spread							
C. Greatest Spread							
D. Inside Spread of MAIN BEAMS	Spread credit may equal but not exceed length of longer antler						
IF Inside Spread of Main Beams exceeds longer antler length, enter difference							
E. Total of Lengths of all Abnormal Points							
F. Length of Main Beam							
G-1 Length of First Point, if present							
G-2 Length of Second Point							
G-3 Length of Third Point, if present							
G-4 Length of Fourth Point, if present							
H-1 Circumference at Smallest Place Between Burr and First Point							
H-2 Circumference at Smallest Place Between First and Second Points							
H-3 Circumference at Smallest Place Between Main Beam and Third Point							
H-4 Circumference at Smallest Place Between Second and Fourth Points							
TOTALS							

ADD	Column 1		Exact locality where killed	
	Column 2		Date killed	By whom killed
	Column 3		Present owner	
TOTAL			Address	Zip
SUBTRACT Column 4			Guide's Name and Address	
FINAL SCORE			Remarks: (Mention any abnormalities)	

I certify that I have measured the above trophy on _____ 19_____
at (address) _____ City _____ State _____
that these measurements and data are, to the best of my knowledge and belief, made in accordance with the instructions given.

Witness: _____ Signature: _____
                                                            Boone & Crockett Official Measurer

INSTRUCTIONS

All measurements must be made with a flexible steel tape to the nearest one-eighth of an inch. Wherever it is necessary to change direction of measurement, mark a control point and swing tape at this point. To simplify addition, please enter fractional figures in eighths. Official measurements cannot be taken for at least sixty days after the animal was killed. Please submit photographs of trophy front and sides.

Supplementary Data measurements indicate conformation of the trophy, and none of the figures in Lines A, B and C are to be included in the score. Evaluation of conformation is a matter of personal preference. Excellent, but nontypical Mule Deer heads with many points shall be placed and judged in a separate class.

A. Number of Points on Each Antler. To be counted a point, a projection must be at least one inch long AND its length must exceed the length of its base. All points are measured from tip of point to nearest edge of beam as illustrated. Beam tip is counted as a point but not measured as a point.

B. Tip to Tip Spread measured between tips of main beams.

C. Greatest Spread measured between perpendiculars at right angles to the center line of the skull at widest part whether across main beams or points.

D. Inside Spread of Main Beams measured at right angles to the center line of the skull at widest point between main beams. Enter this measurement again in "Spread Credit" column if it is less than or equal to the length of longer antler.

E. Total of Lengths of all Abnormal Points. Abnormal points are generally considered to be those nontypical in shape or location.

F. Length of Main Beam measured from lowest outside edge of burr over outer curve to the tip of the main beam. The point of beginning is that point on the burr where the center line along the outer curve of the beam intersects the burr.

G-1-2-3-4. Length of Normal Points. Normal points are the brow (or first) and the upper and lower forks as shown in illustration. They are measured from nearest edge of beam over outer curve to tip. To determine nearest edge (top edge) of beam, lay the tape along the outer curve of the beam so that the top edge of the tape coincides with the top edge of the beam on both sides of the point. Draw line along top edge of tape. This line will be base line from which point is measured.

H-1-2-3-4. Circumferences — if first point is missing, take H-1 and H-2 at smallest place between burr and second point. If third point is missing, take H-3 half way between the base and tip of second point. If the fourth is missing, take H-4 half way between the second point and tip of main beam.

TROPHIES OBTAINED ONLY BY FAIR CHASE MAY BE ENTERED IN ANY BOONE AND CROCKETT CLUB BIG GAME COMPETITION

To make use of the following methods shall be deemed UNFAIR CHASE and unsportsmanlike, and any trophy obtained by use of such means is disqualified from entry in any Boone and Crockett Club big game competition:

I. Spotting or herding game from the air, followed by landing in its vicinity for pursuit;
II. Herding or pursuing game with motor-powered vehicles;
III. Use of electronic communications for attracting, locating or observing game, or guiding the hunter to such game.

I certify that the trophy scored on this chart was not taken in UNFAIR CHASE as defined above by the Boone and Crockett Club.

I certify that it was not spotted or herded by guide or hunter from the air followed by landing in its vicinity for pursuit, nor herded or pursued on the ground by motor-powered vehicles.

I further certify that no electronic communications were used to attract, locate, observe, or guide the hunter to such game; and that it was taken in full compliance with the local game laws or regulations of the state, province or territory.

Date _____ Signature of Hunter _____

OFFICIAL SCORING SYSTEM FOR NORTH AMERICAN BIG GAME TROPHIES

RECORDS OF NORTH AMERICAN BIG GAME COMMITTEE

BOONE AND CROCKETT CLUB

RETURN TO:
N. A. B. G. Awards Program
1600 Rhode Island Ave. N. W.
Washington, D, C. 20036

Minimum Score: 195:45 = 240

NON-TYPICAL MULE DEER

DETAIL OF POINT MEASUREMENT

ABNORMAL		
Points Line E		
R		L
TOTALS		
To E		

SEE OTHER SIDE FOR INSTRUCTIONS	Supplementary Data R.	L.	Column 1 Spread Credit	Column 2 Right Antler	Column 3 Left Antler	Column 4 Difference
A. Number of Points on Each Antler						
B. Tip to Tip Spread						
C. Greatest Spread						
D. Inside Spread of MAIN BEAMS	Spread credit may equal but not exceed length of longer antler					
IF Inside Spread of Main Beams exceeds longer antler length, enter difference						
E. Total of Lengths of all Abnormal Points						
F. Length of Main Beam						
G-1. Length of First Point, if present						
G-2. Length of Second Point						
G-3. Length of Third Point, if present						
G-4. Length of Fourth Point, if present						
H-1. Circumference at Smallest Place Between Burr and First Point						
H-2. Circumference at Smallest Place Between First and Second Points						
H-3. Circumference at Smallest Place Between Main Beam and Third Point						
H-4. Circumference at Smallest Place Between Second and Fourth Points						
TOTALS						

Column 1		Exact locality where killed
Column 2		Date killed By whom killed
Column 3		Present owner
Total		Address
SUBTRACT Column 4		Guide's Name and Address
Result		Remarks: (Mention any abnormalities)
Add Line E Total		
FINAL SCORE		

I certify that I have measured the above trophy on _____ 19_____
at (address)_____ City _____ State_____
and that these measurements and data are, to the best of my knowledge and belief, made in accordance with the
instructions given.

Witness: _____ Signature: _____

Boone and Crockett Official Measurer

INSTRUCTIONS

All measurements must be made with a flexible steel tape to the nearest one-eighth of an inch. Wherever it is
necessary to change direction of measurement, mark a control point and swing tape at this point. To simplify
addition, please enter fractional figures in eighths.

Official measurements cannot be taken for at least sixty days after the animal was killed. Please submit
photographs of trophy front and sides.

Supplementary Data measurements indicate conformation of the trophy, and none of the figures in Lines A, B
and C are to be included in the score. Evaluation of conformation is a matter of personal preference.

A. Number of Points on Each Antler. To be counted a point, a projection must be least one inch long AND its
length must exceed the length of its base. All points are measured from tip of point to nearest edge of beam as
illustrated. Beam tip is counted as a point but not measured as a point.

B. Tip to Tip Spread measured between tips of Main Beams.

C. Greatest Spread measured between perpendiculars at right angles to the center line of the skull at widest
part whether across main beams or points.

D. Inside Spread of Main Beams measured at right angles to the center line of the skull at widest point between
main beams. Enter this measurement again in "Spread Credit" column if it is less than or equal to the length of
longer antler.

E. Total of Lengths of all Abnormal Points. Abnormal points are considered to be those nontypical in shape
or location. It is very important, in scoring nontypical heads, to determine which points are to be classed as
normal and which are not. To do this, study carefully the markings G-1, G-2, G-3 and G-4 on the diagram, which
indicate the normal points. On the trophy to be scored, select the points which most closely correspond to these.
All others over one inch in length (See A, above) are considered abnormal.

Measure the exact length of each abnormal point, over the outer curve, from the tip to the nearest edge of the
beam or point from which it projects. Then add these lengths and enter the total in the space provided.

F. Length of Main Beam measured from lowest outside edge of burr over outer curve to the tip of the main beam.
The point of beginning is that point on the burr where the center line along the outer curve of the beam intersects the burr.

G-1-2-3-4. Length of Normal Points. Normal points are the brow (or first) and the upper and lower forks as
shown in illustration. They are measured from nearest edge of beam over outer curve to tip. To determine nearest edge (top edge) of beam, lay the tape along the outer curve of the beam so that the top edge of the tape
coincides with the top edge of the beam on both sides of the point. Draw line along top edge of tape. This line
will be base line from which point is measured.

H-1-2-3-4. Circumferences — If first point is missing, take H-1 and H-2 at smallest place between burr and
second point. If third point is missing, take H-3 half way between the base and tip of second point. If the fourth
point is missing take H-4 half way between the second point and tip of main beam.

* * * * * * * *

TROPHIES OBTAINED ONLY BY FAIR CHASE MAY BE ENTERED
IN ANY BOONE AND CROCKETT CLUB BIG GAME COMPETITION

To make use of the following methods shall be deemed UNFAIR CHASE and unsportsmanlike, and any trophy
obtained by use of such means is disqualified from entry in any Boone and Crockett Club big game competition:

      I. Spotting or herding game from the air, followed by landing in its vicinity for pursuit;

      II. Herding or pursuing game with motor-powered vehicles;

      III. Use of electronic communications for attracting, locating or observing game, or guiding the
           hunter to such game.

I certify that the trophy scored on this chart was not taken in UNFAIR CHASE as defined above by the Boone
and Crockett Club.

I certify that it was not spotted or herded by guide or hunter from the air followed by landing in its vicinity for
pursuit, nor herded or pursued on the ground by motor-powered vehicles.

I further certify that no electronic communications were used to attract, locate, observe, or guide the hunter to
such game; and that it was taken in full compliance with the local game laws or regulations of the state,
province or territory.

Date_____ Signature of Hunter_____

Photo Credits

All photos are by the author, with the exception of those noted below.

Baker Manufacturing Company: page 207

Erwin A. Bauer: pages 111 (bottom), 115 (top)

Bear Archery Company: page 116

Clarence Beard: page 5

Jon Cates: pages 19 (top left), 47, 52 (bottom), 61 (top), 64, 69, 70, 72 (top), 98, 100, 162, 247, 255

Charles Elliott: pages 110 (bottom), 115 (bottom), 203

Steve Gallizioli: page 19 (top right)

John Hall, Vermont Fish and Game Department: page 97 (bottom)

Illinois Department of Conservation: page 83

David Jensen: page 72 (bottom)

Kentucky Fish & Wildlife Resources: page 174

Earl Kipischke: page 49

Montana Fish & Game: pages 97 (top), 126

Nebraska Game & Parks Commission: pages 110 (top), 211

Oregon Wildlife Commission: page 19 (bottom right)

Primus-Sievert: page 209

Remington Arms Company: pages 198, 199

Leonard Lee Rue III: pages 39, 53, 55, 56, 67, 76, 108, 166, 253

Leonard Lee Rue IV: pages 19 (bottom left), 184, 254

Saskatchewan Government: page 52 (top)

U.S. Forest Service, Southwestern Region: page 32

Winchester Western: page 27

Don Wooldridge: pages 91, 93, 94, 95, 96, 131; 212

Index